Manager's Guide to Excellence in Public Relations and Communication Management

Manager's Guide to Excellence in Public Relations and Communication Management

David M. Dozier
San Diego State University

with
Larissa A. Grunig
James E. Grunig
University of Maryland

The Excellence Study was funded through a grant from the International Association of Business Communicators (IABC) Research Foundation

LAWRENCE ERLBAUM ASSOCIATES, PUBLISHERS
1995 Mahwah, New Jersey   Hove, UK

Lawrence Erlbaum Associates, Inc., Publishers
10 Industrial Avenue
Mahwah, New Jersey 07430

cover design by Mairav Salomon-Dekel

Library of Congress Cataloging-in-Publication Data

Dozier, David M.
    Manager's guide to excellence in public relations and
communication management / David M. Dozier, Larissa
A. Grunig, James E. Grunig.
        p.   cm. -- (LEA's communication series)
    Includes bibliographical references and index.
    ISBN 0-8058-1809-X (acid-free paper). -- ISBN 0-
8058-1810-3 (pbk. : acid-free paper)
    1. Communciation in management.   2. Public rela-
tions.   I. Grunig, Larissa A.   II. Grunig, James E.   III.
Title.   IV. Series.
HD30.3.D69 1995   95-3607
                                                    CIP

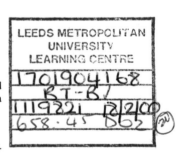
Books published by Lawrence Erlbaum Associates are printed
on acid-free paper, and their bindings are chosen for strength
and durability.

Printed in the United States of America
10 9 8 7 6 5 4 3 2 1

Contents

Preface   **vii**

Acknowledgments   **xi**

1   What is Communication Excellence?   **1**

PART I: COMMUNICATOR KNOWLEDGE BASE

2   Knowing How to Manage Strategically   **23**

3   Knowing Two-Way Communication Practices   **39**

4   Knowing Traditional Communicator Skills   **53**

5   Build Your Knowledge Base   **63**

PART II: SHARED EXPECTATIONS ABOUT COMMUNICATION

6   The Power of the Communication Department   **75**

7   Shared Expectations of Communication   **89**

8   Building Linkages to the Dominant Coalition   **107**

9   What CEOs Should Do About Excellence   **121**

PART III: THE CHARACTER OF ORGANIZATIONS

10   Participation and Authority in the Culture of Organizations   **135**

11   Empowering Women and Culturally Diverse Employees   **149**

12   The Global Qualities of Excellence   **163**

13   Changing the Character of Organizations   **183**

PART IV: PUTTING EXCELLENCE TO WORK

14   Origins of Communication Programs   **195**

15   Using Traditional and Advanced Practices   **207**

16   Communication Excellence Makes a Difference   **217**

Appendix: How the Excellence Study Was Conducted   **237**

Author Index   **251**

Subject Index   **253**

Preface

This book reports the findings of a $400,000, three-nation study of public relations and communication management sponsored by the International Association of Business Communicators (IABC) Research Foundation. As you will learn, the Excellence Study provides communication managers and public relations practitioners with information critical to their own professional growth. The Excellence Study provides tools that help organizations communicate more effectively and build beneficial relations with key publics. Communication excellence is a powerful idea of sweeping scope that applies to all organizations, large or small, that need to communicate effectively with publics on whom the organization's survival and growth depends. The essential elements of excellent communication are the same for corporations, not-for-profit organizations, government agencies, and professional-trade associations; they apply to organizations globally.

Men and women who manage communication for organizations will find much useful information in this book directly relevant to their work. Those who aspire to manage communication for organizations should consider this book an essential professional development tool. If you are a typical communication manager, you are likely mid-career with a decade or more of professional experience in the field. You know the communication profession and you know your organization. Most important, professional development and career opportunities motivate you to improve and expand your expertise; you seek broad managerial responsibilities. You read professional communicator journals such as *Communication World*; you attend professional workshops and seminars. You may study for the accreditation exam or you may already have earned this important professional distinction. You may pursue an advanced degree on the side.

In short, you seek professional advancement rather than rest on your laurels. New ideas in the communication profession interest and excite you, rather than leave you petrified. As communication and public relations enter the 21st century, *change* stands out as the one certain imperative of this emerging profession. You see yourself growing professionally to meet these changes, not counting the years to retirement or looking for a different career.

Other managers and consultants will also find this book valuable in working with communicators and in helping organizations manage communication effectively. Heads of marketing and human resource departments will find this book especially useful, because many professional communicators work in these departments. More important, managers of marketing and human resource departments benefit from strategic alliances with communication or public relations departments to build and maintain beneficial relationships with customers and employees.

Managers involved in strategic planning will also benefit from reading this book. As explained in Parts II and III, excellent communication departments make significant contributions to strategic planning and management in their organizations. As a strategic planner, are you receiving the full contribution that excellent public relations and communication management can make to strategic planning?

Finally, consultants and consulting firms of all kinds will benefit from a clear understanding of communication excellence and how such excellence contributes to overall organizational effectiveness. As major corporations and other organizations become leaner and more responsive to changing markets, publics, and audiences, consultants play an increasingly important role in public relations and communication management. Whether that role helps or hinders organizations in achieving communication excellence will depend, in part, on the knowledge or expertise that consultants bring to organizations. Part I helps consultants understand the expertise needed to achieve excellence in public relations and communication management. Part II helps consultants identify the key linkages with senior management that are necessary to support excellent communication programs. Part III helps consultants understand the culture of organizations that, in turn, nurtures or hinders excellence.

SPHERES OF COMMUNICATION EXCELLENCE

The Excellence Study measured excellence in public relations and communication management. As more fully introduced in chapter 1, these measures are described as the three spheres of communication excellence, one inside the other. Chapter 1 provides a broad introduction to these spheres. The spheres of excellence help organize the presentation of this book.

Part I examines the core or inner sphere of communication excellence: the *knowledge base* of the communication department.

A second sphere surrounds the knowledge core: the *shared expectations* of top communicators and senior managers about the function and role of communication. Part II closely examines these shared expectations.

The two inner spheres are embedded inside the third sphere, the organization's culture. An organization's culture provides the larger context that either nurtures or impedes communication excellence. Part III considers organizational culture and the role culture plays in communication excellence.

The three spheres of communication excellence consider the overall function and role of communication in organizations. But how does an excellent communication department actually *do* public relations and communication management? Part IV examines communication excellence as demonstrated in communication programs developed for specific publics. The last chapter of the book returns to a fundamental question posed at the beginning of the study: What is the value of excellent communication to organizations?

The findings from the qualitative case studies are woven into a common fabric with the survey findings. In particular, the case studies showed how activist publics and turbulent conditions inside and outside organizations push organizations toward excellence. Several organizations exhibiting few qualities of excellence in the 1990–1991 survey had made tremendous strides toward excellence at the time of the 1994 case studies. These findings are also reported.

The appendix provides the interested reader with more details about the actual conduct of the Excellence Study, including the research methods used.

A FEW WORDS ABOUT TERMINOLOGY

"We" refers to the three of us—David Dozier, Larissa Grunig, and James Grunig—the authors of this book. As we write, we also describe the work of other members of the research team—William Ehling, Fred Repper, and Jon White—who did not actively write or edit this book. *Excellence in Public Relations and Communication Management* (Grunig, 1992)[1] includes their original writings regarding communication excellence. We urge readers who would like to know more about communication excellence to read that book, which served as a foundation for this book. When we refer to the *Excellence research team*, or simply the *research team*, we refer to the six of us.

We use the terms *public relations* and *communication* interchangeably. We use these terms to denote the management of communication between an organization and its publics.

The Excellence Study refers to the $400,000, three-nation study funded by the IABC Research Foundation. The Excellence Study includes the survey of 321[2] organizations in Canada, the United Kingdom, and the United States in 1990–1991, the first phase of the research. We refer to this large-scale, quantitative part as the 1990–1991 survey. The Excellence Study also includes a second phase: follow-up case studies in 1994 of 24 organizations that participated in the original survey. We refer to this second phase as the case studies.

Excellence in public relations and communication management, or simply communication excellence, refers to an abstraction or "ideal" that the Excellence

---

[1]Grunig, J. E. (Ed.). (1992). *Excellence in public relations and communication management.* Hillsdale, NJ: Lawrence Erlbaum Associates.

[2]Of the 321 participating organizations, 270 provided completed questionnaires from all three categories of respondents: CEOs, top communicators, and employees. This permitted computation of an overall Excellence Score for these organizations. The other 51 returned partial information, which was used for data analysis when appropriate.

Study sought to measure. *Communication excellence* describes the ideal state in which knowledgeable communicators assist in the overall strategic management of organizations, seeking symmetrical relations through management of communication with key publics on whom organizational survival and growth depends. When we write of excellent organizations or excellent communication departments, we are referring to this ideal.

Like any ideal, no one set of measures can capture all the nuances and subtleties of communication excellence. However, as sketched in chapter 1 and as detailed throughout the rest of the book, the Excellence Study identified a set of indicators that permit the objective measure of communication excellence in organizations. This set of indicators is called the *Excellence Factor*. Each organization in the Excellence Study was assigned a score on each of these indicators that make up the Excellence Factor. An organization's *Excellence Score* is an organization's overall score for all measures on the Excellence Factor.

In the 1990–1991 survey, questionnaires were completed by the top communicator in each participating organization. Those top communicators carried an array of job titles: vice presidents, directors, managers, and supervisors of communication, public relations, public affairs, corporate communications, and so forth.

Throughout the book, we refer to these participants as top communicators and the instruments they completed as top communicator questionnaires. Questionnaires also were completed by top executives in participating organizations, who carried a range of job titles: chief executive officer, executive director, president, and so forth. Throughout the book, we refer to these participants as chief executive officers (CEOs) and the instruments they completed as CEO questionnaires. A sampling of about 12 employees in each participating organization completed employee questionnaires.

We avoided jargon wherever possible. To report findings of scientific research, however, we needed to use an occasional term. Whenever we introduced a technical term, we provided a definition. In addition, we have used examples from the 1994 case studies to help illustrate key points and concepts.

—*David M. Dozier*
— *Larissa A. Grunig*
—*James E. Grunig*

Acknowledgments

Several groups of very special people made this book possible—or made it better—through their contributions. Foremost, board chairs, board members, and contributors to the International Association of Business Communicators (IABC) Research Foundation made the Excellence Study possible. This book reports the findings of that study, the most comprehensive research project ever conducted of public relations and communication management. To all our supporters in the IABC Research Foundation, I express the research team's enduring gratitude.

I also thank the chief executive officers, the heads of communication departments, and over 4,600 employees in the organizations that participated in the Excellence Study. In 1990–1991, these organizations filled out some 28,300 pages of questionnaires. In 1994, 24 of the original organizations participated in follow-up case studies, providing some 100 hours of interviews to the Excellence research team. Each piece of information helped us better understand public relations and communication management.

A second group of people worked hard to help us explain the Excellence Study research findings to communication managers and others in corporations, not-for-profit organizations, government agencies, and associations. As a former newspaper reporter and public information officer, I still strive for active construction, terse sentences, and lucid examples. But 15 years in academe exacts a price. Technical terms and jargon seep into paragraphs. Multiple dependent clauses attach like leeches to simple declarative sentences. Readers miss much of the elegance and power of abstract concepts and models because writers fail to provide concrete examples and cases.

To combat this, this IABC Research Foundation assembled an editorial advisory panel to help write this book. The panel included Robert Berzok, Director of Corporate Communications, Union Carbide, Danbury, Connecticut; Kathleen Bourchier, Corporate Consultant for Strategic Communication, Alcan Aluminum, Montreal, Canada; Cheryl Greene, Associate, The Rodgers Group, Chicago, Illinois; Lester Potter, Communication Account Manager, American Red Cross, Washington, DC; Vicci Rodgers, Principal, The Rodgers Group, Chicago, Illinois; Maire Simington, Systems Director of Communication Services, Samaritan Health

System, Phoenix, Arizona; Nancy Welch, Senior Research Specialist for the Morrison Institute for Public Policy, Arizona State University, Tempe, Arizona; and Louis Williams, President, L. C. Williams and Associates, Chicago, Illinois. The panel read each chapter, providing criticism, suggesting examples, and demanding clarity. As you read this book, the parts you find interesting, cogent, and informative reflect the hard work of the editorial review panel. The rest is my fault.

The Excellence research team itself deserves special recognition. As project director, Professor James E. Grunig, University of Maryland, invested uncounted hours over nearly a decade to bring the Excellence Study to a successful conclusion. The Excellence research team appreciated his symmetrical and participative leadership style. Arguably the world's preeminent scholar of public relations, James Grunig brought his formidable theoretical rigor to the project; the Excellence Study benefited immensely from it. Other Excellence team members brought their own special contributions and expertise to the project: William P. Ehling, Professor, S. I. Newhouse School of Public Communication, Syracuse University (retired); Larissa A. Grunig, Associate Professor, College of Journalism, University of Maryland; Fred C. Repper, Vice President of Public Relations, Gulf States Utilities (retired); and Jon White, Adjunct Faculty, City University of London.

Many others have joined the Excellence research team over the life of the project. For their efforts, I thank Jody Buffington, Linda Childers Hon, Judith K. Meyer, Kenneth D. Plowman, and K. Sriramesh from the University of Maryland; Troy Anderson, Jane Ballinger, Valerie Barker, Brian Ferrario, Danielle Hauck, Nancy Lowden, Susie Maguire, Jo Nell Miettinen, James Ritchey, Natalie Walsh, and Kimberly J. White from San Diego State University; and John M. Blamphin from Rapier Marketing in London.

Three colleagues not affiliated with this book or the Excellence Study exerted considerable influence on my work. Dr. Everett Rogers of the University of New Mexico first taught me the importance of making research findings accessible to people other than college professors. As we braved Rocky Mountain snowstorms in a study of "technology transfer," Ev taught me the importance of diffusing research findings from scholars to practitioners. Dr. Glen Broom and Dr. Martha Lauzen of San Diego State University provide me with an intellectually stimulating environment for teaching and scholarship in public relations.

Two members of the Excellence Study research team helped co-author this book. I thank Larissa and Jim Grunig for the many editorial and conceptual improvements they provided.

On a more personal note, I thank my wife, Lorri Anne Greene, for her toleration and support of my work on the Excellence Study and this book. I also thank my daughters, Sara and Lara, for sharing me with the mainframe computer and word processor.

—David M. Dozier

1

What Is Communication Excellence?

Excellence in public relations and communication management takes many forms, yet a few key characteristics underlie all excellent communication programs. Look for the common thread of excellence in these diverse examples:

- The medical director at a blood bank could see the impact of effective media relations at the peak of the AIDS crisis. Often, the deadly HIV virus passes through blood transferred from an infected person to someone not infected with the virus. In the mid-1980s, many people feared that donating blood was risky. In nearby cities, blood donations dropped 15% to 25%, but donations at this blood bank dropped only 3%. The blood bank's chief financial officer estimated the savings in revenues not lost at $986,000 to $2.1 million. Senior management credits the top communicator with a big part of this success, because her extensive media contacts helped contain and combat unfounded misinformation about donating blood. Another communicator at the blood bank learned research techniques in college. The blood bank uses informal media contacts as well as focus groups, surveys of volunteers who organize blood drives, and survey evaluations of each blood drive to track community perceptions, trends, and issues affecting blood donations and the blood bank. The blood bank built communication excellence, in part, on the knowledge that both communicators bring to the organization.
- The director of corporate communications in a large chemical manufacturing company explained that he plays an active role in strategic management. "If there are strategic issues that require planning," he said, "communication is involved."

Why involve communicators so intimately in strategic management? "Everything you do strategically in a company has to do with relations with the outside world," his boss explained, noting that communication is more than simply transmitting information. "It's a two-way function." He also noted that the Bhopal tragedy in India pushed all chemical manufacturers to change, to become "willing to be more open to the public."

As with many organizations in the Excellence Study, crises and turbulence pushed this organization toward communication excellence. The chemical manufacturing company has built excellence, partly because the organization's sophisticated managers demand excellence from corporate communications. The top communicator understands those expectations and has the expertise to deliver.

• A woman runs a one-person communication department in a small economic development agency in the southern United States. Armed with a master's degree in environmental science with a concentration in community relations, she had been with this organization about six months when we interviewed her. We wanted to talk to people in this organization because it scored low in overall communication excellence among those participating in the 1990–1991 survey. Although only a newcomer at the time of the interview, she already played an important role in strategic management. She was developing programs to monitor the impact of communication programs on the agency's clients. This progress occurred in an organizational culture that the chief executive officer (CEO), a man, described as "traditionally male." Why had there been a change in attitudes toward women?

"Part of the reason I was hired was because I had a much different background from the clerical types [who previously handled communication]," she explained. "Females [communicators] were expected to not only write the press releases but type the envelopes, get the stamps, when we could be spending our time doing management work."

Are stereotypes of women changing?

"The president is rethinking [my role]," she replied. "Others in the organization look at me as a resource for other things . . . other than just writing or editing."

The economic development agency is taking the first steps toward communication excellence by empowering the woman who manages communication for the organization.

• A not-for-profit organization that conducts research and promotes health issues illustrates another side of communication excellence: the culture of the organization itself. "No one is left out," the CEO said of the extensive consultation system at the organization. Department heads share information at weekly liaison meetings. The organization uses its universal voice mail system extensively.

"It's simple," the top communicator said of the organization's highly participative culture, "we talk to each other." In addition, she often spends days with field staff "doing what they do." The top communicator stressed "keeping in touch with the real world" by "working in the trenches" to gather valuable feedback from volunteers and local affiliated associations. This not-for-profit health organization built communication excellence, partly because the nurturing character of the organization encourages participation, teamwork, and two-way communication.

These four organizations provide snapshots of different qualities of communication excellence. We picked them from the organizations that participated in both the initial survey and the case study follow-ups to the Excellence Study. This is the largest, most intensive investigation ever conducted of public relations and communication management. Nearly a decade in the planning, execution, and reporting of results, this $400,000 study will affect communication practices and scholarship well into the 21th century. (See the appendix for details about how the study was conducted.)

In 1990–1991, top communicators, their bosses, and a sampling of employees in 321 organizations in Canada, the United Kingdom, and the United States completed questionnaires. These questionnaires provided over 1,700 separate pieces of information about communication practices in these organizations. In 1994, 24 organizations from the original 321 participated in case studies. These case studies included face-to-face interviews, phone interviews, and an examination of communication materials.

The Excellence Study continues to spawn new research in other nations. Translated versions of all or parts of the questionnaires have been administered in Greece, India, Slovenia, and Taiwan.

KEY CHARACTERISTICS OF COMMUNICATION EXCELLENCE

By sifting and organizing information from the study and by examining it from various perspectives, the research team identified a set of key characteristics that distinguish excellent from less-than-excellent programs.[1] This book provides communicators with powerful tools to pursue communica-

---

[1]The phrase *less than excellent* is used throughout this book to describe organizations with overall Excellence Scores lower than those in "excellent" organizations. These terms are relative, meaning than an organization or group of organizations are "less-than-excellent" in comparison to some other organization or group. No organization studied was fully "excellent" with regard in communication, nor was any organization without some aspects of communication excellence.

tion excellence in their organizations.[2] This is not a cookbook or manual—
you will not find "10 easy steps to communication excellence." It runs
deeper, with a compelling logic that is at once more elegant and less clut-
tered than any 10-step, how-to guide.

To fully appreciate what it is, communication managers should understand what communication excellence is not. Some aspects run counter to
our gut-level expectations.

SURPRISES ABOUT EXCELLENT COMMUNICATION

At speaking engagements in a dozen nations around the world, the research
team has discovered four recurring communicator expectations about what
the Excellence Study would or should show. After we present our findings,
audiences often pose questions or make statements about excellence. Let's
address those first.

"Yes, But What About MY Industry?"

Many people expect concepts of excellence to be different, depending on
the industry, types of organization, or nationality. Instead, we found that
communication excellence is universal—It is no different in Canada, the
United Kingdom, or the United States. It is the same for corporations, not-
for-profit organizations, government agencies, and trade or professional
associations. That is because communication excellence involves knowledge
or expertise that transcends any particular public, organizational division or
unit, industry, organizational type, or national setting. The traditional communicator crafts that a practitioner needs to communicate with employees
in a large manufacturing corporation may differ from the specific communicator crafts that a trade association needs to communicate with legislators or
regulators. Specialized, traditional communicator crafts do not define excellence. Although excellent communication programs do have strong traditional crafts (see chapter 4), communication excellence is something more
than technique.

"Can You Name the Organization with Perfect Communication?"

As mentioned in the introduction, communication excellence represents an
ideal or perfect state that no organization can reasonably expect to achieve
fully. There is no one organization that the Excellence research team can
point to and say: "Communication in that organization is fully excellent in

---

[2]This book does not directly address this audience, although many scholars and students will
find this book informative and useful.

all regards, so go copy it!" In fact, when we looked at how the study's top dozen organizations performed on all of the indicators that made up their overall excellence scores, several measures were only somewhat better than average.

Why? Each organization has multiple measures that, when appropriately weighted and combined, provide an overall measure of communication excellence. If we think of these multiple measures of excellence as an organization's report card, then even the top performers had some Bs. None had "straight As." The statistical tools used to generate report cards for organizations isolated important qualities of excellence from actual organizations studied. Then these qualities were extrapolated to determine what *perfection* would mean for each one. Although every organization studied had some elements of communication excellence, and some achieved higher levels than others, none was perfect. Think of perfect communication as you would think of perfect parenting: a lofty goal to pursue, but probably not fully achievable in the real world.

"Can Our Communication Department Be Excellent When Our CEO Isn't?"

No. We found we could not separate excellence from the role that communication management plays in running organizations. We communicators award gold quills and silver anvils to our outstanding peers. Indeed, such recognition for outstanding performance is an important function of professional associations. But the very phrase *communication excellence* suggests an artificial separation of communication from all the other organizational contributors to overall effectiveness.

As discussed later in the chapter, you can not have communication excellence if you don't have a shared understanding with senior management about communication and its function in organizations. You may have the potential for excellence in your communication department, but unless senior management values communication and supports it, and unless communicators and senior management share a common understanding of communication's function and role, you cannot establish an excellent program.

"Why Are My Writing and Editing Skills Devalued?"

Findings from the Excellence Study do not devalue the traditional skills of professional communicators. Chapter 4 provides a detailed analysis of the important contribution that traditional communicator crafts make to excellence. The study does show that such traditional skills, no matter how highly developed, are alone not enough for communication excellence. Excellence is not an "either/or" choice between traditional skills and new expertise.

Excellence is a matter of "both together," the organic integration of the old and new.

For example, in the chapters that follow, we make distinctions between one-way and two-way models of communication practices, and between the technician and manager roles that communicators play in organizations. Such distinctions are very powerful, because they help us isolate key underlying characteristics of communicator models and roles. In making these distinctions, however, remember that no program is purely one way or two way. No communicator plays the manager or technician role exclusively. In the textured, multilayered complexity of real-world practices, one-way and two-way models of communication practices work in tandem. Most communicators play both manager and technician roles to varying degrees each day.

In case studies of organizations with excellent communication programs, we found that strategic planners worked side by side with highly skilled, artistic specialists in the communication department, individuals who played the technician role predominantly. This synergism was perhaps best described by Lester Potter, communication account manager for the American Red Cross, at the 1994 IABC conference, when he said, "It's not just doing things right; it's also doing the right things." In less-than-excellent communication programs, communicators often do things right: for example, an award-winning photograph or an attractive annual report. The Excellence Study shows that communication excellence will not be achieved by simply improving how you do things right. For example, new desktop publishing software may help a less-than-excellent employee communication program get the newsletter out faster, but that alone will not make a less-than-excellent employee communication program excellent. Excellent programs integrate "doing things right" with "doing the right things." As we indicate in chapter 4, excellence means doing the right things right.

WHAT THE EXCELLENCE STUDY DISCOVERED

Imagine a mountain of questionnaires—some 100 pages of questionnaires from each of 321 organizations studied in Canada, the United Kingdom, and the United States, with over 1,700 pieces of information from each organization's CEO, its top communicator, and a sampling of other employees.[3] How do you find the essential attributes of communication excellence in all this information?

The research team needed to answer that question when we first faced

---

[3]Of the 321 participating organizations, 51 did not provide a complete set of questionnaires from CEOs, top communicators, and employees. However, information was used from these organizations whenever appropriate.

TABLE 1.1
The Communication Excellence Factor

Knowledge Base of Communication Department	Source
• Knowledge to play the communication manager role	TC
• Knowledge to use the two-way symmetrical model	TC
• Knowledge to use the two-way asymmetrical model	TC

Shared Expectations About Communication with Senior Management	Source
• Value dominant coalition (senior management) places on communication	TC
• Support dominant coalition (senior management) gives to communication	TC
• Contributions of communication department to strategic planning	TC
• Top communicator reports playing communication manager role	TC
• Top communicator reports playing senior adviser role	TC
• Perceived demand for two-way symmetrical practices	TC
• Perceived demand for two-way asymmetrical practices	TC
• Support dominant coalition (senior management) gives to communication	CEO
• Value dominant coalition (senior management) places on communication	CEO
• Importance of knowledge–communication with external groups	CEO
• Demand for two-way asymmetrical practices from dominant coalition	CEO
• Demand for two-way symmetrical practices from dominant coalition	CEO
• Demand for communication manager role from dominant coalition	CEO
• Demand for senior adviser role from dominant coalition	CEO
• Contributions of communication department to strategic planning	CEO

Organizational Culture	Source
• Support for female employees in the organization*	TC
• Participative organizational culture	EMP

Legend: TC = Top communicator questionnaire
CEO = CEO (or other dominant coalition member) questionnaire
EMP = Employee questionnaires (answers aggregated for all employees)

*This measure of organizational support for women, as reported by the top communicator, posted a higher factor loading than its placement in this table would indicate. However, this item was placed here because of its logical linkage to organizational culture.

just such a mountain of information in late 1991, as the survey phase of the study drew to a close. All the information was entered into computers and analyzed. The research team successfully isolated 20 key characteristics of communication excellence in organizations. These key characteristics of communication excellence are displayed in Table 1.1, from the most important at the top of the list to the least important at the bottom.

The 20 items[4] in Table 1.1 fall into three rough groupings. The top three items, the best indicators of communication excellence, involve departmental expertise in sophisticated communication practices, as reported on the

---

[4]The term *items* is used loosely here. In most instances, a number of items were summed together to produce an index or scale, rather than rely on a single measure. For example, eight separate items were used to measure the communication department's knowledge to play the communication manager role.

top communicator questionnaire. The next 15 items involve shared expectations about communication, as reported by the top communicator and the CEO. The final two items measure qualities of organizational culture: The first measures the support that organizations provide to female employees; the second measures teamwork, shared decision making, and common goals, as reported by samplings of employees in each organization.

Before examining the Excellence Factor in more detail, let us first consider an important question: How do we know that this particular grouping of questionnaire items is, indeed, a measure of communication excellence?

First, measures were compared to what the theory of communication excellence suggested.[5] The most compelling argument about the Excellence Factor is that the interpretation makes sense, both by the logic of theory and through observation of what communicators, CEOs, and employees reported.

Second, we examined return on investment for communication expenditures for "most-excellent" and "least-excellent" programs.[6] In the survey, CEOs were asked to estimate benefits that their organizations received from the dollars or pounds invested in communication. If the CEO said the organization received one dollar back for each dollar spent on communication, then communication benefits were even with costs. If two dollars in benefits were received for each communication dollar spent, then communication provided the organization with a positive return on investment.

The CEO's evaluation of return on investment is, admittedly, subjective. But consider this: The CEO's judgments about costs and benefits are the very judgments that will determine if your budget and staff increase or decrease next year! Further, no other manager in the organization has the same vantage point as the CEO.

The average return on investment from the CEOs in organizations with most-excellent communication programs was $2.66 for every dollar invested in communication. In contrast, CEOs of organizations with least-excellent communication programs reported only a $1.46 average return on investment for each dollar spent on communication. CEOs with most-excellent communication programs—as defined by the Excellence Study and as isolated in the Excellence Factor—see greater return on investment for communication expenditures than do CEOs with least-excellent programs.

Exhibit 1.1 briefly describes how the research team isolated the Excellence Factor. (The appendix provides a more detailed treatment of the

---

[5]This theory is summarized in chapter 1 of *Excellence in Public Relations and Communication Management* (Grunig, 1992), and detailed throughout the balance of that book.

[6]The 30 organizations with the highest overall Excellence scores, roughly 10% of the participating organizations, were compared to the 30 organizations with the lowest overall excellence scores. This is one way to compare most-excellent to least-excellent communication in organizations. This strategy of comparing the top 10% to the bottom 10% of organizations (based on overall Excellence Scores) is used elsewhere in this book to illustrate key points.

EXHIBIT 1.1
Isolating the Communication Excellence Factor

The first step in isolating the Excellence Factor is to ask the right questions about communication excellence. The research team avoided constructing questionnaires willy nilly. Rather, we met in daylong sessions to identify questions to take maximum advantage of the research findings that came before. We reviewed not only prior works in communication and public relations, but also literature in management, organizational psychology, social psychology, sociology, cognitive psychology, feminist studies, political science, decision making, and culture. This extensive analysis of prior research is reviewed in *Excellence in Public Relations and Communication Management* (Grunig, 1992), the first volume in the series of books spawned by the Excellence Study.

With a detailed understanding of the prior research and a significant theory to test, questionnaires were constructed. Once data were collected and fed into computers, a powerful statistical tool called *factor analysis* was used to help "crunch" the numbers. Basically, this procedure groups or clusters questionnaire items together, based on how people answered the questions. Suppose you report on a questionnaire that you "frequently" make communication policy decisions in your organization. Lower in that same questionnaire, you report you "frequently" are held accountable for the success or failure of communication programs in your organization. Another communicator working for another organization reports "rarely" making communication policy decisions, nor being held accountable for communication program success or failure. These two questions, one addressing decision-making authority and the other addressing accountability, seem to "vary" together. That is, a person answering "rarely" to one question is likely to answer "rarely" to the other question as well. Another person answering "frequently" to one is likely to answer the other question in the same way. Of course, the pattern is not perfect. These two answers do not necessarily "vary" together for everyone else in the survey. But factor analysis is sensitive to patterns and trends in the data not readily visible to us if we were to leaf through a stack of questionnaires, looking for such patterns in the responses.

After considerable analysis (and many computer runs), a single factor was extracted. As indicated, this factor consisted of 20 items (see Table 1.1), grouped together by the way top communicators, CEOs, and other employees responded to items on the questionnaire. Prior research and theory building suggested which items ought to group or cluster, but the men and women who participated in the survey determined which measures actually belonged together. A more detailed explanation is available in the *Initial Data Report and Practical Guide* (IABC Research Foundation, 1991).

research design and execution of the Excellence Study.) The three groupings of items on the Excellence Factor displayed in Table 1.1 are considered in detail next.

THE THREE SPHERES OF COMMUNICATION EXCELLENCE

Think of communication excellence as three spheres, one inside another. These spheres, which graphically represent and summarize the essence of the Excellence Factor, are displayed in Fig. 1.1. Viewed this way, the structure is quite simple.

At the core—the sphere at the center—is the knowledge base of the communication department. Surrounding the core is a larger sphere in which the core knowledge base is embedded.

This middle sphere represents a set of shared expectations about communication between top communicators and senior managers in organizations. These shared expectations create linkages between the communication department and those powerful people who run organizations and make

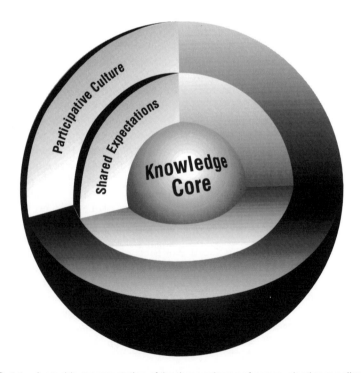

FIG. 1.1   A graphic representation of the three spheres of communication excellence.

strategic decisions. One linkage is the demand for communication excellence from senior management. A second reciprocal link is the delivery of such excellence from the communication department.

Both the knowledge core and the sphere of shared expectations are embedded in a larger sphere of organizational culture. Generally, participative cultures based on teamwork and broad-based decision making tend to nurture communication excellence. One important quality of organizational culture is the support that organizations provide to female employees. Organizations that support such employees also nurture communication excellence.

The Core Sphere of Communicator Knowledge

Most communication departments have creative technicians[7] who can write and edit, handle technical aspects of production, and know about photography and graphics. These communicators are often asked to edit, for grammar and spelling, the writing of others in the organization. Both excellent and less-than-excellent communication programs have such creative, skilled technicians. In itself, enhancing these technical skills does not lead to excellence.

Rather, the core knowledge base that distinguishes excellent from less-than-excellent communication involves management role playing, especially strategic management. Does your communication department have the expertise to contribute to strategic planning? Do you all have the knowledge base to make communication policy decisions and then be held accountable for program success and failure? Can you outline communication program alternatives and guide senior management through a logical problem-solving process? Does the top communicator in your department consider him- or herself to be the organization's communication expert? How do other managers regard the expertise of the top communicator? More important than anything else that contributes to communication excellence, the communication department's expertise to play the communication manager role is paramount.

In most communication departments, there are technicians who know how to generate publicity for the organization. There are those who know how to handle media inquiries, provide sources and collateral materials,

---

[7]The term *technician* has a special meaning throughout this book, which is considered from several perspectives in parts I and II. *Technician* describes the predominant role of the individual communicator to provide communication products or services, usually at the direction of others. This role is not related to the decision-making processes involved in selection of the goals and objectives served by those communication activities. For this reason, a technician can be alternately described as a tactician, in contrast with other communicators who play roles as strategists.

deflect potentially damaging news about the organization, and "get our side of the story out there." These are essentially one-way communication strategies, with the communicator providing information from the organization to various publics, but not the other way around. Both excellent and less-than-excellent communication programs have such expertise. Improving one-way communication expertise, by itself, does not lead to communication excellence.

The knowledge that distinguishes excellent from less-than-excellent communication programs involves two-way communication. Does anyone in your department know how to moderate a focus group and interpret the information collected? Does your department have the expertise to put together an unbiased questionnaire that will provide the information needed to make decisions? Do you know how to sample publics, administer the questionnaire, and analyze the results? Can anyone in the communication department help other managers make sense of the survey results? Do communicators know how to monitor phone and mail complaints as a tool to keep senior management posted about emerging trends and issues that affect the organization? Do the communicators know how to act as your organization's eyes and ears?

Most forms of two-way communication involve specialized knowledge about formal and informal research.[8] However, two-way communication may be either symmetrical or asymmetrical, reflecting two distinctly different assumptions or worldviews about the nature of relationships between organizations and publics. Exhibit 1.2 provides a brief synopsis of the distinctions between two-way symmetrical and two-way asymmetrical communication.

At one extreme, two-way asymmetrical communication can help organizations persuade publics to think and behave as your organization desires. Using this model, the scope of the communication function does not include persuading senior management to change its thinking and behavior about a particular policy or issue. In terms of game theory, organizations play asymmetrical communication as a "zero-sum" game: Your organization "wins" only if the public or publics "lose."[9]

---

[8]We use the term *research* in its widest sense. Citizen advisory panels, informal meetings with activist leaders, the "Speak Up" section of an employee newsletter, and employee–management forums can all serve as forms of research to detect communication and public relations problems. These activities become research when they are seen as mechanisms for gathering information about publics. Likewise, listening to senior managers or members of the board of directors discuss policies, procedures, or proposed actions can also be regarded as research.

[9]Some adherents to this model suggest that organizations persuade publics to behave in a manner that is in everybody's best interest. Health campaigns, for example, attempt to persuade people to stop smoking or reduce the fat in foods they eat. The assumption that the organization knows what's best for the publics they manipulate is a dangerous one, as documented by the numerous innovations that later turned out to have dangerous unintended effects.

EXHIBIT 1.2
Distinguishing Two-Way Symmetrical and Two-Way Asymmetrical
Communication

Four models of communication and public relations practices are recognized. The press agentry and public information models of communication and public relations practices are one-way models, emphasizing the flow of information outward from an organization's senior managers to various publics. Communicators using these models do not serve as channels of information from publics back into management decision making.

The two-way asymmetrical model is more sophisticated than the one-way models of communication practices, because the communicator plays an important role in gathering information about publics for management decision making. Using this model, communicators develop messages that are most likely to persuade publics to behave as the organization wants. Under the two-way asymmetrical model, the information communicators collect about publics is not used to modify the goals, objectives, policies, procedures, or other forms of organizational behavior.

The two-way symmetrical model also requires the sophisticated use of knowledge and understanding of publics to counsel senior management and execute communication programs. However, such two-way communication seeks to manage conflict and promote mutual understanding with key publics. Under this model, communicators seek to negotiate solutions to conflicts between their organizations and key publics. To use an overworked phrase properly, communicators practicing the two-way symmetrical model seek "win–win" solutions to conflicts with publics. Communicators play a somewhat paradoxical role as advocates of the organization's interests in negotiations with key publics but advocates of the publics' interests in discussions with the organization's strategic planners and decision makers.

On the other extreme, two-way symmetrical communication serves as a tool for negotiation and compromise, a way to develop "win–win" solutions for conflicts between organizations and publics. Specifically, senior management may change what it knows, how it feels, and the way the organization behaves as a result of symmetrical communication. In game theory, organizations play symmetrical communication as a positive sum game. Both your organization and the publics involved can win as a result of negotiation and compromise.

Arguably, symmetrical communication provides one foundation for ethical practices, because communicators play an active role as advocates of the publics' interests in strategic decision making. When symmetrical communication practices prevail, communication and public relations make valuable contributions to society as a whole.

In the rough-and-tumble, everyday world, however, communicators alternately negotiate and persuade, depending on the situation. The excellent communicator advises senior management and knows how to use both the symmetrical and asymmetrical models of communication. Indeed, game theorists suggest that public relations and communication management is more practically viewed as a mixed motive game. The organization and its publics realize that pursuing a strict zero sum game strategy is destructive to the interests of all parties. At the same time, all parties will seek to better their own special interests when situations permit.

To practice two-way communication, communicators need a body of knowledge about research methods and interpretation derived from the social sciences. Research (the other half of two-way communication) can serve both symmetrical and asymmetrical outcomes. Deciding when to persuade publics and when to negotiate and compromise with publics is more art than science. Given this, you and your department might benefit from the Communicator's Serenity Prayer: "Grant us the serenity to compromise with publics we cannot change, the courage to persuade publics we can change (when it is socially responsible to do so), and the wisdom to know the difference."

Middle Sphere of Shared Expectations

At its core, the communication department must have communicators with the knowledge to play the manager role, contribute to strategic decision making, and execute two-way communication programs.[10] Communicator expertise, the necessary foundation of excellence, cannot build excellence in isolation. To build excellent programs, communicators must forge partnerships with the organization's dominant coalition. The dominant coalition is the group of individuals in organizations with the power to set directions. Exhibit 1.3 provides a brief explanation of dominant coalitions as examined in the Excellence Study.

Communicators are linked to dominant coalitions in organizations with excellent programs by a specific set of shared understandings or expectations about the following questions: What is communication management? What should communication do for this organization? What role does communication play in the overall management of this organization? In what ways can communication benefit this organization? In the Excellence Study, CEOs with excellent communication programs answered these questions differently than did CEOs with less-than-excellent programs.

In organizations with excellent communication programs, dominant coalitions value communicators for their input before decisions are made. In this strategic role, the communicator acts as boundary spanner, environ-

---

[10]Not every communicator in the department must have the expertise to perform all of these functions. Rather, the department as a whole must have such expertise among its full-time and part-time employees, including consultants.

EXHIBIT 1.3
About Dominant Coalitions

The phrase *dominant coalition* comes from management science and organizational theory, identifying that group of people with the power to set directions and affect structure in organizations. We used the phrase *senior management* as a substitute for *dominant coalition*, in the introduction, but the phrase *senior management* is not strictly a synonym for *dominant coalition*.

The dominant coalition is the group of individuals within an organization with the power to affect the structure of the organization, define its mission, and set its course through strategic choices the coalition makes. Top levels of the organizational chart typically identify some dominant coalition members, but dominant coalitions are often informal alliances. Such coalitions can include others who are low on the organizational chart or missing from it altogether. Individuals who control a scarce and valued resource can be included in dominant coalitions, as can those who are central to the network of decision makers in organizations. Communicators may be members of dominant coalitions, even though the organizational chart indicates otherwise. Among organizations with excellent communication programs, CEOs often identified the top communicator as a member of the dominant coalition, although this was not always the case.

In the Excellence Study, we asked CEOs and top communicators to identify the group of powerful people in their organization who are represented in this power elite. This allowed the research team to ask questions about dominant coalitions, to see if top communicators and CEOs held a common or shared understanding about what dominant coalitions want from communicators and the communication department.

---

mental scanner, and an "early warning system." Such communicators tell the dominant coalition what publics know, how they feel, and how they may behave relevant to strategic decisions under consideration. In a sense, communicators act as advocates for publics, articulating those external points of view as they counsel dominant coalitions. When decisions are made, excellent communicators design programs and craft messages to effectively communicate in a fashion that achieves the dominant coalition's desired outcomes among targeted publics. To play this role as a two-way communicator, the top communicator sits at the decision-making table with other senior managers, either formally or informally. That is, the top communicator plays the manager role. After all, how could informed strategic decisions be made that affect relationships with key publics, if the organization's expert on relations is not at the table? The top communicator contributes to strategic management and planning.

In organizations with less-than-excellent communication programs, dominant coalitions see communication essentially as one way: from top management to publics. Communicators, hired largely for their technical expertise

FIG. 1.2. The demand–delivery linkage for communication excellence.

as writers and such, are brought in after decisions are made. Their expertise is sought solely to help disseminate information in support of dominant coalition objectives. The dominant coalition sees no value in sitting a skilled craftsperson such as the top communicator at the decision-making table. After all, they reason, what could such a technician or tactician in a support function like communications contribute to strategy?[11]

If the dominant coalition understands the meaning of communication excellence, and if the communicators have the knowledge base to provide such excellence, then critical linkages evolve between the communication department and the dominant coalition. We can think of the dominant coalition as demanding excellence from the organization's communicators. When communicators understand that demand and are able to deliver excellence in response, a demand–delivery linkage is established. This demand–delivery linkage, which is displayed in Fig. 1.2, describes an ongoing relationship between communicators and dominant coalitions. Over time, expectations and performance reinforce each other. When dominant coalitions expect communicators to think strategically to solve a problem or conflict with a key public, that reinforces the knowledge or expertise in the communication department to deliver communication excellence. When communicators respond strategically to help solve a problem important to

---

[11]The term *communications* (with a trailing *s*) is used here to distinguish *communication* as a management function from *communications* as discrete sets of messages fashioned by technical support staff to implement communication policy decisions made by other managers in the organization.

the dominant coalition, that reinforces the strategic view of communication in the dominant coalition. The dominant coalition comes to value and support the communication department. Such political support from the dominant coalition is integral to the set of shared expectations that lead to communication excellence.

The Outer Sphere of Participative Culture

Every organization has its own history, its own approach to decision making, its own way of treating its employees, and its own way of dealing with the world outside. Despite this uniqueness, the character or culture of organizations is not idiosyncratic. Indeed, regular patterns underlie seemingly diverse organizations and their cultures. In the Excellence Survey, 4,620 employees in the participating organizations answered questions about their organization's culture. The research team based the measures of organizational culture on a thorough review of prior research.[12] Two basic forms of organizational culture emerged from our analysis: participative and authoritarian. Each organization has attributes of both participative cultures and authoritarian cultures. However, the values of one culture—participatory or authoritarian—typically predominate in each organization.

Organizations with predominantly participative cultures infuse their employees with shared values, pulling employees together as a team to accomplish a common mission. Open to outside ideas, these organizations favor innovation and adaptation over tradition and domination.

Participative cultures provide a superior setting for excellent communication. Such cultures provide nurturing conditions for excellent programs. Organizations that value teamwork, widely involve employees in decision making, and are open to ideas from outside the organization are more likely to have excellent programs. A participative culture is one of the characteristics that make up the Excellence Factor.

Theory suggests that authoritarian organizations—closed to outside ideas, with worldviews favoring asymmetrical communication—would place little value on excellent public relations and communication management. The degree to which an organization's culture is authoritarian, however, does not seem to make much difference to communication excellence. Participative organizational cultures provide a favorable environment for excellent communication, but excellent communication departments and programs sometimes occur in organizations with predominantly authoritarian cultures. Fig. 1.3 provides a graphic representation of the participative and authoritarian cultural values that exist in varying degrees in every organization.

---

[12]See chapter 21 in Grunig (1992).

FIG. 1.3.   Participative and authoritarian cultures in organizations.

What sense can we make of this? Communicators build excellent communication programs when they have the knowledge base to do so. Dominant coalitions help them build such programs by sharing an understanding of the communication function and by demanding excellence. The performance of communicators—the delivery of two-way communication in a department managed strategically—completes the linkage. As noted previously, participative culture is more conducive to excellence than is an authoritarian culture. But organizational culture is more peripheral to communication excellence, the outer sphere in our model in Fig. 1.1. The nurturing environment of a participative culture cannot create sophisticated expertise in communication departments, nor cause dominant coalitions to demand strategic, two-way programs from communicators.

Professional communicators should pay special attention to one aspect of an organization's culture and values: the treatment of women and related issues of ethnic diversity. In 1994, the U.S. Department of Labor reported that about 60% of American communicators and public relations practitioners are women, up from 25% in the 1960s. Similar shifts are occurring in Canada and the United Kingdom. Reflecting a profession in which the majority are women, the status and power of communication departments in organizations are closely linked to the status of women in those organizations. Theoretically, progressive organizations take steps to make optimum use of all human resources, including women and those from culturally diverse backgrounds. When organizations actively support the advancement of women and those from culturally diverse groups, they are more likely to build excellent communication programs.

Data from the Excellence Survey support this logic. The treatment of women, from basic support (flex time, child-care assistance) to nondiscrimination policies to advancement programs (mentoring, training), is part of the Excellence Factor. Organizations that provide basic support and enhance the professional growth of female employees posted higher overall communication excellence scores than organizations that did not.

The Excellence Factor, as represented in Fig. 1.1, provides a concrete measure of the theory of communication excellence described in chapters 1 and 3 of *Excellence in Public Relations and Communication Management* (Grunig, 1992). The theory of excellence in that book only suggested the right questions to ask. The research team in the Excellence Study uncovered and extracted the Excellence Factor from patterns in the answers provided by communicators, CEOs, and other employees in the organizations that participated. In short, the Excellence Factor was constructed by the participants in the study. The representation of communication excellence in Fig. 1.1 simply restates what study participants told us about excellence.

This chapter provides a terse summary of communication excellence. In part I of this text, the core sphere of communication excellence—the expertise or knowledge in the communication department—is analyzed in greater detail. Part II analyzes the complex set of shared understandings and expectations about communication between top communicators and dominant coalitions in organizations. Part III examines the role that organizational culture plays in communication excellence. Related to culture and communication excellence is the support and opportunities for women and culturally diverse groups as employees of organizations. In part IV, the three spheres of communication excellence are linked to the execution of specific programs for specific publics.

REFERENCES

Grunig, J. E. (Ed.). (1992). *Excellence in public relations and communication management.* Hillsdale, NJ: Lawrence Erlbaum Associates.

IABC Research Foundation. (1991). *Initial data report and practical guide.* San Francisco: Author.

Part I

Communicator Knowledge Base

In this first part of the book, we consider the inner core of communication excellence: the knowledge base of the communication department. In the chapters that follow, we examine the expertise in communication departments to play a senior-level strategic role in managing communication and public relations programs, as well as contributing to the overall strategic management of the organization. This knowledge we call *manager role expertise.*

Intricately wrapped up with manager role expertise is departmental knowledge to use cutting-edge practices that position communicators as the eyes and ears of organizations, as well as spokespersons. A key quality of excellence is two-way communication, with communication departments using formal and informal research to gather information about publics to interpret and share with senior management. Senior managers can use such information to manipulate or persuade publics to do as organizations want them to—that's asymmetrical communication. Alternatively, managers can use that information to negotiate and compromise, seeking win–win solutions to conflicts that build long-term relationships, benefiting both organizations and publics—that's symmetrical communication. Departmental knowledge to play the manager role is insufficient without the expertise to practice two-way symmetrical and two-way asymmetrical communication. Fig. I.1 displays the three components of the knowledge base of an excellent communication department.

What about the traditional communicator craft? The ability to write, edit, take photographs, work with graphics, and handle the myriad aspects of production are an important part of excellent communication and public

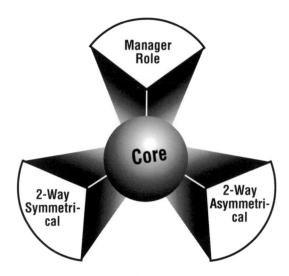

FIG. I.1.   The three components of the knowledge base of an excellent communication department.

relations departments. Excellent communication departments have greater expertise in these technical areas than do less-than-excellent departments. However, such technical expertise alone is not what makes excellent programs excellent: The best communication programs achieve excellence through the strategic use of such craft expertise to solve important problems or create important opportunities for senior management.

We wrap up part I by considering steps communicators can take to increase personal and departmental knowledge to practice excellent communication.

2

Knowing How to Manage Strategically

Of all the measures made of participating organizations, one set does the best job of measuring communication excellence.[1] That set measures knowledge of those individuals in the communication department to play the role of communication manager. The expertise to play the manager role is closely tied to expertise in engaging in two-way practices. We think that manager role knowledge is necessary but not sufficient by itself to establish excellent communication programs. The research team developed five questionnaire items to determine this expertise, and included those items in the top communicator's questionnaire. These items are shown in Table 2.1.

Two items in Table 2.1 directly measure strategic expertise. Two other items measure the department's expertise to use research in managing the communication function. The final item, knowledge to prepare the department's budget, reflects an operational aspect of manager expertise with strategic implications.

Since the 1970s, communication and public relations scholars have studied the roles that communicators play in organizations. Exhibit 2.1 provides a brief overview of the communication manager role. In the Excellence

---

[1]The Excellence Factor is made up of many measures of excellence. Some measures of communication excellence have higher factor loadings than do others. We interpret high factor loadings to indicate a high correlation of the item with the underlying dimension (excellence) that the factor measures. In this sense, the item with the highest factor loading is a closer or even a better indicator of the underlying dimension of excellence than are the other items. In this case, the item is actually an index, made up of five items from the top communicator questionnaire that were summed to create a single measure of "knowledge of manager role." See Exhibit 1.1 for a more detailed explanation of factor analysis and the Excellence Factor.

TABLE 2.1
Department Expertise or Knowledge to Play Communication Manager
Role*

The Tasks

- Manage the organization's response to issues
- Use research to segment publics
- Develop goals and objectives for your department
- Conduct evaluation research
- Prepare department budget

---

*On their questionnaires, top communicators were asked about "tasks requiring special expertise or knowledge that is available in some public relations or communication departments but not in others." Top communicators were asked to report "the extent to which your department or someone in the department has the expertise or knowledge to perform each task."

EXHIBIT 2.1
About the Communication Manager Role

The communication manager role is an abstraction of a set of repeated behaviors of professional communicators in organizations. Roles of communicators typically are measured by asking respondents how frequently they engage in a number of organizational activities. The manager role actually consists of three conceptually distinct activities, as first theorized by Broom (1982). The first, the expert prescriber role, is similar to the traditional doctor–patient role. The expert prescriber is an acknowledged expert on communication in the organization, best informed about communication issues, and best qualified to answer communication and public relations questions. The second role, the communication facilitator role, means acting as a go-between, facilitating communication between management and publics. Finally, the problem-solving process facilitator role means helping management think through problems and issues systematically to find a solution.

The notion of communication manager was introduced when factor analysis of several communicator surveys showed that the expert prescriber, communication facilitator, and problem-solving process facilitator roles are played interchangeably by the same communicators. Subsequent research over the last 10 years has consistently has shown that the communication manager role is the most parsimonious way to think of expert prescription, communication facilitation, and problem-solving facilitation in communication roles. Communicators who predominantly play the manager role tend to earn higher salaries than communicators who predominantly play the technician role, even with equal years of professional experience. Those predominantly playing the communication manager role participate more frequently in dominant coalition decision making. In the 1980s, several studies indicated that women were less likely than men to predominantly play the manager role, even when they had equal years of professional experience. However, at least one study from the 1990s indicates that such gender discrimination may be waning (Dozier & Broom, 1995).

Study, we wanted to examine role knowledge or expertise, as well as actual role playing.

WHY DEPARTMENTAL KNOWLEDGE IS SO IMPORTANT

Before examining the measures of communication knowledge in detail, let us keep in mind three key points about communicator expertise. First, the knowledge base is primary, providing the necessary foundation for all other aspects of communication excellence.[2] Second, knowledge or expertise is a characteristic of the department, not necessarily of a single individual.[3] Third, knowledge alone cannot establish excellent communication programs.[4]

The idea of manager role playing takes several forms in the Excellence Factor. The degree to which the top communicator actually plays the manager role is one such indicator of excellence. So, too, are the manager role expectations of the top communicator from the organization's dominant coalition. However, these other aspects of manager role playing cannot occur unless individuals in the department have the knowledge base to perform the tasks of a communication manager.[5]

This important finding empowers communicators by placing the most central aspects of excellence directly under their control. As detailed in chapter 5, communicators can build excellence by becoming more expert in the emerging, more sophisticated aspects of communication practices.

---

[2] As several case studies indicated, however, the ability of communicators to deliver excellence and the sophistication within the dominant coalition to demand excellence operate in a circular manner, making it difficult for those involved to determine which came first, the expertise or the demand for it.

[3] Of course, one-person communication departments require much from a single communication professional. Hiring outside consultants to provide needed expertise to the communication department on an as-needed basis may be one way to expand departmental expertise.

[4] The qualities of excellence do not and cannot operate in isolation. Although knowledge to play the manager role is an essential and necessary requirement for communication excellence, manager role knowledge by itself does not lead to excellent communication programs. As detailed in part II, understanding and support from the dominant coalition is also critical. As explained in part III, participative organizational cultures also enhance the opportunities for excellent communication programs to flourish.

[5] A role closely related to the manager role is that of the senior adviser. Senior advisers require levels of expertise similar to those of managers. They differ from managers in their authority to make communication policy decisions and accountability for the success or failure of the resulting communication programs. For this reason, separate knowledge measures were not developed for the senior adviser role. However, top communicators were asked the degree to which they played the senior adviser role, and CEOs were asked if they expected senior adviser role playing from their top communicators.

The example that follows helps illustrate the importance of communicator knowledge in moving an organization toward excellence. An arts funding organization (with low overall scores on the Excellence Factor) participated in a case study follow-up in 1994. Much in this organization had changed since the Excellence Survey in 1990–1991. The top communicator at the time of the survey was assigned to the department without any previous experience in this area. The resulting communication program emphasized technical aspects of events promotion and internal communication.

In 1994, the chief executive officer (CEO) told the Excellence team that the arts organization had wanted a different approach to public relations, hoping to favorably influence public opinion in a politically conservative state generally intolerant of contemporary trends and lifestyles in artistic circles. Changes toward excellence in the arts funding organization started with a change in top communicators. The new top communicator brought sophisticated managerial expertise to the organization. As detailed in the next section, the expertise of the new top communicator set in motion a series of changes in relationships with key publics that directly benefited the organization's bottom line.

In other organizations, excellence evolved over time, with incremental increases in departmental expertise as communication personnel changed. Excellence involves the collective knowledge of the communication department. Not all managerial knowledge in the department needs to belong to a single "renaissance" communicator who is expert in all aspects of traditional and emerging communication sophistication. As the knowledge base of the profession grows, excellent departments likely will consist of complementary communicators who hold different forms of expertise but work well together.

For example, a blood bank with a high score on the Excellence Factor in 1990–1991 participated in a case study follow-up. The top communicator regarded herself, and was so regarded by others in the organization, as expert in media relations. Her college education in the 1970s reflected traditional emphasis on the technical aspects of public relations, including media relations. Another communicator in the department complemented this traditional area of expertise. Attending college in the 1980s, the subordinate had learned a new set of communicator skills, such as setting measurable goals and objectives for communication programs, conducting research to detect emerging public relations problems, segmenting publics, and measuring the effectiveness of communication programs.

In describing their working relationship, both communicators were quick to acknowledge the importance of the other's contribution to the department's overall effectiveness. Each communicator had primary areas of responsibility, based on what each knew best and what each liked best to do. In addition, some duties were swapped back and forth, depending on time demands, with both communicators being equally expert.

The CEO gave high marks to the communication department; it mattered little which communicator had the expertise. The important point, he felt, was that the department had the expertise to provide communication excellence. Emerging communicator expertise in strategic planning and research does not replace or diminish the importance of traditional communicator skills in writing, editing, graphics, media relations, and so forth. Rather, the new expertise is added to the traditional communicator's skill set to build a well-rounded, excellent communication department.

The vice president for strategic planning in a large chemical manufacturing company, who supervises corporate communications, echoed the same perspective in an interview with the Excellence team. "If I hadn't had a couple of talented communication managers," he said, "I couldn't have done anything. You can't make a silk purse out of a sow's ear."

As detailed in part II of this book, communicator expertise alone is not enough. Dominant coalitions also need to understand excellence in order to enter into a set of shared expectations with the top communicator. Organizations achieve communication excellence only when dominant coalitions value and support communication departments. Such dominant coalition support must be based on shared expectations regarding manager role playing and two-way communication practices, both symmetrical and asymmetrical. Such shared expectations presuppose new communicator expertise.

What is this new expertise? The measures of manager role expertise used in the Excellence Study are like the tip of an iceberg. These items that tap strategic knowledge and research knowledge are indicators of a much larger body of knowledge. This cutting-edge knowledge will advance the practice of public relations and communication management into the 21st century.

STRATEGIC KNOWLEDGE

Two items measuring expertise to play the manager role involve knowing how to manage communication strategically. These items measure knowledge or ability to:

- Manage the organization's response to issues.
- Develop goals and objectives for your department.

Both items involve the strategic management of relationships with publics. By *strategic management*, we mean the balancing of internal processes of organizations with external factors. The overall strategic management of organizations is inseparable from strategic management of relationships, traditionally the responsibility of the public relations or communication department.[6]

The vice president for strategic planning in a large chemical company shared this perspective with us in an interview: "In fact, everything you do strategically in a company has to do with relations with the outside world. It has to do with your relationship to the customer, your competitors, your suppliers. . . . So it's perfectly logical for the public relations function to be directly tied to the strategic function."

Sometimes, top communicators play a cutting-edge role in helping the rest of the dominant coalition tackle strategic issues more systematically. For example, a state hospital association with an excellent program (top 3% in the Excellence Study) hired a new top communicator. The CEO told us in an interview that the "core function" of his association is to understand and address issues important to member hospitals. However, the new top communicator introduced the dominant coalition to a "whole new science." He said: "When [the top communicator] came into our organization, she brought in a whole new view and way of thinking with her knowledge of communication. Then we realized how much we needed her." The new top communicator, who told us she likes to "think big," plays a leadership role in the strategic planning of her organization.

To play this senior role, communicators must know how to manage the organization's response to issues and the knowledge to set goals and objectives. This means that communicators must have the expertise to identify the desired relationships an organization seeks to build and maintain with key stakeholders or publics. Communicators specify these desired relationships through the goals and objectives of communication programs.

Often, desired relationships are affected by the organization's response to issues important to key publics. By managing responses to issues strategically, desired relationships can be built or maintained with key stakeholders. The arts organization mentioned earlier illustrates both strategic measures of manager role expertise.

Managing Responses to Issues

The arts funding organization sought to communicate benefits of strong community arts programs to the positive social development of "at-risk" youths. Successful communication of this message helped change the exist-

---

[6]This perspective comes from several scholars of organizations. For example, see Higgins (1979), who defined *strategic management* as "the process of managing the pursuit of the . . . organizational mission coincident with managing the relationship of the organization to its environment" (p. 1).

ing relationship of the arts funding organization with state legislators—key stakeholders with the power to approve or reject arts funding.

In the past, the arts funding organization had failed to connect the arts with combating juvenile delinquency. Through its support of community arts programs, the organization found a way to connect with legislators who could see political benefits of combatting juvenile delinquency, rather than the political costs of supporting artists with unconventional lifestyles and progressive viewpoints. The issue of at-risk youths provided the framework for a new relationship between the arts organization and legislators.

Strategic Goals and Objectives

The communication department set goals and objectives to increase funding levels for the arts organization, a clear, bottom-line measure of communication performance for an organization such as this. Contrast this strategic knowledge with tactical knowledge in communication. Traditional expertise in communication involves tactical knowledge. Tactical knowledge involves the expertise to target messages to publics through appropriate media. What is the best way to package key message points? If we want to communicate with state legislators, as the arts funding organization did, should we have one-on-one meetings or a leadership breakfast? If we want to communicate with community arts program participants throughout the state, should we use a newsletter or a videotape magazine format?

Such tactical decisions are important. Tactical knowledge of communication aided the arts funding organization in the execution of communication programs. In the final analysis, however, excellence of the arts funding communication program must be judged by the relationships it established or maintained, not by the quality of communication products as an end in themselves.

Tactical knowledge cannot operate in a vacuum and still achieve communication excellence. Tactical knowledge comes to the fore after strategic knowledge has been employed to make decisions about the relationships desired with key publics. All too often, communicators write tactical goals and objectives: the number of issues of the employee publication to be produced next quarter, or the number of news releases to be produced during the next budget cycle. Called *process measures*, such goals and objectives confuse means and ends. Strategically speaking, communication products are not an end in themselves—they are tools used in the pursuit of desired relationships with key publics. Tactical decisions about messages and media remain important, but clearly subordinate to the consequence of strategic decisions reflected in the goals and objectives for communication programs.

RESEARCH KNOWLEDGE

Another two items that measure manager role expertise involve research. These items asked top communicators about departmental expertise to:

- Use research to segment publics.
- Conduct evaluation research.

In communication, research takes many forms. Some organizations use formal and informal techniques to identify emerging issues that may affect their organizations, tracking public opinion regarding those issues. Some organizations seek to define publics dynamically, based on how publics are affected by the organization and how they may behave toward the organization. Some organizations hold communication programs accountable by asking communicators to evaluate the impact of programs on the awareness, knowledge, opinions, and behaviors of publics. All of these are examples of research applications.

We view research as an innovation in the public relations profession, a new idea spreading through the ranks of professional communicators. With changes in national accrediting standards that came in the early 1990s, higher education has begun to place greater emphasis on basic research training for future communicators. Professional communicator associations such as the International Association of Business Communicators (IABC) and the Public Relations Society of America (PRSA) offer one- and two-day workshops on research.

Despite these efforts, the use of research in public relations and communication management remains an infrequent practice (Dozier, 1990). The recent advent of research training in colleges and universities provides only one explanation. Also important is individual communicator resistance to learning research methods. As individuals who have high verbal skills but, frequently, lower interest and aptitude in quantitative skills, many communicators have a profound distaste for anything mathematical or statistical.[7] Despite this, research techniques are skills essential for communication managers.

Research to Segment Publics

The knowledge to use research is critical to communication excellence. Specific to playing the manager role, communication departments need the research expertise to, among other things, segment publics and evaluate

---

[7]As teachers of research to future communicators, we have learned that an important milestone is achieved in any communication research methods course when the student overcomes an initial resistance to research and discovers how interesting and useful its applications are in public relations and communication management.

programs. As detailed in chapter 3, research also plays an important role in two-way practices, both symmetrical and asymmetrical.

Nine ways have been identified to segment publics (Broom & Dozier, 1990). Some strategies, such as identifying publics by organizational membership, geographic area, or demographic characteristics (age, gender, income, education, and so forth), require minimal research.[8] Other strategies, such as segmentation by psychographics,[9] covert power,[10] and role in relevant decision-making processes, require detailed research before segmentation can occur.

One powerful strategic method for segmenting publics is based on a situational theory that argues that organizations create publics when their actions have consequences for other organizations or groupings of people. "Publics come and go," Grunig and Hunt (1984) asserted, depending on "what an organization does and how people and organizations in the environment react to that organizational behavior" (p. 138). When organizations or groups of individuals in the environment are not affected in any way by an organization's behavior, they are a nonpublic. If they are affected by organizational behavior, but are not aware of this, they are a latent public. Once those affected realize they have a common problem, they become an aware public. When they organize to do something about their common problem, they become an active public.

To segment publics according to Jim Grunig's situational theory, communicators must conduct research on individuals and organizations to determine if they are affected in any way by organizational behavior, to learn if those affected are aware of this impact of organizational behavior, and to learn if those affected are communicating and organizing with each other to do something about it. Research is needed on those affected to segment them as latent, aware, or active publics.

Because active publics are the only ones that generate consequences for organizations, communicators might be tempted to ignore latent and aware publics. However, as publics become more active, communication from the organization is handled differently. Rather than simply processing information about an issue in a passive way, active publics seek out information on the organization and the issue. Active publics also evaluate messages from the organization with a critical eye. As Gossen and Sharp (1987) argued in

---

[8]That is, specifying geographic or demographic definitions of publics requires minimal research. Substantial secondary research is required to better understand publics segmented in these ways, in order to construct a useful situation analysis of who is involved or affected by the identified problem, issue, or opportunity that motivates the communication program.

[9]*Psychographics* is a term used to describe psychological and lifestyle characteristics of individuals which can be used for grouping or clustering purposes.

[10]Covert power is the unofficial influence of individuals in a community who exert considerable covert or unofficial influence over community decisions in a variety of settings and contexts.

their discussion of dispute resolution, the leadership of an activist public may stake out a rigid position in opposition to the organization, making negotiations difficult. Proactive communicators seek to communicate with latent and aware publics while there's still room for negotiation.[11]

Research to Evaluate Communication Programs

One characteristic of the communication manager role is that managers take responsibility for the success or failure of their organization's communication programs. Others in the organization likewise hold communication managers accountable for success or failure of their programs. To determine this, the communication manager must be able to do research that evaluates its impact.

The strategic success or failure of communication programs is determined by relationships between organizations and key publics. Are members of a key public knowledgeable or even aware of the organization's position on an issue of mutual concern? Do members of that public agree or disagree with the organization's position or behavior? How do members of that public behave toward the issue or the organization? Have lawsuits increased or decreased? Is employee turnover increasing or decreasing, compared to the benchmark?

To answer these questions, the communication manager must be a sophisticated practitioner—or at least a sophisticated consumer—of evaluation research. To measure the strategic effectiveness of a communication program, strategic goals and objectives first must be established that focus on relationships. Although no single design fits all evaluation settings, a minimal design for evaluation research measures the awareness, knowledge, opinions, and behaviors of members of a target public both before the communication program is executed and after the execution.[12] An initial survey of the target public provides a benchmark of awareness, knowledge, opinions, and behavior against which subsequent studies can be compared.

When communication programs incorporate a symmetrical worldview, the target public is not the only party to the relationship that is expected to change: The goals and objectives of symmetrical communication programs

---

[11]These issues are discussed in greater detail in chapter 7 of *Excellence in Public Relations and Communication Management* (Grunig, 1992). As detailed in that book, research is critical to segmenting publics in a dynamic, proactive manner.

[12]Such a minimal design is called a *one-group pretest–posttest design*. It is not strong at isolating communication program effects from other factors and influences that may also affect the target public at the same time. More powerful evaluation designs use control groups or comparison groups to control or minimize these other influences. For a more detailed discussion, see chapter 5 in Broom and Dozier (1990).

also seek to change (or maintain) awareness, knowledge, opinions, and behavior of the organization's dominant coalition. Dominant coalitions, as many communicators know from their own professional experiences, often create conflicts with key publics out of ignorance. Dominant coalitions develop ways of looking at the outside world from an insider's perspective. For example, a logging corporation may think of forests as "tree farms," emphasizing the one attribute of these complex ecosystems that best fits the corporate mission. A symmetrical communication program for such a corporation would seek to move the dominant coalition's perceptions in the direction of latent, aware, or active publics who do not regard forests as farms.

A communication specialist for a chemical manufacturing corporation in the United States encountered similar issues when she was sent to Switzerland to meet with company representatives: "They has some real issues with corporate. . . . We're ethnocentric. We use our own kind of examples. We talk about baseball, and they don't know anything about baseball. I came back and said, 'These people don't think we're attuned to their needs. And we weren't.'"

Research provides one way for dominant coalitions to become attuned to strategic publics. As detailed in chapter 3, research is essential for two-way communication, both symmetrical and asymmetrical. Focus groups and surveys are as much channels of communication as are news releases, press conferences, and internal publications. The frugal communicator can use the same focus groups and surveys of publics to set an evaluation benchmark, while educating the dominant coalition in the process. The focus of strategic symmetrical communication programs is on relationships, a coming together of the dominant coalition and members of strategic publics around issues of mutual interest. Evaluating relationships requires sophisticated expertise in research methods.

For example, a large oil company with excellent communication programs (top 3% in the Excellence Study) depends extensively on research. The oil embargo of the 1970s and the Exxon *Valdez* oil spill put all oil companies on the defensive. In response, the oil company began to hire more researchers, legislative analysts, and communicators with research sophistication. The company also began to make better use of the research talent it already had on staff. Said the research director in the communication department: "The idea kind of hit the industry by surprise, being blamed for embargoes imposed by Middle East countries. That sort of started all this. . . . We gave more recognition to the [research] profession and the importance of spending money and resources to be prepared [for] future crises."

Large companies are not the only ones conducting research. A small economic development agency with only one communicator on staff is implementing a monitoring program to measure the impact of communication on the attraction and retention of clients.

Contrast strategic evaluation of communication programs with tactical program evaluation. Communicators too often set program goals that are actually tactical objectives to produce and distribute communication products. These "process" goals and objectives are attractive, because producing communication products is largely under the control of communicators. Evaluating such tactical goals and objectives also is attractive, because evaluation may simply mean counting communication products such as news releases and internal publications and comparing the totals to those originally projected. Questions about program impact on problems, opportunities, or issues remain unanswered.

The problem with tactical communication alone is that savvy dominant coalitions will not settle for processes that do not affect the bottom line. At the chemical manufacturing company in the Excellence Study, corporate communications provides support to other departments. A "request to communicate" is sent to corporate communications from the requesting department, asking for such services as videotape productions or report preparation. Recently, the procedure was changed to include an "alignment check" by the vice president for strategic planning and public affairs. The procedure ensures that communication products serve common strategic goals. Are message points consistent? Is the audience adequately identified? Is the desired behavior defined? What are the benefits? The procedure discourages generating messages for the sake of generating messages. Rather, messages must attempt to do something.

Nearly 20 years ago, Robert Marker (1977) provided a vivid account of a dominant coalition's emerging intolerance of "safe" program evaluations that count communication products. As the press services manager at the Armstrong Cork Company, Marker was asked by a senior executive to explain the company's benefits from dollars spent on communication. Armed with a massive clip file from the previous year, Marker explained to the executive that if all the copy were laid end to end, favorable publicity would stretch from one end of the building to the other. Marker thought the executive was impressed. "I leaned back in my chair, feeling confident that the day was won. And then it came, the question no one had ever asked before: 'But what's all this worth to us?'" (p. 51).

That same question drives the Excellence Study. That short question has produced a long answer between the covers of this book. The answer, in part, is that communication processes can help organizations build strategic relationships with key publics. These relationships, in turn, are crucial to the effectiveness of organizations and, in many instances, do have measurable monetary impact.[13] The first step in linking communication to the bottom line is planning programs that focus on outcomes (relationships), and then evaluating by measuring the maintenance or change in relationships.

KNOWLEDGE OF BUDGETING

Knowledge of budgeting techniques is essential. The more strategic the communication department is, the more sophisticated budgeting issues become.[14] That is because excellent communication departments constantly adjust and restructure programs to respond dynamically to changing relations with strategic publics. Contemporary trends of downsizing and outsourcing in corporations and other organizations add additional wrinkles of complexity to budgeting communication departments and programs.

Contrast this strategic notion of structure and budgeting with "historicist" structure and budgeting (Broom, 1986). Some organizations strongly depend on "what we did last year" to make plans for next year. In these organizations, the communication department came about because of some significant event in the past. Perhaps a crisis—strike, boycott, restrictive regulations, or hostile takeover attempt—prompted the dominant coalition to create the communication department. Perhaps the department was created on the whim of a past CEO. Once created, the communication department and its budget are perpetuated over time, because "that's what we did last year."

Such routine favors departmental budgets built around costs of specific communication products and services: the annual report, the employee and stockholder magazines, the media relations staff, and so forth. Organizations like historicist routine, because such routine decisions require less effort, and less emphasis is put on justifying the communication department's existence. Our justification is simply that we were here last year. For communicators, historicist routines mean that communication programs can run year after year, like a perpetual motion machine. The process of communicating becomes an end in itself; the budget is justified by promising to do as much communicating next year as this year. The communication department's budget survives as a matter of historical routine.

Programs produced through historicist budgeting routines typically can-

---

[13]See especially chapter 16, which addresses this question in detail.

[14]In chapter 14 of *Excellence in Public Relations and Communication Management* (Grunig, 1992), we argued that the optimal communication department is organized dynamically—the department's internal structure "is flexible, configured to meet the special demands. . . . As the situation changes, as new problems are identified and new publics defined, the . . . structure changes" (p. 403).

not satisfy savvy dominant coalitions demanding strategic relevance from communication. As Robert Marker discovered when he tried to justify his budget with pounds of newspaper clippings, measures of communication process cannot answer one critical question from the dominant coalition: What is all this worth to us?

The communication manager needs to know how to budget strategically. Program planning starts with identification of the most strategic publics and the kinds of relationships that dominant coalitions want to establish and maintain with those publics. Managers build program goals and objectives around the desired relationships sought. Budgets are zero based, designed to implement the most efficient programs for the most strategic publics.[15]

Such strategic thinking can be seen at the chemical manufacturing company discussed earlier, where corporate communications was whittled down during the recession of the early 1990s, along with other departments in the organizations. As a consequence, limited resources are directed to activities where they have the most strategic impact. "When things get cut back," the top communicator of this company said, "I sacrifice quantity but not quality."

SUMMARY

Five items on the top communicators' questionnaire measured knowledge or expertise in the department to play the communication manager role. These items included the strategic expertise to both manage organizational responses to issues and set goals and objectives, the research expertise to segment publics and evaluate programs, and budgeting expertise. These items measure only the tip of the iceberg, for the knowledge base of the communication manager role runs deep. Such expertise can be spread among the entire staff of the communication department. It permits the strategic management of the communication department and its programs, focusing on relationships with key publics as outcomes rather than treating communication activity as an end in itself.

REFERENCES

Broom, G. M. (1982). A comparison of sex roles in public relations. *Public Relations Review, 8*(3), 17–22.
Broom, G. M. (1986, May). *Public relations roles and systems theory: Functional and historicist*

---

[15]In chapter 23 of *Excellence in Public Relations and Communication Management* (Grunig, 1992), we provided a more conceptual argument for this approach to strategic budgeting and planning.

causal models. Paper presented at the meeting of the Public Relations Interest Group, International Communication Association, Chicago.

Broom, G. M., & Dozier, D. M. (1990). *Using research in public relations: Applications to program management.* Englewood Cliffs, NJ: Prentice-Hall.

Dozier, D. M. (1990). The innovation of research in public relations practices: Review of a program of studies. In L. A. Grunig & J. E. Grunig (Eds.), *Public relations research annual* (Vol. 2, pp. 3–28). Hillsdale, NJ: Lawrence Erlbaum Associates.

Dozier, D. M., & Broom, G. M. (1995). Evolution of the manager role in public relations practice. *Journal of Public Relations Research, 7*(1), 3–26.

Gossen, R., & Sharp, K. (1987). Workshop: How to manage dispute resolution. *Public Relations Journal, 43*(12), 35–37.

Grunig, J. E. (Ed.). (1992). *Excellence in public relations and communication management.* Hillsdale, NJ: Lawrence Erlbaum Associates.

Grunig, J. E., & Hunt, T. (1984). *Managing public relations.* New York: Holt, Rinehart & Winston.

Higgins, H. M. (1979). *Organizational policy and strategic management: Texts and cases.* Hinsdale, IL: Dryden.

Marker, R. K. (1977). The Armstrong/pr data measurement system. *Public Relations Review, 3*(4), 51–59.

3

Knowing Two-Way
Communication Practices

To play the manager role, communicators must know advanced practices that rightfully treat communication as a two-way process. Communicators act as eyes and ears of organizations, spanning organizational boundaries with one foot firmly planted inside their organizations and the other outside. Sometimes communicators use what they know about publics to persuade those publics to act as dominant coalitions want. Such advanced practices are called *two-way asymmetrical communication*. Other times, communicators use what they know about publics to negotiate win–win solutions to conflicts, building mutually beneficial relations with publics. These advanced practices are called *two-way symmetrical communication*.

Measures of expertise in two-way asymmetrical and two-way symmetrical practices complete the knowledge sphere, the core sphere of communication excellence. This expertise is measured with items on the top communicator questionnaire that tap departmental knowledge to practice these two sophisticated forms of public relations and communication management. Knowing how to practice communication using both models makes an important contribution to overall communication excellence.

The tools of two-way communication range from simple, informal techniques to sophisticated, scientific methods. An organization with excellent communication (top 5% of the Excellence Study) provides services to the disabled. The top communicator conducts no formal research, but every phone conversation with the organization's clients is used to update an informal database on client issues. Communicators routinely ask: "Where did you get information on [disabled] services?" and "How can we provide you with better information?" Focus groups are occasionally conducted.

In contrast, a large oil company with excellent communication programs (also top 5% of the Excellence Study) has 120 professional communicators on staff and its own internal communication research department. The research department conducts ongoing public opinion surveys, using state-of-the-art polling techniques and advanced computer analysis of data.

In both organizations, communicators serve as key conduits of information about publics to senior managers. Despite striking differences between these two organizations, their communication departments have the knowledge base to act as their organizations' eyes and ears, and the expertise to practice two-way communication.

ABOUT MODELS OF COMMUNICATION AND PUBLIC RELATIONS PRACTICES

Just as roles describe patterns in the activities of individual communicators in organizations, models describe the values and a pattern of behavior (practices) that communication departments use to deal with publics. The press agentry/publicity and the public information models involve the generation of messages about organizations that are distributed to audiences or publics. These unsophisticated, one-way models date to the turn of the 20th century. The sophisticated, two-way models are evolving with the communication profession itself.

As with sophisticated roles, ignorance of the tools used in the more sophisticated models preclude their use. This, in turn, reduces the department's responsiveness or effectiveness in building and maintaining desired relationships with key publics. Exhibit 3.1 provides a brief history of public relations and communication management based on the models that guide practices. Note how sophistication and purposes of communication practices shift with each model.

As Exhibit 3.1 shows, public relations and communication practices have come a long way since railroad baron William Vanderbilt supposedly declared "The public be damned!" when its interests conflicted with his powerful corporate interests. In those early days, the Vanderbilts and the companies they owned hired communicators to help write beneficial "news." Practices today differ both in sophistication and purpose. Consider these two organizations from the Excellence Study: One organization, an insurance company, posted an overall Excellence Score in the bottom 10% of participating organizations; the other, a utility in the Midwest, posted an overall Excellence Score in the top 1%.

"We are pretty much one way, unfortunately," said the top communicator for the insurance company, noting that public relations is a support unit for the marketing department. "But we do so little public relations in the first place. And because we do not focus on public relations, the result is one-way communication. Basically, we disseminate brochures, direct mail, and press releases."

EXHIBIT 3.1
A Brief History of Models of Communication and Public Relations
Practices

A model is an abstraction, a "map" of reality that captures the important features but leaves out much of the detail. Grunig and Hunt (1984) and Cutlip, Center, and Broom (1994) traced early forms of public relations and communication management to ancient civilizations in India, Greece, and Rome.

• The earliest model of public relations practices identified by Grunig and Hunt (1984) is the publicity/press agentry model. Predominant in the late 1800s, the publicity/press agentry model emphasizes generation of media coverage of an organization or individual by any means necessary, including deception and trickery. Publicist P. T. Barnum's claim that there is "a sucker born every minute" seemed an especially appropriate critique of media gatekeepers of his time. Believing that there is no such thing as bad publicity, practitioners of this model used publicity stunts of all kinds to generate "ink."

• An innovation in the early 1900s, the public information model favors truthful disclosure of information to the media, though damaging information may not be volunteered. Good media relations generate favorable publicity in the long run. The communicator acts as a journalist, prompting the label "journalist in residence" for communicators using the public information model.

Both the publicity/press agentry model and the public information model are one-way models. Communication flows one way, from the organization through media channels to target publics.

• In the 1920s, Edward Bernays is credited with the next innovation, the two-way asymmetrical model. To "engineer consent," the communicator gathers information from target publics in order to devise effective media and message strategies. Such information gathering from publics makes organizational communication two way. But communicators might use such feedback from publics to persuade or even manipulate them into compliance with the organization's objectives.

• The next innovation in practices, the two-way symmetrical model, emerged in the late 20th century. Arthur W. Page, former vice president of public relations for AT&T, was an early practitioner of the model, combining sophisticated research with a symmetrical worldview, as captured in the quotation: "All business in a democratic country begins with public permission and exists by public approval" (Broom & Dozier, 1990, p. xi).

In both two-way models, research provides feedback from publics to management, closing the loop and making communication two way. Whereas asymmetrical communicators use research to persuade and even manipulate malleable publics to the unbending objectives of dominant coalitions, symmetrical communicators use dispute resolution techniques to negotiate mutually beneficial outcomes, involving give and take from both publics and dominant coalitions.

"We do a lot of surveying, a lot of focus group analysis, to stay on top of where the customer is," said the senior communication specialist for the utility. "Last year, I probably went to 50 focus groups in 20 cities across our system."

"In survey after survey, our employees have said they prefer to get their information from their supervisors," said the top communicator for the utility. "We decided to take the hard way around and start training our supervisors to be better communicators . . . to their employees because that's the best way to get the information out and meet their goals."

One-way and two-way communication are starkly contrasted in these two organizations, which differ widely in the purpose and sophistication of their communication practices. Refer to these two organizations as we consider these differences in greater depth.

SOPHISTICATION MEANS STRATEGIC RESEARCH

We distinguish the two-way models from the publicity/press agentry and the public information models. The two-way models are professional because they are based on a body of knowledge and a set of techniques used for strategic purposes: to manage conflicts and build relationships with publics. The one-way models are "craft," meaning that communication techniques are used to generate messages, as if messages were ends in themselves.

The more sophisticated professional models require a form of expertise that the less sophisticated craft models do not. To practice either two-way model, the communication department needs expertise regarding strategic research. By *strategic research*, we mean the ability to systematically collect reliable information about large and small publics that affect the organization, organize that information into a manageable form, and share that information with the dominant coalition to improve strategic decisions. As indicated in the examples of the disabled services organization and oil company cited earlier, organizations differ widely in the kinds of research they conduct. However, knowledge about strategic research allows sophisticated departments to make the most of minimal and informal opportunities to gather information about publics.

Strategic research differs from the tactical research familiar to most communicators. *Tactical research* means the ability to gather information in order to generate or distribute messages. Checking facts for a news release or gathering library information to help write the annual report are forms of tactical research. Tactical research even includes doing a scientific survey ("How many North Americans sleep in the nude?") to generate news releases and media coverage. Although the study may precisely estimate the percentage of nude and pajama-clad sleepers in North America, the purpose is tactical—to generate media coverage.

TYPES OF STRATEGIC RESEARCH

Strategic research gathers information about publics to improve strategic decision making. Such research consists of both formal (scientific) and informal methods or techniques. In reviewing a number of communicator surveys and studies (Dozier, 1990), we found that scientific research correlated with the two-way asymmetrical model and, to a lesser degree, to the two-way symmetrical model. Scientific research involves both scientific scanning (research to detect environmental turbulence—e.g., new competition, strikes, boycotts, and regulations), and scientific evaluation (research to see if strategic communication programs worked). Exhibit 3.2 explains the difference between scanning and evaluation research.

Techniques of scientific research include surveys to track issues, the use

EXHIBIT 3.2
Scanning and Evaluation Research

Communicators use research to "scan" the organization's environment, helping to sensitize dominant coalitions to changes and potential threats to relationships with key publics. Environmental scanning is a part of the larger management function of strategic planning. An organization's environment is made up of many groups of people and organizations that affect an organization's autonomy. For corporations, government regulations can sharply curtail their ability to make profits for stockholders. One oil company that participated in the Excellence Study carefully monitors pending legislation both at the national level and in the state where corporate headquarters is located. For not-for-profit organizations, events and issues can affect members and their relationship to the organization. One not-for-profit organization in the Excellence Study promotes health issues through various means, including local chapters. The top communicator gathers valuable feedback from volunteers and local chapters by spending days with them in the field. Both the communicator monitoring pending legislation for the oil company and the communicator listening to volunteers in the field are doing environmental scanning.

Communicators also use research to measure the impact of communication programs on relationships with key publics. For example, a blood bank that participated in the Excellence Study evaluates each blood drive through a questionnaire completed by blood donors. The essence of communication evaluation is: Did we accomplish what we planned to accomplish with this program? To contribute strategically, communication evaluation must focus on measures of outcomes. Regarding blood drives, outcomes are units of blood donated. Evaluations do not measure anything of inherent value to organizations when they focus on such communication process measures as the number of flyers distributed or the number of news releases written and/or published. These process or implementation measures become meaningful to dominant coalitions when they are coupled with outcome measures—awareness, knowledge, opinions, and behaviors of publics that affect the organization.

of public opinion research agencies, and monitoring other research in the public domain, such as the Gallup or Harris polls. Mixed research consists of both scientific techniques (i.e., formal analysis of media content and complaints by phone or letter) and informal techniques (i.e., media contacts). Informal research involves keeping in touch with members of publics, calling back people attending an organization's presentation, and checking with field personnel.

Communicators use informal research most frequently, followed by mixed research. Communicators use scientific research least often. Measures of usage probably reflect the greater cost and time it takes to do more rigorous forms of research. We think of the three types of research—scientific, mixed, and informal—as a cluster of techniques from which communicators can choose selectively, depending on the circumstances.

KNOWLEDGE OF TWO-WAY MODELS AND RESEARCH USAGE

In the Excellence Study, top communicators in the participating organizations reported on their questionnaires six measures of strategic research use. Three items tapped the use of formal information gathering and three measured informal methods. These items are shown in Table 3.1.

We tested to see if knowledge of the two-way models affected research usage. Indeed, communication departments with the expertise to practice the two-way models used research much more extensively than did departments with little knowledge of two-way practices. Significantly, departments with the knowledge to practice the two-way models used both formal and informal research much more frequently than did departments without two-way expertise.

TABLE 3.1
Department Research Contributions to Strategic Management*

Formal Information Gathering

- Regularly conducted and routine research activities
- Specific research conducted to answer specific questions
- Formal approaches to gathering information for use in decision making other than research

Informal Information Gathering

- Informal approaches to gathering information
- Contacts with knowledgeable people outside the organization
- Judgment based on experience

*On their questionnaires, top communicators were asked to "estimate the extent to which your department makes its contribution to strategic planning and decision making through each of the . . . activities [above]."

Findings from the Excellence Study meshed with what we expected. Research is the extra tool communicators need to close the loop, providing channels for publics to "talk back" to dominant coalitions. Traditional communication education and work experiences favor development of one-way tools, allowing dominant coalitions to send messages to publics through pamphlets, brochures, news releases, press conferences, annual reports, employee magazines, and—more recently—video news releases, electronic mail, and video "magazines" for distribution through controlled media. Only recently have communicators begun to learn research techniques to gather information about what publics know, the way they feel, and how they might behave. By gathering such information and organizing it such that dominant coalitions can understand it, communicators master the requisite skills for practicing two-way models.

MEASURING KNOWLEDGE OF TWO-WAY MODELS

Table 3.2 displays the four items used to measure knowledge of two-way symmetrical practices. The word research does not appear in any of these items, yet the knowledge to perform these tasks is deeply rooted in research. The task of helping management understand publics assumes that communicators have such understanding to share. From where did such communicator understanding come? Strategic research! Measuring public reactions to the actions of organizations is another source of communicator expertise. Negotiation with activist publics and the use of conflict resolution involve a detailed understanding of publics involved, obtained through strategic research.

For example, the arts funding organization discussed in chapter 2 needed to develop more strategic relationships with state legislators, who controlled the purse strings for public support of the arts. The organization received only "default funding" from public sources, a phrase the top communicator used in a case study interview with us to describe nominal sums they typically received from the state. Informal research showed that legislators would sit up and take notice if the arts funding organization could show that strong community arts programs reduced the delinquency of at-risk youths by giving them other choices. Of course, more strategic research was needed to convince legislators that arts funding would, in fact, help reduce delinquency.

By targeting messages to legislators about community arts programs and at-risk youths, the funding request to the state legislature resulted in a $300,000 grant, the first state grant of this magnitude in the organization's history. The legislature granted an additional $25,000 to fund a one-year study of the potential impact of an additional $1 million grant targeted specifically to community arts programs for at-risk youths. Legislators found

TABLE 3.2

Department Expertise to Practice Two-Way Symmetrical Communication*

The Tasks

- Negotiate with an activist public
- Use theories of conflict resolution in dealing with publics
- Help management to understand the opinion of particular publics
- Determine how publics react to the organization

*On their questionnaires, top communicators were asked about "tasks requiring special expertise or knowledge that is available in some public relations or communication departments but not in others." Top communicators were asked to report "the extent to which your department or someone in the department has the expertise or knowledge to perform each task."

a politically safe way to fund arts programs in a state hostile to the arts by pointing to the positive impact of community arts programs in reducing juvenile delinquency. The arts funding organization found a way to build new relationships with state legislators, improving chances for more funding in the future. This is an example of a win–win solution.

Table 3.3 displays the four items in the top communicator questionnaire measuring knowledge of two-way asymmetrical practices. These items emphasize persuasion—getting publics to do what management wants them to do. By persuading publics to the organization's position on issues, getting them to behave as management wishes, and manipulating publics scientifically, communicators practice a sophisticated form of public relations and communication management.

Symmetrical and asymmetrical communication use different processes to achieve different kinds of outcomes. In symmetrical practices, communicators use theories and techniques of conflict resolution and negotiation to increase dominant coalition understanding of publics. In asymmetrical practices, communicators use attitude theory, persuasion, and manipulation to shape public attitudes and behaviors. Although both models involve two-way communication, two distinctly different worldviews are incorporated in

TABLE 3.3

Department Expertise to Practice Two-Way Asymmetrical Communication*

The Tasks

- Persuade a public that your organization is right on an issue
- Get publics to behave as your organization wants
- Manipulate publics scientifically
- Use attitude theory in a campaign

*On their questionnaires, top communicators were asked about "tasks requiring special expertise or knowledge that is available in some public relations or communication departments but not in others." Top communicators were asked to report "the extent to which your department or someone in the department has the expertise or knowledge to perform each task."

each. (Refer to Exhibit 1.1 for a more detailed treatment of two-way symmetrical and two-way asymmetrical models of communicator practices.)

MAKING SENSE OF SYMMETRY AND ASYMMETRY

Prior to the Excellence Study, we thought that excellent communication programs needed expertise to practice the two-way symmetrical model. Indeed, findings of the 1990–1991 survey support our view. Departmental knowledge of two-way symmetrical practices is second only to manager role expertise as the best measure of communication excellence. However, departmental knowledge of two-way asymmetrical practices ranks third in the Excellence Factor.

Knowledge of symmetrical and asymmetrical practices, it seems, goes hand in hand to help communication departments and organizations achieve communication excellence. Yet, in many respects, symmetry and asymmetry represent opposites. How can knowledge of both be so important to excellence?

The answer lies in rethinking symmetry and asymmetry. Symmetrical practices reflect important values about how organizations ought to behave in society. The two-way symmetrical model provides a framework for ethical communication practices, without making moral or ethical judgments about organizations themselves. Communicators practicing the two-way symmetrical model play key roles in adjusting or adapting behaviors of dominant coalitions, thus bringing publics and dominant coalitions closer together. In a society that often brands public relations as unethical, the two-way symmetrical model provides a coherent framework for socially responsible practices.

Murphy (1991) used game theory to suggest that organizations play public relations as a "mixed-motive" game. In mixed-motive games, both sides pursue their own interests, but both sides also realize that the game's outcome (the relationship in this context) must be satisfactory to both sides. A player in a mixed-motive game benefits from the ability to see conflicting issues from the other player's perspective. Communicators provide valuable services to dominant coalitions when they help senior managers see their organizations and behaviors from the publics' viewpoints.

In thinking of symmetrical and asymmetrical practices as parts of a common mixed-motive game, knowledge of both models makes sense. As organizations pursue their own interests in relations with publics, communicators try—from time to time—to persuade publics that their organizations are right on an issue. At times, communicators try to convince publics to behave as their organizations want. Sometimes, communicators use attitude theory and research to manipulate publics scientifically. Indeed, activist publics likewise will follow similar asymmetrical strategies to persuade, convince, and manipulate organizations.

However, organizations and publics also need to find an equilibrium, a middle position, between the desired outcomes of each. Such an equilibrium must be sufficiently satisfactory so that neither publics nor organizations have cause to regret their actions, given how the other side would have responded. Publics and organizations can be described as cooperative antagonists, looking for a compromise around an issue in which true differences exist between parties. They do not trust each other, nor do they believe everything communicated by the other side. However, they trust each other enough to believe that each will abide by any agreement reached.

The findings of the Excellence Study suggest a new way of organizing the model of two-way practices, which is displayed in Fig. 3.1. In the model, organizations and publics are viewed as holding separate and sometimes conflicting interests. Nevertheless, negotiation and compromise permit organizations and publics to find a common ground, the win–win zone in Fig. 3.1. The model suggests that a number of outcomes are possible within the win–win zone. Unsatisfactory and unstable relationships exist on either side of the win–win zone, with one party exploiting the other. To the left of the win–win zone, the organization's position dominates to the public's disadvantage. To the right, the public's position dominates to the organization's disadvantage.

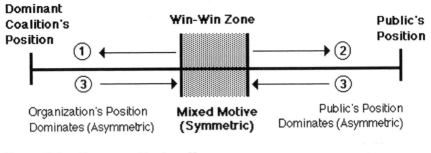

Type of Practice	Explanation
① **Pure Asymmetry Model**	Communication used to dominate public, accept dominant coalition's position
② **Pure Cooperation Model**	Communication used to convince dominant coalition to cave in to public's position
③ **Two-Way Model**	Communication used to move public, dominant coalition, or both to acceptable "win-win" zone

FIG. 3.1.   New model of symmetry as two-way practices.

Communication can be used to manipulate or persuade publics to accept the dominant coalition's position. This is indicated by Arrow 1 in Fig. 3.1. Instead of negotiating for a relationship in the win–win zone, communicators try to take advantage of publics. Such practices are the zero-sum or win-lose game played by communicators practicing pure two-way asymmetrical communication.

Communication can be used by publics to persuade the organization's dominant coalition to accept the public's position outside the win–win zone. When communicators in the organization try to help publics in this endeavor, the communicators use the pure cooperation model. This practice is indicated by Arrow 2 in Fig. 3.1. Dominant coalitions are unlikely to appreciate communicators who persuade the organizations they work for to accept clearly undesirable positions that benefit publics at the expense of organizations.

Some have argued (Murphy, 1991) that the two-way symmetrical model most closely matches the pure cooperation practices shown in Fig. 3.1. However, we think symmetry is better represented by the practices indicated by Arrow 3 in Fig. 3.1. That is, communicators negotiate with both publics and dominant coalitions to reach a position (outcome, relationship) in the win–win zone. In communicating to publics, communicators try to persuade publics to move toward the organization's position. In communicating with dominant coalitions, communicators try to persuade dominant coalitions to move toward the public's position. These practices are called the *two-way model*, because it subsumes the former models of two-way symmetrical and two-way asymmetrical practices. Asymmetrical tactics are sometimes used to gain the best position for organizations within the win–win zone. Because such practices are bounded by a symmetrical worldview that respects the integrity of long-term relationships, the two-way model is essentially symmetrical.

Practically speaking, the two-way model means treating dominant coalitions as another public influenced by communication programs. The corporate communications director at a chemical manufacturing company described the mixed-motive nature of symmetrical practices. Regarding publics, this top communicator recognized the persuasive intent of his communication strategies. "We don't want to just inform and educate everybody for the sake of saying we've done our good deed," he told us. "We want to inform and educate them with the intent of buying our stock, of being a safer employee, of coming to work more than being absent, and in seeing a better article in the press. Those are the desirable behavioral outcomes."

At the same time, the chemical manufacturer's dominant coalition is also persuaded by this top communicator. "I see management as being one of our audiences," he continued. "Changing perceptions on the part of management is a desired behavioral outcome."

Unfortunately, the use of asymmetrical tactics to achieve mutually beneficial outcomes in the win–win zone creates considerable ambiguity for observers in the larger society. Are we using asymmetrical tactics within the framework of a larger symmetrical philosophy, or are we simply going for the jugular in a purely asymmetrical win–lose game?

We asked the research director for a large oil company during a case study interview how his company made choices between symmetrical and asymmetrical practices. He said that, generally speaking, symmetrical practices build the best long-term relationships with publics, but symmetrical practices are expensive (compromises usually are) and sometimes the risks of alternative asymmetrical practices are low. Under those circumstances, the oil company might pursue its own interests according to the asymmetrical model. "To be frank," the research director for the oil company said, "I think it would depend on what you could get away with."

ETHICAL IMPERATIVES VERSES PRAGMATIC CONSEQUENCES

The two-way model suggests another way to select symmetrical or asymmetrical practices: Such selection is based on an ethical commitment by professional communicators to place greater emphasis on mutually beneficial, long-term relationships than other parties might (e.g., leadership of activist publics or dominant coalitions). In game theory terms, the communicator is a cooperative antagonist that seeks to preserve the integrity of the game, often at the expense of a short-term advantage.

In the interest of building long-term relationships with key publics, communicators may choose to forego asymmetrical practices as an investment in future returns in the form of more symmetrical behavior from the publics involved. In this way, professional communicators can view intermittent, short-term asymmetrical practices as necessary tactics for pursuing organizational self-interest in a mixed-motive game. Professional communicators must subordinate such practices, as well as the asymmetrical worldview they support, to a broader, symmetrical worldview. That larger symmetrical worldview is implicit in communicator Arthur W. Page's declaration that "All business in a democratic country begins with public permission and exists by public approval" (Broom & Dozier, 1990, p. xi).

SUMMARY

Knowledge to practice two-way symmetrical and two-way asymmetrical communication joins manager role expertise to form the core of communication excellence. Two-way communication means that communicators act as eyes and ears of their organizations, conduits for information from publics to dominant coalitions. Two-way communication is based on the use of formal (scientific) and informal research. Communication departments with the knowledge to practice two-way communication conduct more research than do communication departments without such knowledge.

Excellent communication departments know how to practice both symmetrical and asymmetrical communication. This finding led the research team to conclude that the two-way symmetrical model and two-way asymmetrical model actually make up a single mixed-motive model. This mixed-motive model involves the short-term use of asymmetrical practices within the context of a broad symmetrical philosophy. This provides the basis for ethical public relations and communication practices.

REFERENCES

Broom, G. M., & Dozier, D. M. (1990). *Using research in public relations: Applications to program management.* Englewood Cliffs, NJ: Prentice-Hall.

Cutlip, S. M., Center, A. H., & Broom, G. M. (1994). *Effective public relations* (7th ed.). Englewood Cliffs, NJ: Prentice-Hall.

Dozier, D. M. (1990). The innovation of research in public relations practice: Review of a program of studies. In L. A. Grunig & J. E. Grunig (Eds.), *Public relations research annual* (Vol. 2, pp. 3–28). Hillsdale, NJ: Lawrence Erlbaum Associates.

Grunig, J. E. & Hunt, T. (1984). *Managing public relations.* New York: Holt, Rinehart & Winston.

Murphy, P. (1991). The limits of symmetry: A game theory approach to symmetric and asymmetric public relations. In L. A. Grunig & J. E. Grunig (Eds.), *Public relations research annual* (Vol. 3, pp. 115–132). Hillsdale, NJ: Lawrence Erlbaum Associates.

4

Knowing Traditional
Communicator Skills

Members of the research team have spoken at scores of meetings of professional communicators in Canada, the United Kingdom, and the United States, as well as to communicators in other nations. Most communicators react enthusiastically to findings of the Excellence Study, asking questions about how they can incorporate the results into their work. Some communicators, however, wonder about the relationship between excellence and traditional communicator skills, such as writing, editing, graphic design, production techniques, media relations, and so forth. Sometimes anxious, sometimes angry, these communicators want to know the role of communicator craft in excellence.

We use *craft* to name the range of traditional communicator skills associated with the technician role and the press agentry/publicity and public information models of public relations and communication practices. The good news is that organizations with excellent programs have strong communicator craft. The bad news is that traditional skills are not what make them excellent. This chapter addresses traditional craft and its role in communication excellence.

The chief executive officer (CEO) of a state hospital association understood the relationship between traditional craft and excellence. His association has an outstanding communication department, scoring in the top 5% of organizations in the Excellence Study. When health care became more competitive and more closely scrutinized in the early 1990s, his thinking about public relations and communication management changed. "The whole mission changed," he told us in a case study interview. "I realized the importance of communication with the public. I insisted on hiring new people with strong skills, both in writing and speaking and in management."

Compare this CEO's view with that of a senior vice president at an insurance company. The insurance company posted an overall Excellence Score in the bottom 10% of organizations studied. "The communication department and its employees weigh very much toward the technical aspects of communication," he said.

The company's top communicator concurred, describing the communication department's mission as wholly technical. "[Communication] provides technical support to the marketing functions," she told us.

Both organizations have strong communicator craft in their departments. How such craft is used accounts for the glaring differences in overall communication excellence.

HOW TECHNICIAN ROLE EXPERTISE WAS MEASURED

In the survey portion of the Excellence Study, top communicators reported the extent to which their departments have the expertise to perform certain tasks. The eight items measuring knowledge to play the communication technician role are displayed in Table 4.1.

As conceptualized, communicators in the technician role provide technical communication services. Period. Technicians do not help with strategic planning or the consequences of decisions. Scholars (Broom & Smith, 1979) studying roles called such communicators *journalists-in-residence*, hired away from media because of their communication skills and mass media experience.

The eight items in Table 4.1 measure tasks that qualified communication technicians know how to do. The first three measure writing expertise; the fourth measures knowledge of print production. Two items measure com-

TABLE 4.1
Department Expertise to Play the Communication Technician Role*

The Tasks

- Write news releases and feature articles
- Write an advertisement
- Write speeches
- Produce publications
- Produce audio/visuals (graphics, slide shows, videos, radio spots)
- Take photographs
- Create and manage a speakers' bureau
- Coordinate a press conference or arrange media coverage of an event

* On their questionnaires, top communicators were asked about "tasks requiring special expertise or knowledge that is available in some public relations or communication departments but not in others." Top communicators were asked to report "the extent to which your department or someone in the department has the expertise or knowledge to perform each task."

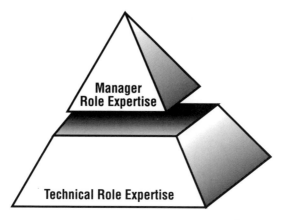

FIG. 4.1. A hierarchical view of manager and technician role expertise in communication departments.

municators' visual expertise regarding photography and audio/visuals. The final two items measure "events" expertise regarding press conferences and speakers' bureaus.

Departmental expertise to play the communication technician role is strong in those departments that have the expertise to play the manager role. Expertise in the technician role also is strong in departments that know how to practice two-way models. In fact, knowledge of the technician role in communication departments is stronger for organizations with high overall Excellence Scores, compared to organizations with lower Excellence Scores. Put succinctly, departments with the knowledge base to establish excellent communication programs also have high levels of technical expertise.

As explained in part II of this book, organizations have less-than-excellent communication when traditional technical expertise is all the department has. This shows up when the organization's top communicator primarily plays the technician role. In some cases, top communicators play this role because the dominant coalition expects it. In other cases, top communicators play this role because they lack the knowledge to play any other.

Knowledge of traditional communicator craft, as indicated by technician role expertise, helps excellent communication departments work. In case study interviews, the research team confirmed that even the most strategically managed department still must possess the expertise to implement communication programs, using the technical expertise within the department. We thought most departments would be organized in a traditional hierarchy with senior-ranking managers supervising technicians in subordinate positions (see Fig. 4.1).

However, case study interviews indicated that some organizations use a more organic approach to roles. Tasks are assigned according to the strengths

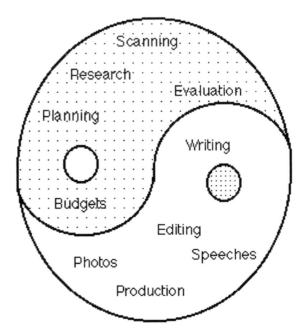

FIG. 4.2.   An organic view of manager and technician role expertise in communication departments.

of individual communicators, without great regard to who is the supervisor and who is the subordinate. For example, we conducted case study interviews with communicators at a blood bank, which the survey portions of the Excellence Study placed in the top 10% of participating organizations. The interviews indicated that the top communicator and her subordinate passed roles back and forth, based on preferences and knowledge.[1] "Writing is strong for both of us," the top communicator said. "But I've done media relations for so long, I tend to handle the touchy issues. [Her subordinate] handles the planning aspects. She likes to plan."

Her subordinate indicated that she enjoyed planning and budgeting. Because she also has the appropriate training, the subordinate also coordinates research activities. Both described their work as collaborative, with the top communicator verbalizing concepts and ideas with her subordinate. The subordinate then commits those ideas to paper.

Swapping of manager and technician roles between the two in this excellent organization suggests that a rigid hierarchical model may be inappropri-

---

[1]That is, the communicators shared and swapped tasks associated with the manager and technician roles. The case studies confirmed a pattern in the survey data that showed top communicators playing multiple roles.

ate. We think the yin and yang concept provides a better metaphor: Manager and technician role expertise can be thought of as two fundamentally different principles of communication that work best in tension and balance with each other. Fig. 4.2 captures this sense of balance and tension.

HOW EXPERTISE TO PRACTICE ONE-WAY COMMUNICATION WAS MEASURED

Just as technician role expertise complements manager role expertise in excellent communication departments, the technical aspects of traditional one-way practices in public relations and communication management complement two-way practices. In excellent communication departments, knowledge of the press agentry/publicity model and the public information model is generally stronger than in less-than-excellent departments.

Table 4.2 displays the four items used to measure departmental expertise to practice the press agentry/publicity model. Top communicators were asked the extent to which their departments had the expertise to perform the four tasks listed in Table 4.2. These tasks focus on the press agentry imperative to generate publicity. Only the last one, keeping bad publicity out of the media, deals with the favorable quality of the information. The other three concentrate on generating media coverage, regardless of content.

These items were combined to create a single measure of press agentry/publicity expertise. The greater the department's expertise to practice the two-way symmetrical and two-way asymmetrical models was, the greater the department's expertise to practice the press agentry/publicity model. Organizations with higher overall excellence scores also posted higher scores on press agentry/publicity expertise.

Table 4.3 displays the items measuring knowledge of public information

TABLE 4.2
Department Expertise to Practice the Press Agentry/Publicity Model*

The Tasks

- Convince a reporter to publicize your organization
- Get your organization's name into the media
- Get maximum publicity for a staged event
- Keep bad publicity out of the media

* On their questionnaires, top communicators were asked about "tasks requiring special expertise or knowledge that is available in some public relations or communication departments but not in others." Top communicators were asked to report "the extent to which your department or someone in the department has the expertise or knowledge to perform each task."

TABLE 4.3.
Department Expertise to Practice the Public Information Model*

The Tasks

- Perform as journalists inside your organization
- Understand the news values of journalists
- Prepare news stories that reporters will use
- Provide objective information about your organization

---

* On their questionnaires, top communicators were asked about "tasks requiring special expertise or knowledge that is available in some public relations or communication departments but not in others." Top communicators were asked to report "the extent to which your department or someone in the department has the expertise or knowledge to perform each task."

practices—tasks that measure the technical expertise expected from a journalist-in-residence. Knowledge of public information practices emphasizes the communication department's ability to operate as a journalistic unit, understanding the news values of reporters and using that understanding to write stories that reporters will use. Objectivity is one such journalistic value incorporated into products of the communication department.

The research team combined the four items into a single measure of public information expertise. Departments with high levels of expertise regarding the more sophisticated two-way practices also reported high levels of expertise in practicing the public information model. Organizations with higher overall communication excellence scores also had higher levels of public information expertise, when compared to organizations with less-than-excellent programs.

WHY TRADITIONAL CRAFTS ARE NOT ENOUGH

Mark Twain once wrote to a newspaper that had published his obituary by mistake, complaining that the news of his death was greatly exaggerated. The Excellence Study shows that traditional craft skills are alive and well in excellent communication departments. Excellent communication departments still need to know how to write, edit, take photos, make graphics, handle communication production, run news conferences, maintain media relations, and organize speakers' bureaus. Not only do excellent communication departments have this capacity, but their knowledge of tradition communicator craft is superior. Although the traditional crafts are not obsolete, they are not enough.

Traditional communication craft deals only with implementation; missing from the list of technician role expertise, press agentry/publicity expertise, and public information expertise is any sense of purpose. In other words, departments that are missing the knowledge to play the manager role or practice two-way models lack a sense of direction. They churn out messages like perpetual motion machines.

Cutlip, Center, and Broom (1994) used the cuttlefish as a metaphor to analyze what happens when traditional communication crafts are used in a purposeless manner. This squidlike marine mollusk squirts an inklike substance indiscriminately whenever it encounters something threatening. Linking the mollusk to traditional communicator crafts, Cutlip, Center, and Broom said: "Some public relations programs are routinized to the point that, regardless of the problem . . ., the response is to get out a press release "telling our story. . . ." Maybe the cuttlefish's strategy for squirting ink at problems is not unique to that species" (p. 216).

The authors do not object to the "ink"—to well-crafted communication. They object to the discharge of communicator ink in so witless a manner, without a clear understanding of what such messages seek to accomplish in building or maintaining relationships with publics.

Discussions of roles and practices too often focus on what individual communicators know, rather than on the knowledge base of the entire communication department. As detailed in Part II, the role behavior of the top communicator becomes crucial to communication excellence in organizations, because communication excellence requires top communicators to play the manager role more often than not. The types of communication practices that dominant coalitions expect also help or hinder communication excellence. Communication excellence occurs when organizations demand two-way practices from their communication departments. Top communicators understand these demands for sophisticated two-way practices.

Within excellent departments, individuals with strong creative talents in traditional communication crafts play an important role. The best-laid plans of dominant coalitions and top communicators mean nothing without traditional communication skills to implement them.

Consider, for example, our case study of an economic development agency in the southern United States. This small organization has 15 employees and 1 communicator. Regarding communication excellence, the development agency scored in the bottom 5% of organizations participating in the Excellence Study. Thus, the research team was surprised to find considerable progress toward communication excellence in the 1994 case study. The communicator who completed the 1990–1991 questionnaire left the organization in 1993, and was replaced by a more talented communicator. Within fewer than seven months on the job, the new communicator had instituted several important innovations. The communicator now participates in the agency's strategic planning, ending what the CEO described as the "splendid isolation amongst the top management" that had prevailed before. The communicator has proposed a two-year plan for the agency to monitor attraction and retention of clients, using ongoing evaluation techniques to keep track of successes and failure of program goals. The communicator will play a leadership role as the agency implements a total quality management program.

Because the organization has only one communicator, she must play both manager and technicians roles. Her manager role expertise comes from her master's degree in environmental science with a concentration in community relations, as well as previous work experience in marketing communications. Her technical role expertise comes from undergraduate studies in communication courses, followed by high school teaching. This example provides a vivid sketch of the range of expertise required for communication excellence in a one-person department.

Larger departments permit areas of selective specialization for communicators. For example, a large oil company participated in the original survey, scoring in the top 10% in overall excellence. A follow-up case study showed considerable specialization within the department. Of interest to the research team was the communication department's extensive internal research unit. Of special relevance, however, was the company's highly diverse department, with experts in graphics, speech writing, media relations, and so forth.

Presently, as professors at our respective universities, members of the research team teach future communicators how to write and edit, as well as the other elements of traditional communicator craft. In the past, we have worked as journalists and public relations practitioners. We believe we understand the practice as well as the theory of public relations and communication management. At the core of any communication department is the expertise to perform traditional communication crafts. At the core of an excellent communication department, these traditional crafts complement cutting-edge expertise to manage the department strategically and utilize two-way communication practices.

SUMMARY

Traditional communication crafts—writing, editing, photography, graphics, media relations—play an important role in excellent communication departments. Indeed, excellent communication departments tend to have greater technical expertise than do less-than-excellent departments. However, traditional communication craft is not what makes excellent departments excellent; increasing departmental expertise in traditional craft areas does little to bring about overall communication excellence. What do departments and organizations do with traditional craft skills? It is the application of communicator craft to the pursuit of strategic goals that separates excellent from less-than-excellent communication programs.

REFERENCES

Broom, G. M., & Smith, G. D. (1979). Testing the practitioner's impact on clients. *Public Relations Review, 5*(3), 47–59.

Cutlip, S. M., Center, A. H., & Broom, G. M. (1994). *Effective public relations* (7th ed.). Englewood Cliffs, NJ: Prentice-Hall.

5

Build Your Knowledge Base

We hope the previous chapters have convinced you that the first and most important step toward communication excellence starts with what you and your colleagues know. The Excellence Study identified 16 areas of specialized expertise that communication departments need for excellence. These areas permit communicators to play the manager role and engage in two-way practices. In Table 5.1, these 16 areas are grouped under four major areas of knowledge: strategic and operational management, research, negotiation, and persuasion.

As detailed in part II, communicator knowledge or expertise alone is not enough to build communication excellence in your organization. The dominant coalition—those powerful people in your organization that set the mission and goals—must understand communication excellence and demand the same through a series of shared expectations. As part III indicates, the broad cultural values in your organization provide either a fertile or inhospitable setting for communication excellence.

However, excellence begins at home, in the knowledge or expertise that communicators bring to their work. Without expertise for excellence in the communication department, the expectations of the dominant coalition matter little. If your communication department is devoid of needed expertise, even the most demanding chief executive officer (CEO) will not be able to squeeze excellence from it.

In this chapter, seven strategies are explored for increasing a communicator's expertise to achieve excellence. We start with the least invasive strategies, those that require less effort, fewer resources, and minimal institutional support. We end this chapter with strategies requiring significant resources and large institutional change. The advantages and

TABLE 5.1
Knowledge for Communication Excellence

Strategic and Operational Management Knowledge
- Develop strategies for solving public relations and communication problems
- Manage the organization's response to issues
- Develop goals and objectives for your department
- Prepare a departmental budget
- Manage people

Research Knowledge
- Perform environmental scanning
- Determine public reactions to your organizations
- Use research to segment publics
- Conduct evaluation research

Negotiation Knowledge
- Negotiate with an activist public
- Help management to understand the opinions of particular publics
- Use theories of conflict resolution in dealing with publics

Persuasion Knowledge
- Persuade a public that your organization is right on an issue
- Use attitude theory in a campaign
- Get publics to behave as your organization wants

TABLE 5.2
Advantages and Disadvantages of Five Strategies
for Acquiring Knowledge for Excellence

Strategy	Advantages	Disadvantages
Knowing the business	• Credibility with management • Understand challenges facing industry	• Not transferable • Not a substitute for communication expertise
Self-study	• Inexpensive • Flexible • Self-paced	• Requires personal time • Self-motivation necessary
Professional association seminars	• Intensive • Interactive	• Requires employer support
Mentoring	• Part of work routine • Like personal tutor	• Requires competent mentor
Department training	• Accomplished on company time and with company money • All in department learn	• Accomplished on company time and with company money! • Careful preplanning necessary
Accreditation	• Exposure to knowledge base	• Very demanding
Higher education	• In-depth knowledge	• Time consuming

disadvantages of each strategy are summarized in Table 5.2. This chapter reflects both our perspective and the viewpoints of communicators whom we interviewed. Take this chapter as a starting point for discussions with your colleagues.

KNOWING THE BUSINESS

In case study interviews, several communicators who run excellent communication programs stressed the importance of knowing the business. This means becoming knowledgeable about your employer's specific business or industry.

The vice president for public affairs at an oil company told us that his knowledge of company operations was key to his success. The oil company posted an overall Excellence Score in the top 5% of organizations in the Excellence Study. Both the CEO and the top communicator had advanced from line manager positions. This gave the top communicator a special rapport with the CEO that a pure generalist would not enjoy.

The top communicator at a chemical manufacturing company stressed the importance of knowing the chemical industry, as well as communication management. The chemical company scored in the top 25% of organizations in the Excellence Study.

The advantages of knowing the business include greater understanding of the challenges and opportunities facing your organization. This translates into greater credibility with senior managers, who expect all top-level people in the organization to understand the business. On the downside, such expertise is not transferable to other organizational settings outside the industry; nor can knowledge of the industry substitute for knowledge of those areas required for communication excellence.

SELF-STUDY

The top communicator we interviewed at a chemical manufacturing company said that he supplements his formal education and extensive knowledge of the chemical business with regular reading of scientific and research journals. He listed *Communication Research* and the *Journal of Communication* specifically. Another communicator expanded his knowledge by studying major texts in public relations, as well as participating in International Association of Business Communicators (IABC) seminars and workshops. Each of these communicators is pursuing his or her own program of self-study.

Self-study is inexpensive, flexible, and self-paced. On the other hand, self-study requires motivation and the commitment of personal time. A

number of books provide introductory, intermediate, and advanced information regarding topics directly related communication excellence. The
four major topic areas displayed in Table 5.1 are most relevant to advancing
your knowledge of communication excellence. Our book, *Excellence in
Public Relations and Communication Management* (Grunig, 1992), provides
a valuable gateway into each topic area. Each chapter of that book has an
extensive list of other references and sources of valuable information.

PROFESSIONAL ASSOCIATION WORKSHOPS AND
SEMINARS

The International Association of Business Communicators, the Public Relations Society of America (PRSA), the Canadian Public Relations Society
(CPRS), the Institute of Public Relations (IPR), the Arthur Page Society,
the Institute for Public Relations Research and Education, the Public Relations Symposium, and other professional communicator organizations offer
workshops and seminars to both their members and nonmembers (the latter
at a higher fee). Contact your local chapter or the national/international
office for more information about seminar topics and schedules. Seminars
and workshops are offered at regional, national, or international conven-
tions.

Professional development workshops and seminars provide a way to
hone your expertise for communication excellence. Workshops and seminars provide intensive instruction in various topic areas related to excellence. In seminars and workshops, you can interact with instructors and
other participants. This interaction is the major advantage of workshops and
seminars over self-study. Books and articles are notoriously inarticulate
when fielding questions from their readers. On the other hand, professional
development workshops and seminars generally require the active support
of your employer.

Several top communicators we interviewed said the workshops and seminars offered by professional associations played an important role in their
professional development. A public utility scored in the top 1% of organizations participating in the Excellence Study. The top communicator reported
that her involvement with professional associations, such as IABC, had
provided an important supplement to her higher education and mentoring
on the job. She said case studies provided by professional associations were
especially beneficial. Her company also sends her to workshops and seminars sponsored by professional associations.

Another top communicator completed her master's degree with an emphasis in public relations while preparing for the IABC accreditation exam.
She sends junior members of her staff to IABC workshops and seminars at
company expense.

Many colleges and universities offer workshops and seminars of interest and value to communication professionals; other colleges and universities would offer them as well if you and other communication professionals expressed an interest in them. Contact the extension studies office of your nearest college or university and ask for the current schedule of extension offerings. Also ask how new workshops and seminars can be initiated. Some extension courses are offered for academic credit; others are not. Certificate programs and advanced degrees are discussed later in this chapter.

Organizers of workshops and seminars tend to respond to demands from participants, so the quality of content and instruction depends on sophisticated consumers like yourself. A hefty price tag does not, in itself, translate into a quality learning experience. If the brief course descriptions do not answer all your questions, call the sponsor or talk to the instructor of the course. When examining available offerings, use your professional network to talk to others who have attended that particular seminar or workshop. Find out all you can about the instructor. Check around.

Most important, consider the content of what you will learn in the workshop or seminar. Not every workshop or seminar offered will provide you the knowledge or expertise necessary for communication excellence. Many workshops are designed to increase your technical expertise to practice the one-way press agentry/publicity or public information models. Many communicators demand such workshops to enhance their traditional communicator crafts. Chapter 4 showed that excellent communication departments have high levels of traditional craft expertise, but such expertise alone does not make them excellent. The first four chapters of this book prepared you to be a discerning consumer of workshops and seminars of professional communicators. Rather than take traditional craft instruction, look for workshops and seminars that advance your knowledge in the 16 areas detailed in Table 5.1.

MENTORING

Mentoring is the structured or unstructured training of junior communicators to learn the ropes in an organizations and develop advanced expertise, provided by a superior or another appropriate individual in the organization.

The top communicator at an association promoting heart health said that mentoring was "critical to success." The association posted overall Excellence Scores in the top 1% of organizations in the study.

A public utility also scored in the top 1% of organizations in the Excellence Study. Its top communicator told us that mentoring from her current supervisor proved invaluable to her professional growth.

The director of sales at a direct-marketing firm said she learned through "hands on" experiences at work, including learning by "osmosis" from the company's past president. She said she "listened to him on the phone and listened to him talk to people. He was a great trainer and a great leader."

One advantage of mentoring is that it occurs on the job as a regular part of the work routine. Further, having a competent mentor is like having a personal tutor to train you in advanced practices. Mentoring, however, requires a competent mentor with the interpersonal skills, content expertise, and organizational juice to make mentoring a positive experience.

WORKSHOPS FOR YOUR COMMUNICATION DEPARTMENT

Self-study and professional association workshops and seminars are valuable sources of information for communication professionals. Another method for increasing the knowledge base of the communication department is specialized training for the entire department. This approach has the advantage of increasing the knowledge level of the entire unit. For example, individuals with a strong preference for traditional communication crafts can learn how those crafts can be interwoven with manager role expertise and knowledge of two-way practices to increase the overall excellence of the department. From the case studies, we discovered that the best departments do not segregate traditional expertise and the new expertise of excellent communication. In these departments, different forms of expertise work well together, like a well-oiled machine. On the other hand, departmental training requires the active support of management, including time and monetary resources.

For such departmental workshops to work most effectively, they should be carefully preplanned and tailored to the special needs of your organization. A knowledge base inventory should be conducted of all members of the department. The top communicator, in consultation with others in the department and in the dominant coalition, should select topic areas for departmental training that maximize immediate benefits. Remember that the demands on the communication department will not take a vacation while the staff is in training. Therefore, time in training should be intense and provide maximum "bang for the buck."

PROFESSIONAL ACCREDITATION

The most important benefit of accreditation is the careful study of public relations and communication management by individuals preparing for the exam. Professional recognition is also an important benefit. The value of accreditation studies cannot be underestimated. Professional communicators are required to step back from the day-to-day bustle of their work and reflect on communication and public relations as an intellectual discipline and a profession. Studying for accreditation exams requires carefully reviewing the evolving body of knowledge in our field, a demanding requirement.

The Excellence Study already has stimulated wide-ranging discussions of accrediting standards for Accredited Business Communicators (ABC), the accreditation program of IABC. Other professional organizations are also reviewing their standards for accreditation, due to rapid growth in knowledge in the communication field.

Changing the accrediting standards raises a number of thorny issues that professional communicators (rather than college professors) are best positioned and equipped to resolve. We pose them here as a series of questions. These questions are not directed toward the IABC accreditation standards, but instead toward accrediting standards of all professional communication associations:

- Should more stringent accrediting standards apply to communication professionals already accredited?
- Should there be two levels of accreditation, with the lower level based on current standards and the higher level based on new expertise required for communication excellence?
- Should accreditation require ongoing professional development activities after accreditation? What should those professional development activities include?
- Is accreditation a precursor to licensing of communication professionals, or will accreditation always remain a voluntary affiliation?
- If accreditation will always remain a voluntary affiliation, how can a professional organization encourage its members to undergo the rigors of the accrediting process?

The Excellence Study has greatly expanded the knowledge base of professional communicators. Now professional communicators must decide how to hold each other accountable for this new body of knowledge.

HIGHER EDUCATION

Colleges and universities play an important role in the long-term diffusion of the knowledge to practice communication excellence. As we educate communicators of tomorrow, programs that train these professionals would benefit from a careful review of the Excellence Study findings. In time, these findings will make their way into the curricula of these programs. Studies at the undergraduate and graduate levels, thus, provide another venue for acquiring the knowledge base for communication excellence. Seeking a bachelor's or advanced degree is a demanding and time-consuming process. Of all the strategies, however, studies in higher education provide the most in-depth knowledge.

A number of communicators we interviewed considered higher education in public relations and communication management pivotal to their careers. One highly successful communicator said that higher education played a key role in her success. She told us in a case study interview that she supplemented her broad training in communication with supplemental coursework in marketing and management. She supplemented these areas with specialized training in a content area related to the business itself. Her business education has given her clout with senior managers.

Among the positive innovations in higher education is the *Design for Undergraduate Public Relations Education* (1987), authored by team member William Ehling and Betsy Plank. This document outlines five core content areas for undergraduate education in public relations and communication management:

- Principles, practices, and theory of public relations.
- Public relations techniques.
- Public relations research for planning and evaluation.
- Public relations strategy and implementation.
- Supervised public relations experience.

This curriculum provides a strong knowledge base for communication excellence.

An important recommendation of the Commission on Undergraduate Public Relations Education was that the departmental affiliation of the degree program was not crucial. Most important is the content of the degree coursework. The courses recommended earlier provide a sufficient framework for introduction of communication excellence in the college curriculum of future public relations practitioners and communication managers. Findings of the Excellence Study belong in the principles, practices, and theory course and in the research and strategy courses.

Change in institutions of higher learning occurs at glacial speed. Educators consider an inch forward in a year to be rapid change. Moreover, institutions of higher learning may well be bastions of academic freedom, able to consider sweeping change and reform in the larger society, including the professions we serve. However, college professors tend to be extremely conservative about change in their own courses and degree programs. In other words, do not expect too much, too fast.

One communicator we interviewed suggested moving public relations education out of journalism and communication departments and into business schools. Such a move would permit educating business majors about communication and public relations as a management function. "Business schools are where our future CEOs are being trained," she said. "They will only consider important that which they too have had to master."

We agree that business management and marketing majors would benefit from instruction in public relations and communication management. However, efforts to move public relations education to another academic unit, in our view, do little to advance excellence in public relations.

Our concern is that educators in business schools will share many of the same misconceptions about communication and public relations as do dominant coalitions in less-than-excellent organizations. In 1989, the public relations firm of Nuffer, Smith, Tucker, together with San Diego State University, sponsored a colloquium to bring together top educators and professional communicators to clarify the similarities and differences between marketing and public relations. Research team member William Ehling from Syracuse University represented public relations and communication management educators. Philip Kotler of Northwestern University represented marketing educators. Professor Kotler's initial position was similar to what many business administration and marketing educators think: Public relations (publicity) is one of several dissemination channels available to support the management function of marketing.

Educators of public relations and communication management, such as Professor Ehling, subscribe to a different conceptualization of public relations and communication management. One popular definition[1] of public relations and communication management (Cutlip, Center, & Broom, 1994) is: "the management function that establishes and maintains mutually beneficial relationships between an organization and publics on whom its success or failure depends" (p. 6).

This definition differs markedly from marketing (Cutlip, Center, & Broom, 1994), which is: "the management function that identifies human needs and wants, offers products and services to satisfy those demands, and causes transactions that deliver products and services in exchange for something of value to the provider" (p. 6).

By the end of the two-day colloquium, Professor Kotler had expanded his definition of public relations and communication management somewhat. Similar enlightenment would be needed throughout business schools before communication excellence could be taught there.

---

[1]In the Excellence Study, we defined *public relations* as the management of communication between organizations and its publics (Grunig, 1992), which places a greater emphasis on communication's role in the process of building and sustaining relationships. The conceptual framework of public relations and communication management, as used in the Excellence Study, is consistent with the Cutlip, Center, and Broom definition.

On a practical level, reorganization of departments and schools in higher education proceed much more slowly than in the corporate world. Institutional values, such as academic freedom and tenure, do not make institutional change easy. The symbolic value of having public relations and communication management taught in a prestigious business school setting is not so important as is upgrading the substance of the curriculum, regardless of departmental affiliation.

A related issue is the clamor among some educators for "integrated marketing communication" or simply "marketing communication." The notion is that public relations, advertising, and marketing should be combined in some way to train students for careers as "integrated communicators." Indeed, future professional communicators do benefit from cross-training in marketing and advertising. In substance, however, much of integrated marketing communication in higher education would destroy the core of communication excellence. A majority of marketing specialists conceptualize public relations and communication management as a technical support function (publicity and direct mail) for marketing. When this is the case, integrated marketing communication dooms future communicators to the kind of technical support roles they now play in less-than-excellent organizations.

SUMMARY

The knowledge base to practice communication excellence can be acquired in at least seven ways: learning the business, self-study, workshops and seminars, mentoring, departmental training, preparation of accrediting exams, and higher education. In the short term, learning the business, self-study, mentoring, and workshops/seminars provide maximum flexibility and lowest cost for individual communicators to build their expertise. In the long run, accreditation and higher education play important roles in providing communicators with the tools for communication excellence.

REFERENCES

Cutlip, S. M., Center, A. H., & Broom, G. M. (1994). *Effective public relations* (7th ed.). Englewood Cliffs, NJ: Prentice-Hall.

Ehling, W. P., & Plank, B. (1987). *Design for undergraduate public relations education.* Chicago: Commission on Undergraduate Public Relations Education.

Grunig, J. E. (Ed.). (1992). *Excellence in public relations and communication management.* Hillsdale, NJ: Lawrence Erlbaum Associates.

Part II

Shared Expectations About Communication

Recall from Fig. 1.1 that communication excellence consists of three spheres that represent different qualities of excellence. In Part I, we considered the different components of the most inner sphere: the knowledge base of the communication department.

In this second part of the book, we consider the middle sphere of communication excellence: the shared expectations that communicators and senior managers hold about communication. Communication departments may have the core knowledge to practice excellent communication, but senior management also must share a common understanding about the role and function of communication.

The middle sphere of communication excellence involves communicator relations with the dominant coalition, that group of powerful individuals in organizations who set organizational goals and make strategic decisions. The middle sphere of shared expectations has three components, which are displayed in Fig. II.1.

The first component of excellence in this middle sphere is departmental power, the ability to influence members of the dominant coalition. This is reflected in how CEOs think their dominant coalitions value and support communication. Sometimes, top communicators are members of dominant coalitions, participating directly in strategic management and planning. Often, top communicators exert informal influence as providers of information and as process facilitators to dominant coalitions.

The second component of excellence in this sphere is the demand-delivery loop. Senior managers demand two-way practices from their communicators to persuade and negotiate, and top communicators are aware of this.

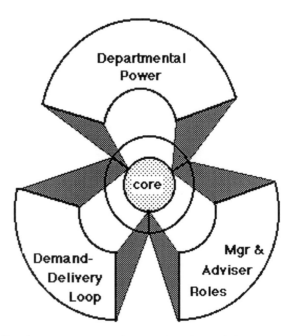

FIG. II.1.   The three components of the middle sphere of shared expectations for communication excellence.

Further, excellent communication departments have the savvy to deliver. This sets up a loop of repeated behavior, with senior management demanding and communicators delivering excellent communication programs.

The third component of excellence in this sphere is the organizational role played by the top communicator. Top communicators may have formal decision-making authority for communication policy; they may be responsible for program success or failure. On the other hand, top communicators may play a more informal role as senior advisers who outline options and provide research information needed for decision making by other senior managers. Both manager and senior adviser role playing contribute to communication excellence.

6

The Power of the Communication Department

Power is the capacity to exert influence, a transaction in which you get others to change their behavior as you intended. We show power when we get others to act differently than they would otherwise. Traditionally, communicators have described the power of a particular communication strategy or campaign to influence publics. We often describe particularly effective communication products (e.g., a corporate advocacy advertisement, a public service announcement) as powerful. By itself, this notion of power reflects a one-way view of communication and power. Excellent communication programs incorporate another dimension of power: the communicator's ability to influence decisions about an organization's goods and services, its policies, and its behavior. The communication department must have power and influence within the dominant coalition to help organizations practice the two-way symmetrical model.[1]

Powerful communication departments are valued and supported by dominant coalitions. Where do power, value, and support come from? The source of these three qualities of excellent departments was succinctly summarized by a senior communication specialist we interviewed: strategic contributions. This communicator worked for a public utility that ranked in the top 1% of organizations in the Excellence Study. "Top management comes to accept you when they see work coming out of your department that meets their strategic objectives," he told us in a case study interview. "You've got

---

[1]We use the two-way symmetrical label as synonymous with the mixed-motive, two-way model detailed in chapter 3.

to be adding value in their eyes. Then you'll get a place at the table. You've got to start thinking in strategic terms."

In this chapter, we consider the power of communication departments in organizations, represented by the value and support that communication departments receive from dominant coalitions. Communication departments need power within senior management in order to make strategic contributions. These contributions, in turn, lead to greater power and influence in management decision making.

WHY WE NEED POWERFUL COMMUNICATION DEPARTMENTS

We believe that communication departments, as represented by top communicators, must be powerful players in organizational decision making.[2] Our interest in the power of communication departments has little to do with "protecting turf" or enhancing the "image" of communication as an important organizational function; rather, power is important in order to implement excellent communication programs. Lacking the ability to influence the strategic decision making of dominant coalitions, communication departments must execute less-than-excellent communication programs. Such less-than-excellent programs seek to influence publics on issues important to dominant coalitions, but cannot exert a reciprocal influence on dominant coalitions on behalf of publics.

The power of communication departments is frequently informal. This means that excellent communication departments, usually through top communicators, influence the decision making of dominant coalitions without having any formal power or authority to do so. Some top managers have formal power explicitly spelled out in organizational charts—a capacity to influence others whether they choose to exercise such authority or not. Communicators, on the other hand, are influential only to the degree that they actually influence decisions of dominant coalitions. The power of communicators is dynamic, found in the "doing" of senior management decision making.

The dominant role played by top communicators, either manager or technician, provides key indicators of the communication department's power. Serving in the manager role means that top communicators influence key strategic decisions of dominant coalitions. Serving in the technician role

---

[2]The argument in favor of organizational power for communication departments is described in greater detail in chapters 4, 6, and 18 of *Excellence in Public Relations and Communication Management* (Grunig, 1992).

means that top communicators implement, as service providers, decisions made by other senior managers. When top communicators play the technician role predominantly, much can be deduced about how dominant coalitions regard the communication function. We address role enactment by top communicators in greater detail in chapter 8.

Logically, a powerful communication department can play an important role in mutual adjustments of dominant coalitions and publics. Symmetrical practices among communicators require that the communicators act as advocates of their organization's viewpoint when communicating with publics, and as advocates of public interests when communicating with their dominant coalitions.[3] Communicators help organizations and publics negotiate mutually acceptable resolutions to disputes, building long-term relationships. Weak communication departments are limited to implementing decisions of others. One-way models of press agentry/publicity and public information largely define the range of practices of weak communication departments. Just as communication flows one way, so too does influence.

POWER AND EMPOWERMENT

Organizations exhibit two basic forms of culture: authoritarian and participative. Authoritarian cultures emphasize centralized control and decision making by a few powerful managers. Participative cultures emphasize teamwork, with wide participation in decision making.

Every organization exhibits characteristics of both authoritarian and participative culture. The authoritarian side of an organization's culture emphasizes power rooted in formal authority. The participative side of an organization's culture emphasizes influence—the informal power to persuade others involved in decision making.

One problem with authoritarian culture is that centralized control and decision making often leaves many employees powerless. Employees may be accountable or responsible for performing some task or achieving some outcome, but they lack sufficient authority over resources to get the job done. This leads to job dissatisfaction. Communicators are especially subject to such dissatisfaction from powerlessness. They are responsible for organizational relationships with publics, but can not influence the decisions of dominant coalitions that shape those relationships.

The solution is to empower employees, giving them sufficient control over needed resources to complete the job. The empowerment value runs

---

[3]Of course, advocacy is not all that symmetrical communicators do. Listening to both public and senior management is also an important and necessary quality of two-way communication.

deep in participative culture. The total quality management (TQM) philosophy, in all its myriad forms, seeks to empower employees, decentralizing some aspects of decision making.

As detailed in Part III, participative culture provides a nurturing soil in which communication excellence can grow. The top communicator is more likely to be excluded when a few top managers make centralized decisions by virtue of formal authority. As decision making expands to include other contributors without formal authority, top communicators are more likely to be influential. Top communicators need such informal power—a form of empowerment for communication departments—for communication excellence.

DOMINANT COALITION SUPPORT FOR COMMUNICATION

In the Excellence Study, both chief executive officers (CEO) and top communicators were asked to assess the degree to which dominant coalitions supported their communication departments. In the CEO questionnaire, these top managers were asked to identify the "group of powerful people" in their organizations called the *dominant coalition*. Immediately following this question, CEOs were asked to indicate the extent to which the dominant coalition they had just identified supported the public relations or communication function in the organization. The CEOs were further instructed: "In this case, 0 would indicate no support at all, 100 would indicate the average extent to which organizations support public relations, and a higher score would indicate strong support." As with other measures, CEOs could assign as high a score as they wished. This measure of support for communication and public relations is one of the 20 measures of communication excellence. (See Table 1.1.)

To provide an indication of how excellent communication programs differed from less-than-excellent programs, the average level of support in the top 10% of organizations was computed and compared to support for the communication function in the bottom 10%.[4] CEOs in the bottom 10% placed dominant coalition support for the communication and public relations function at 113, slightly above the hypothetical average score of 100. For the top 10%, however, CEOs placed dominant coalition support for the communication function at 290, almost three times above the support for an average communication function.

The same question was posed in the same manner to top communicators.

[4]The top 10% were the 30 organizations (out of 321) with the highest overall Excellence Score on the Excellence Factor. See Exhibit 1.1 for a brief description of the Excellence Factor. See the appendix for a more detailed description of the Excellence Study.

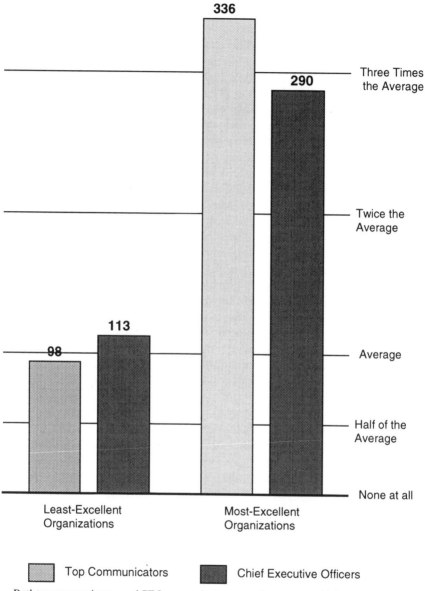

Both top communicators and CEOs were asked to report the extent to which the organization's dominant coalition supports the communication and public relations function. A score of 0 means no support at all, a score of 100 is average support, and scores greater than 100 indicate strong support. The scores given here are the averages for the most-excellent and least-excellent organizations, based on their overall scores on the Excellence Factor.

FIG. 6.1.   Level of dominant coalition support for the communication function among most-excellent and least-excellent organizations.

After identifying the dominant coalition in their organization, they were asked to estimate the support of the dominant coalition for the communication or public relations function. The answers from the top 10% of organizations in the study were compared to the bottom 10%. Top communicators in the bottom 10% of organizations placed this support at 98, two points below the score for an average communication function. Top communicators in the top 10% of participating organizations placed dominant coalition support at 336, over three times the support for the average communication function. Fig. 6.1 displays support scores for the communication function, as reported by CEOs and top communicators for the most-excellent organizations (top 10% of overall communication Excellence Scores) and least-excellent organizations (bottom 10% of overall Excellence Scores).

Generally, CEOs and top communicators provided similar assessments of dominant coalition support for the communication function in their respective organizations. In the least-excellent organizations, CEOs and top communicators reported average support for the function. In the most-excellent organizations, CEOs and top communicators report dominant coalition support to be roughly three times the support given to the function if it were only average. This is the first of many shared expectations or understandings between top communicators and CEOs that define communication excellence. Communicators in organizations with the top 10% of overall Excellence Scores know that the communication function has strong support from the dominant coalition. CEOs in those same organizations recognize that same strong support for the communication function.

THE RELATIVE VALUE OF THE COMMUNICATION DEPARTMENT

CEOs and top communicators answered a similar set of questions to assess the value of the communication and public relations department, relative to other departments in the organization. The support-of-function questions discussed earlier tap support for the function among dominant coalitions in the abstract, somewhat separate from actual performance of communicators in the organization. Recall that "average" support meant the average extent to which organizations support the communication and public relations function.

Departmental value, on the other hand, measures the value "that you think *your* public relations or communication department has in *this* organization." This concrete measure of value was asked of the top communicator in two ways. First, the top communicator was asked to give "*your* rating of the value of the public relations/communication department." Zero meant no value at all; 100 meant the average value for a typical department in the same organization; 200 meant twice the average value; 300 meant three times average; and so forth. Next, top communicators were asked how the *dominant coalition* would rate the value of the communication department.

CEOs were asked a slightly different question. As members of the dominant coalition, the CEOs were asked to think about the "value that you think your public relations or communication department has to this organization." CEOs were asked to compare the communication department to other, typical departments in the same organization. A score of 0 meant no value at all; 100 meant the communication department was of average value, when compared to other departments in the organization; 200 meant twice average; 300 meant three times average; and so forth.

Responses to these value questions were compared for least-excellent organizations and most-excellent organizations, based on their overall communication Excellence Scores. Among least-excellent organizations, self-evaluations of the top communicators placed the communication department's value at about one-and-a-half times the average value of departments in their organizations. However, these same top communicators said dominant coalitions would score the value of the communication department at slightly below average. In fact, CEOs in these least-excellent organizations placed the value of their communication departments at slightly above average.

Among most-excellent organizations, self-evaluations by top communicators placed departmental value at over two-and-a-half times the value of an average department in their organizations. These same top communicators thought the dominant coalition would score the department's value at slightly below their own self-evaluations. On average, CEOs in these most-excellent organizations valued their communication departments the same as did their top communicators: over two-and-a-half times the average. Fig. 6.2 displays the actual averages for most-excellent and least-excellent organizations.

How much CEOs and dominant coalitions value their communication departments affects the power of top communicators to retain or expand the departmental budget. When we conducted our case studies in 1994, we found that the recession of the 1990s had negatively affected even excellent communication departments. One not-for-profit organization posted an overall excellence score in the top 5% in the survey. When we interviewed the top communicator in 1994, she indicated that only the communication department and the development department had been spared layoffs and budget reductions. In other, for-profit corporations with high overall excellence scores, communication budgets had been reduced, but not as much as in other departments. In short, when the communication department is viewed as relatively valuable by the CEO, the department does relatively well in times of tighter budgets.

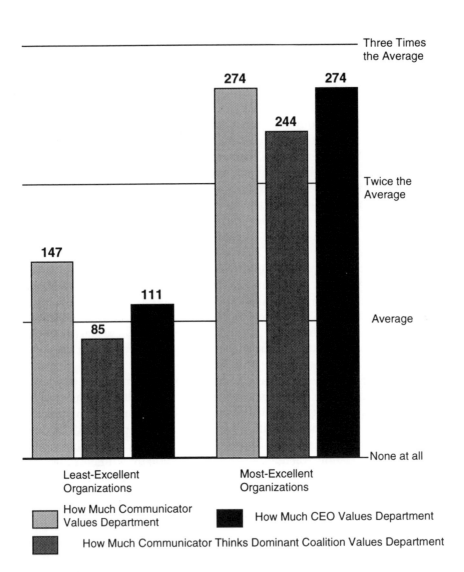

Both top communicators and CEOs were asked to report the value that they think their communication and public relations department has to the organization. A score of 0 means no value at all, a score of 100 is average value in comparison to other departments in the organization, and scores greater than 100 indicate greater than average value. In addition, top communicators were asked how much they thought their dominant coalitions valued the communication and public relations department in their organization. The same scale was used. The scores in the table are the averages for the most-excellent and least-excellent organizations, based on their overall scores on the Excellence Factor.

FIG. 6.2. The relative value of the communication department as perceived by top communicators and dominant coalitions among most-excellent and least-excellent organizations.

TOP COMMUNICATORS IN DOMINANT COALITIONS

Communication departments are more likely to be excellent when top communicators are members of dominant coalitions. Recall that dominant coalitions are informal alliances that include individuals and units not formally recognized as powerful on organizational charts. (See Exhibit 1.3 for a more detailed explanation of dominant coalitions.) In order to capture the membership of dominant coalitions, CEOs were asked to indicate who was in the dominant coalition in their organizations. Of special interest to the research team was whether the organization's top communicator was in this powerful coalition of decision makers.

Must We Be in the Dominant Coalition?

After studying the data, we can say that top communicator membership in the dominant coalition is not necessary for communication excellence—but it sure helps. We looked at organizations with overall excellence scores in the top 10%. In these most-excellent organizations, 76% of the top communicators were identified by their CEOs as members of the dominant coalition. The other 24% of top organizations achieved excellence without their top communicators in dominant coalitions. As a basis for comparison, we examined organizations with overall excellence scores in the bottom 10%. In these least-excellent organizations, only 10% of the top communicators were members of the dominant coalition. Such membership in the dominant coalition is a key measure of departmental power. The most-excellent organizations have powerful communication departments, typically with top communicators as members of the organization's powerful elite, the dominant coalition.

Reporting Relationships

We thought that reporting relationships also provided a way to measure the power and influence of the communication and public relations departments. We reasoned that top communicators who report directly to CEOs would have more influence than would top communicators lower in the organizational hierarchy, so we asked CEOs if their top communicators reported directly to them. If they did not, we asked if top communicators had an indirect reporting relationship to CEOs on some important matters, but not others. If the answers to both questions were no, we asked about two-step reporting relationships in which top communicators report to another manager who, in turn, reports to the CEO.

When we compared reporting relationships to overall excellence scores, we were surprised by the weak relationships we found. Indeed, top communicators who report directly to CEOs have slightly higher overall excellence scores for their organizations than do top communicators who report to CEOs through a longer chain of command. However, the difference in overall excellence scores was small.

We examined the top 10% and bottom 10% of organizations to see if they could help illuminate these puzzling findings.[5] Among least-excellent organizations, 57% of top communicators reported directly to their CEOs. Among most-excellent organizations, 76% of top communicators reported directly to their CEOs. With the majority of top communicators in both most-excellent and least-excellent organizations reporting directly to their CEOs, reporting relationships are not very good indicators of excellence. We might think of direct communicator–CEO reporting relationships as somewhat necessary but hardly sufficient for communication excellence.

As we puzzled over the findings, we realized that we had become overly enamored with organizational charts and formal reporting relationships. After all, an administrative assistant in the CEO's office and the senior vice president for finance may both report directly to the CEO. The reporting relationship tells us little about the degree of influence these two individuals have on decision making by the dominant coalition.[6]

The top corporate communicator with a chemical manufacturing company said it best. The critical factor, he told us in a case study interview, "is not who you report to but rather whether you have access. As a communicator, I have access to any of the [corporate] officers at will."

Concerning membership in the dominant coalition, a more fluid and informal arrangement of organizational power and influence provides a strong indicator of communication excellence.

THE CONTRIBUTION OF COMMUNICATION TO STRATEGIC PLANNING

Strategic management and planning involve the exercise of organizational power at the highest level, because an organization's mission and long-term goals are "on the table" when dominant coalitions plan strategy. The very purpose and direction of an organization can be recast when top managers plan strategically. Exhibit 6.1 provides a more detailed explanation of strategic management and planning.

---

[5]The top 10% and the bottom 10% of organizations were identified by their overall Excellence Scores on the Excellence Factor.

[6]These examples are used because they contrast large differences in formal organizational power in similar reporting relationships. However, we are not suggesting that the administrative assistant in this example is powerless. Indeed, the power-control perspective in organizational theory suggests that the administrative assistant may be very influential by virtue of network centrality, or "being where the action is." Our point is simply that reporting relationships alone tell us little about the influence of individuals on dominant coalition decision making.

EXHIBIT 6.1
Strategic Management and Planning

Strategic management and planning are high-level organizational functions tightly linked to excellence in public relations and communication management. Higgins (1979) defined *strategic management* as the "process of managing the pursuit of the accomplishment of organizational mission coincident with managing the relationship of the organization to its environment" (p. 1). That is, the purpose and direction of an organization (its mission) is affected by relationships with key constituents (publics) in the organization's environment. These relationships affect an organization's autonomy to pursue its mission and accomplish its goals. Dominant coalitions engage in strategic planning when they make strategic decisions in a proactive manner. Steps in strategic planning include determining the organization's mission, developing an organizational profile, assessing the external environment, matching the organizational profile with environmental opportunities, identifying best options consistent with mission, choosing long-term goals, developing short-term objectives, implementing programs, and evaluating success or failure. Public relations and communication management can play a key role as the dominant coalition's "eyes and ears," a reliable source of information about what's going on in the organizational environment. Communication becomes a strategic management function when communication programs help manage relationships with key publics that affect organizational mission, goals, and objectives. According to Steiner, Miner, and Gray (1982), strategic management differs from operational management precisely because of the growing influence of external environments on internal decision making. By the same token, strategic public relations and communication management differs from tactical or functionary communication. Strategic public relations and communication management involve top communicators in the highest management roles in an organization, and help dominant coalitions assess the external environment and respond appropriately to it. Top communicators are qualified to play this role because their departments practice two-way models of communication. Communicators provide two-way channels of communication from dominant coalitions to publics and back again. Such feedback loops from publics to dominant coalitions are crucial to dominant coalition assessment of organizational environments and appropriate responses to them. Tactical or functionary communication, on the other hand, involves nonstrategic dissemination of messages from organizations to frequently poorly defined and understood publics. Under such conditions, top communicators need not be managers. A supervising technician, with routine budgeting and personnel supervision skills, will suffice. At best, such one-way practices execute strategies chosen and planned by others in the organization. At worst, one-way communication is simply functionary, the generation of messages as an end in themselves, a perpetual motion machine, squirting ink. The reason for such communications may have some long-forgotten historical basis (Broom, 1986), but current practices simply reflect an imperative to "do this year what we did last year."

In some organizations, the top communicator plays an important role in strategic management and planning. In others, the top communicator is not involved. Two key measures of communication excellence are the contributions of communication departments to strategic planning, as reported by CEOs and top communicators.

When a state arts organization hired a new top communicator, he immediately sought access to management decision making. "I explained to them that I needed to sit in on the big meetings to be truly effective," he told us in a case study interview. "I need to know the issues from the beginning, not simply crank out press releases."

In time, the top communicator proved his worth in strategic planning. His power increased because he successfully obtained significant increased funding for the organization. "He has been invaluable in heightening the organization's awareness," the CEO told us. "Most of the infighting has quieted down."

CEOs were asked to describe the "extent to which your [communication and] public relations department makes a contribution to the *strategic planning function* of your organization." A score of 0 meant no contribution at all, 50 meant half the contribution of an average communication department, 100 meant a contribution equal to that of an average communication department, and scores above 100 were described in the questionnaire as "highly significant contributions."[7] The question was phrased in an identical fashion on the questionnaire for top communicators.

To help illustrate the relationship between communication excellence and strategic planning contributions, the least-excellent and the most-excellent organizations were compared.[8] Among least-excellent organizations, top communicators reported communication department contributions to strategic planning at 38; CEOs in these same organizations placed communicator contributions at 35. In least-excellent organizations, therefore, both CEOs and top communicators provide nearly identical assessments of communication's contribution to strategic planning. That contribution falls well below half the contribution one would expect from an average public relations and communication department.

Among the most-excellent organizations, both CEOs and top communicators reported that communication departments make "highly significant" contributions to strategic planning. However, CEOs did not place depart-

---

[7]A score of 200 meant twice the contribution of an average department; 300 meant three times the average contribution; and so forth.

[8]That is, the top 10% and the bottom 10% of organizations were identified by their overall Excellence Scores on the Excellence Factor. Average scores for contributions to strategic planning were compared for CEOs and top communicators.

mental contributions as high as did top communicators. On average, CEOs in the most-excellent organizations placed the contribution of communication departments to strategic planning at 185, nearly twice the level of contributions CEOs would expect from an average communication department. Top communicators in those same organizations placed the contributions of communication departments at 293, nearly three times the contribution of average communication departments.

The discrepancy between CEOs and top communicators may lie in the meaning of *strategic planning* to different participants. The blood bank was one of the most-excellent organizations that participated in the case studies. The top communicator reported much higher levels of contribution to strategic planning than did the chief financial officer, who completed the CEO questionnaire. The top communicator and her subordinate in the communication department reported that someone from communication participated in daily half-hour senior management meetings, in which strategy and tactics were discussed. The chief financial officer, however, indicated that most strategic planning involved the medical director, key board members, and herself. The communication department played only an indirect role in formal strategic planning. Arguably, the blood bank conducts much work of a strategic sort, as well as handling operational issues, in its daily senior management meetings. Imprecise differentiation between strategic and tactical planning could contribute to different perceptions of contributions. Subtle ambiguity in terminology did not matter much in the least-excellent organizations. Whatever strategic planning might mean, CEOs and top communicators agreed that the communication department was not contributing.

In the findings from our case studies, we concluded that participation in strategic planning and management was among the most powerful predictors of overall excellence. In case after case, the most-excellent communicators we interviewed played important roles in strategic planning, whereas communicators in least-excellent organizations played little or no role in strategic planning.

How do top communicators earn a place at the table where strategic decisions are made? "You have to earn it," the top communicator at a financial services company told us. "Show them what you're worth. If you bring value to the equation, you will be recognized and the [dominant coalition] will seek your input."

"You have to be comfortable working with senior management and showing them you have the necessary skills to be an asset as an expert in . . . decision making," another communicator with a medical products company told us.

Once a top communicator is established as a key player, his or her power and influence grows. "My opinion is being solicited and I am being listened to by the people who are in charge," the top communicator at an engineering research firm said.

SUMMARY

The power of communication departments come from dominant coalitions—that powerful elite that sets mission and goals and calls the shots in organizations. The power of communication departments is seen in their contributions to strategic planning. Communicators cannot influence the strategic decisions of dominant coalitions unless the membership of that coalition values and supports communication. As several communicators told us, value and support come to those communication departments that prove their worth to senior management by their strategic contributions. Influence, then, is circular. Power is necessary to be given the opportunity to contribute. Strategic contributions, in turn, increase the value and support dominant coalitions give to communication departments.

For each "power" measure of communication excellence, both CEOs and top communicators must agree. Ambiguity and uncertainty about the value and support of communication diminishes the department's ability to contribute. In fact, it is hard to imagine a powerful communication department if the CEO and dominant coalition did not view communication in the same way. The next chapter considers the relationship between the demand for excellence from the dominant coalition and the delivery of excellence from communication departments.

REFERENCES

Broom, G. M. (1986, May). *Public relations roles and systems theory: Functional and historicist causal models*. Paper presented at the meeting of the International Communication Association, Chicago.

Grunig, J. E. (Ed.). (1992). *Excellence in public relations and communication management*. Hillsdale, NJ: Lawrence Erlbaum Associates.

Higgins, H. M. (1979). *Organizational policy and strategic management: Texts and cases*. Hinsdale, IL: Dryden.

Steiner, G. A., Miner, J. B., & Gray, E. R. (1982). *Management policy and strategy* (2nd ed.). New York: Macmillan.

7

Shared Expectations of Communication

Organizations that achieve excellence have communication departments with the expertise for both advanced and traditional practices. (By *advanced practices*, we mean two-way communication to negotiate and persuade both senior management and publics toward mutually beneficial relationships.) Knowledge of advanced practices is not enough, however. To put such expertise to use, communication departments need CEOs and dominant coalitions that understand such practices and expect them from their communication departments. Under such conditions, communication becomes essential to strategic management and the smooth operation of organizations.

Consider this perspective from a vice president in an economic development agency. He had recently hired a new communicator with expertise to practice two-way communication. "We look at communication as being a critical component of the system," he told us. "If you pull one chunk out, the system doesn't function properly."

One association we encountered in the study promotes heart health through a top-ranked communication program. The top communicator practices two-way communication extensively with local volunteer chapters and other key constituents. "Maybe some companies see a communication department as just a nice thing to have and not a necessity," she said. "Our [CEO] has great regard for communication."

Two-way communication means that communicators serve as eyes and ears for their organizations. It also means that communicators act as go-betweens, reducing conflicts between senior management and publics through negotiation and persuasion.

The top communicator for a state arts organization clearly understood this important responsibility. "One of my roles is to bridge the gap between the different mentalities held by people in the arts organization and the state and federal legislators who definitely have a different perspective on things," he told us. "I help both understand each other."

Such advanced, two-way practices require the understanding and support of dominant coalitions. In some organizations, communicators with the expertise for excellence find their dominant coalitions equally receptive.

The top communicator for a Midwest gas and electric company said that the communication department "is blessed with leaders who believe in what we [in communication] are doing. Communication is an important part of what *they* [senior managers] are doing."

In organizations with less-than-excellent communication, dominant coalitions often view communication as a narrow technical support function. "Some CEOs don't have the broad scope of communication," the vice president at an insurance company told us. He supervises a communication department that ranked in the bottom 10% of organizations participating in the Excellence Study. "They have tunnel vision," he continued, referring to the CEO of his own company. "They refuse to change bad habits."

Narrow vision is not a malady of CEOs alone—sometimes communicators regard themselves as technicians in support of other organizational functions. A communicator for one division of a hotel chain viewed communication as a support function for marketing. "I don't spend a lot of time justifying our existence or defending our area," he explained. "[Communication] is not the most important thing our company does. PR just fits into a whole lot of other things." Reflecting on communication's narrow support role in many organizations, he added, "There are many more crucial issues in the business world."

Other communicators have wider and higher vision. They see the need for advanced practices and are trying to educate senior managers. "As members of the International Association of Business Communicators, we are more educated about where communication belongs," the publications editor of an engineering research agency told us. In the agency, communication has found an ally in a new deputy director, who shares the department's vision for advanced practices. "The deputy director represents new leadership," the publications editor explained. "It will be an ongoing educational process for [senior management] about communication's role."

Regarding excellence, it clearly takes two to tango.

In the survey portion of the Excellence Study, we asked both partners—the CEO and the top communicator—about what is expected from the communication department. The Excellence Factor includes two sets of measures of advanced practices. One set measures two-way symmetrical practices; a second set measures two-way asymmetrical practices. We asked CEOs if their dominant coalitions expected two-way practices—both symmetrical and asymmetrical—from their communication departments. We asked top communicators what senior management expected from their departments. Did their dominant coalitions expect advanced, two-way practices? Taken together, the four measures (two from CEOs and two from top communicators) allowed us to study the shared expectations of communication. We theorized that excellence occurs when dominant coalitions expect their communication departments to practice the two-way models, and top communicators understand those expectations.[1]

HOW SHARED EXPECTATIONS WERE MEASURED

CEOs and top communicators were asked which practices dominant coalitions in their organizations expected from the communication department. In the CEO questionnaire, the question was asked as follows:

> The senior administrators who run an organization—the dominant coalition you were asked to identify—generally have a prevailing idea about how public relations, public affairs, or communication management should be practiced. Please use the open-ended scale to indicate how you think the dominant coalition in this organization *believes public relations should be practiced.*

In the top communicator questionnaire, the question was asked in a slightly different way:

> The senior administrators who run an organization—the dominant coalition you were asked to identify—generally have a prevailing idea about how public relations, public affairs, or communication management should be practiced. *Sometimes that idea differs from that of the public relations department.*[2] Please use the open-ended scale to indicate the extent to which the *dominant coalition* in this organization *believes public relations should be practiced.*

Following these instructions were 16 items, four each for the press agentry/ publicity model, the public information model, the two-way symmetrical model, and the two-way asymmetrical model.

CEOs and top communicators were asked to score each item using a scale in which 0 meant that the item did not describe the expectations of the

---

[1]The expectations of the dominant coalition regarding two-way symmetrical and two-way asymmetrical practices were reported by the CEO, one member of the dominant coalition. Top communicators were asked to report what they thought their dominant coalitions expected regarding advanced, two-way practices. Overall Excellence Scores on the Excellence Factor increased as both CEOs and top communicators reported that the expectations of their dominant coalitions were high for advanced, two-way practices.

[2]This additional instruction was added to the top communicator questionnaire to clarify that we were interested in their perceptions of what dominant coalitions expect, rather than what top communicators prefer or practice.

dominant coalition at all, 100 meant average expectations, 200 meant twice the average, and so forth. We computed mean scores for each of the four models for CEOs and top communicators.[3]

SHARED EXPECTATIONS REGARDING TWO-WAY SYMMETRICAL PRACTICES

Table 7.1 shows the four items that measured two-way symmetrical practices. These items emphasize negotiated solutions to conflicts between publics and senior management in which *management also changes*. Rather than persuading, manipulating, and dominating publics, communicators seek mutually beneficial relationships based on understanding. In their roles as mediators, communicators act as go-betweens. At times, communicators act as advocates of their organizations' positions when communicating with publics. At other times, communicators act as advocates of public interests when communicating with members of their dominant coalitions.

Research is both explicit and implicit in two-way symmetrical practices. To act as effective mediators, communicators must understand the positions of their dominant coalitions and those of key publics. "Research" on dominant coalition positions is conducted through the active participation of top communicators in strategic management. Research on publics involves both formal (e.g., surveys or focus groups) and informal techniques. Mutual understanding by dominant coalitions and publics requires that communicators understand the positions of both parties.

To illustrate the role that shared expectations play in excellence, organizations with high overall Excellence Scores were compared with organizations with low overall Excellence Scores.[4] CEOs and top communicators in the most-excellent organizations said their dominant coalitions had high expectations for two-way symmetrical practices. On average, CEOs in organizations with high overall Excellence Scores placed expectations for two-way symmetrical practices at over one-and-a-half times average.[5] Top communicators in the top organizations reported scores slightly lower than did their CEOs, but well above average. Fig. 7.1 displays these findings.

---

[3]The scores on each of the four items for each model were added together, then divided by four. This strategy kept the meaning of the scores the same: a mean of 0 still meant not at all, 100 still meant average, and so forth.

[4]Using the Excellence Factor, organizations with overall communication Excellence Scores in the top 10% were compared to organizations with overall scores in the bottom 10% of those participating. Average two-way symmetrical expectations were computed for both CEOs and top communicators in the most-excellent and least-excellent organizations.

[5]*Average* in this context means the average level of dominant coalition expectation for any "typical" practice from any of the four models of communication practices.

TABLE 7.1
Measures of Two-Way Symmetrical Practices

- The purpose of public relations is to change the attitude and behavior of management as much as it is to change the attitudes and behavior of publics.
- Public relations should provide mediation for the organization—to help management and publics negotiate conflicts.
- The purpose of public relations is to develop mutual understanding between the management of the organization and publics the organization affects.
- Before starting a public relations program, surveys or informal research should be done to find out how much management and our publics understand each other.

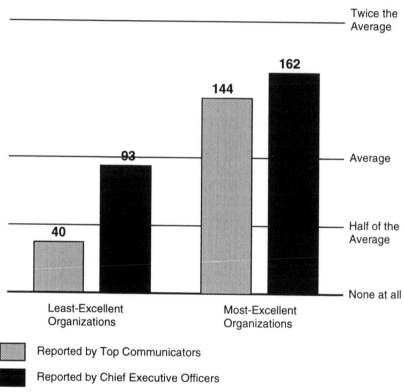

Both top communicators and CEOs were asked to report the extent to which the organization's dominant coalition expects two-way symmetrical practices from the communication function. A score of 0 means none at all, a score of 100 is average demand (relative to all types of practices), and scores greater than 100 indicate above average demand for two-way symmetrical practices. The scores in the table are the averages for the most-excellent and least-excellent organizations as determined by their overall score on the Excellence Factor.

FIG. 7.1. Level of dominant coalition demand for two-way symmetrical practices among most-excellent and least-excellent organizations.

Among those with overall excellence scores in the lowest 10% of participating organizations, CEOs reported higher expectations for two-way symmetrical practices than did top communicators in the same organizations. CEOs in the least-excellent organizations said their dominant coalition would place their preferences for two-way symmetrical practices at 93, slightly below an average score of 100. Top communicators in the same organizations placed expectations of those same dominant coalitions for two-way symmetrical practices at 40, closer to "none at all" than "average."

Poor understanding of dominant coalition expectations in the least-excellent organizations may have resulted, in part, from the isolation of top communicators from strategic planning and decision making. Recall from chapter 6 that only 10% of top communicators in these least-excellent organizations are members of their dominant coalitions. In these least-excellent organizations, both top communicators and their CEOs agree that communication departments make minimal contributions to strategic planning.

Even if top communicators in these least-excellent organizations clearly understood that the dominant coalition prefers two-way symmetrical practices, their departments could not deliver. In the least-excellent organizations, top communicators reported little expertise to practice the two-way symmetrical model. On a scale in which 0 is "no expertise at all" and 100 is "average" expertise across all areas of practices, top communicators in least-excellent organizations reported a score of 34 regarding their knowledge of two-way symmetrical practices. These communication departments simply lack the knowledge necessary to provide the advanced practices that their dominant coalitions expect to a moderate degree.[6]

SHARED EXPECTATIONS REGARDING TWO-WAY ASYMMETRICAL PRACTICES

Table 7.2 displays the four items used in both the top communicator and CEO questionnaires to measure demand by dominant coalitions for two-way asymmetrical practices. Three of the four items mention research explicitly. The top item succinctly states the purpose of asymmetrical practices: to persuade publics to behave as organizations want them to behave.

---

[6]CEOs in least-excellent organizations reported dominant coalition expectations of 93 on the two-way symmetrical practices scale, which is slightly below the average for all practices, both traditional and advanced. That is, CEOs reported an average level of demand for two-way symmetrical practices, which is not a strong demand. However, the demand is stronger than the next-to-nothing demand their top communicators reported. The assumption is that CEOs, as members of dominant coalitions in their organizations, have a better understanding of these expectations than do top communicators, who are typically not coalition members in these least-excellent organizations.

TABLE 7.2
Measures of Two-Way Asymmetrical Practices

- In public relations, the broad goal is to persuade publics to behave as the organization wants them to behave.
- Before beginning a public relations program, one should do research to determine public attitudes toward the organization and how they might be changed.
- Before starting a public relations program, one should look at attitude surveys to make sure the organization and its policies are described in ways its publics would be most likely to accept.
- After completing a public relations program, research should be done to determine how effective this program has been in changing people's attitudes.

When research is done, the purpose is to learn how to change unfavorable public opinions, to learn how to "position" the organization so as to make it acceptable to publics, and to measure the success of such persuasive efforts.

Expectations about asymmetrical practices are illustrated in Fig. 7.2. Among organizations scoring in the top 10% of participants, CEOs and top communicators said their dominant coalitions expected two-way asymmetrical practices at about one-and-a-half times average. In organizations with overall Excellence Scores in the bottom 10% of participants, CEOs placed the preferences of the dominant coalition for asymmetrical practices at 81, below an average expectation of 100. However, top communicators in those same organizations placed expectations for two-way asymmetrical practices at only 38, closer to no expectation at all than average expectations.

Ignorance probably causes the expectation gap between CEOs and top communicators in least-excellent organizations. Top communicators in these least-excellent organizations are isolated from senior management decision making. Further, communication departments in these least-excellent organizations do not have the expertise to deliver two-way asymmetrical practices. When asked to report departmental knowledge of two-way asymmetrical practices, top communicators in least-excellent organizations reported an average level of 32, closer to 0 (no expertise at all) than to average expertise at 100.

Symmetrical practices emphasize changes in management opinions and behavior, as well as those of publics. Asymmetrical practices, on the other hand, emphasize changing the opinions and behavior of publics, without similar changes in the opinions and behavior of dominant coalitions. Both practices emphasize feedback from publics to senior management, using research as a communication tool.

As noted in chapter 3, excellent communication departments know research practices. However, such research serves both symmetrical and asymmetrical purposes through a mixed-motive model. At times, organizations attempt to persuade publics to change, without making corresponding changes in organization behaviors. At other times, organizations negotiate

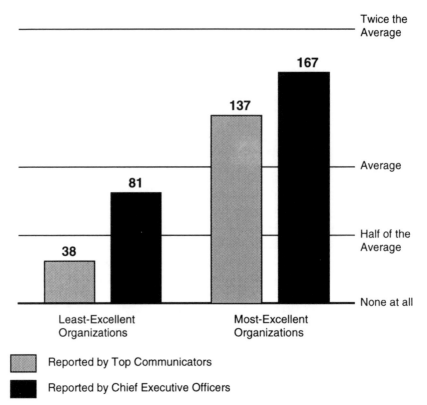

Reported by Top Communicators

Reported by Chief Executive Officers

Both top communicators and CEOs were asked to report the extent to which the organization's dominant coalition expects two-way asymmetrical practices from the communication function. A score of 0 means none at all, a score of 100 is average demand (relative to all types of practices), and scores greater than 100 indicate above average demand for two-way asymmetrical practices. The scores in the table are the averages for the most-excellent and least-excellent organizations as determined by their overall score on the Excellence Factor.

FIG. 7.2.   Level of dominant coalition demand for two-way asymmetrical practices among most-excellent and least-excellent organizations.

and seek to resolve disputes by moving both organizations and publics toward a common ground, what we called the *win–win zone* in chapter 3.

In organizations with excellent communication programs, the use of symmetrical and asymmetrical practices seems paradoxical. Two-way symmetrical practices provide an ethical basis for public relations and communication management. Purely asymmetrical practices, on the other hand, simply provide more sophisticated tools for manipulating publics. Symmetrical and asymmetrical practices seem driven by opposing worldviews. The solution to this seeming paradox is achieved by subordinating asymmetrical to symmetrical practices. Game theory suggests that cooperative antagonists seek short-term tactical advantage through asymmetrical practices, as organizations and publics jockey for position and advantage while they play their mixed-motive game. However, such short-term manipulation of the other party must not jeopardize the overall integrity of the game itself.

Raiffa (1982) said cooperative antagonists—the players in mixed-motive games—have the following characteristics suggestive of asymmetrical practices:

- Parties have different interests.
- Parties are not altruistic.
- Parties are primarily concerned with their own interests.
- Each party expects the other side to make a good case for itself and indulge in strategic posturing.
- Each party expects the other side to be less than candid.

On the other hand, all of these characteristics of cooperative antagonists operate within a larger framework suggestive of symmetrical practices:

- Parties have no malevolent intent.
- Each party would like to be truthful.
- Parties would like to reach a compromise.
- Parties expect power to be used gracefully.
- Parties expect both sides to abide by the law.
- Parties expect all joint agreements will be honored.

As Murphy (1991) argued, public relations practices can be viewed as a mixed-motive game, a "sliding scale of cooperation and competition in which organizational needs must of necessity be balanced against constituents' needs, but never lose their primacy" (p. 127). Does primacy of the organization mean that each cooperative antagonist plays an asymmetrical game? No—cooperative antagonists use asymmetrical tactics when they make a good case for their own side and when they engage in strategic posturing. However, these tactical moves cannot jeopardize the larger cooperative framework of the game itself. Asymmetrical tactics cannot undermine overall symmetrical goals to reach compromises—to collaborate in reaching binding joint agreements that both sides believe the other will respect.

Consider again the comment of the communicator at a major oil company who said that decisions to use asymmetrical practices are based on what the organization can "get away with" (see chapter 3). In a zero-sum game, such a statement would seem to justify massive lapses in the social responsibility of organizations. In a mixed-motive game, asymmetrical tactics in pursuit of organizational interests are bounded by symmetrical presuppositions. Two examples illustrate the difference between asymmetrical tactics in a mixed-motive game and unbounded asymmetrical practices in a zero-sum (win–lose) game.

When customers buy automobiles, both auto dealers and customers dicker with each other, pursuing self-interest and posturing for strategic advantage. Each party assumes the other is less than candid. The customer's interest lies in buying the most automobile for the least amount of money; the dealer's interest lies in moving merchandise at the highest possible price. Nevertheless, both want to make a deal—to reach an acceptable compromise. Buying an automobile, as described, is a mixed-motive game.

The decision to continue manufacturing an unsafe car, as in the famous case of the Ford Pinto, was based on the zero-sum strategy that settlement of lawsuits charging injury and wrongful death was less expensive than recalling unsafe automobiles. As described, the Ford Motor Company violated the symmetrical presuppositions of long-term relations between the company and its customers. The integrity of the game suffered from the graceless use of power and the violation of an implicit agreement between the auto maker and customers about the safety of automobiles.

Customers buy new food products because they may satisfy a perceived need or want. Companies manufacture food products and introduce them into new markets in hopes of capturing an adequate share of the new market so that such exchanges are profitable. In this relationship, customers and food manufacturers pursue their own interests regarding price. In such a mixed-motive game, the customer wants the lowest price possible; the manufacturer wants the highest price possible. The food manufacturer will use advertising and other communication to convince customers of the product's virtues. Customers regard these messages with skepticism. The food manufacturer and customer are cooperative antagonists. A compromise is reached when the customer decides to try the company's product, purchasing it at a certain price.

Nestlé Company, however, followed an asymmetrical, zero-sum strategy when it aggressively marketed infant milk formula in developing nations, as the sale of such products leveled and slumped in the industrialized nations. Consequences included malnourishment, illness, and even death of infants fed inadequate quantities of the formula mixed with contaminated water. Subsequent international boycotts of Nestlé's products provided impetus for a 1981 regulation by the World Health Organization of marketing activities for infant formula (Grunig & Hunt, 1984). Again, graceless use of marketing power violated the symmetrical presuppositions of the mixed-motive games played by cooperative antagonists. In this context, Nestlé's marketing of infant formula in developing nations was not simply an unsuccessful zero-sum strategy; the company's behavior undercut the public's assumptions about the absence of malevolent intent, undermining the integrity of the mixed-motive game.

How do communicators select symmetrical or asymmetrical practices? How should communicators select symmetrical and asymmetrical practices? Within the range of possible, mutually beneficial relationships, both organizations and publics seek positions of relative advantage. That is, organizations and publics use asymmetrical tactics to better their respective positions, so long as those tactics do not violate the basic integrity of long-term relationships.

As professionals,[7] communicators play special roles in strategic management to ensure that asymmetrical tactics do not violate the underlying integrity of the mixed-motive game. Put another way, communicators must protect the integrity of long-term relationships with key publics against inappropriate asymmetrical practices. Communicators seek relationships in the win–win zone.

Communicators are best equipped for this special role in strategic management because they understand the difference between symmetrical purposes and mixed-motive practices. Publics expect organizations to pursue organizational interests; publics do not expect altruism. Publics expect organizations to make their best case (persuasion) and to posture strategically. However, communicators need to know the acceptable boundaries (i.e., within the win–win zone) for such asymmetry, the limits on pursuing short-term self-interest in order to protect the larger integrity of long-term relationships with specific constituents and with society as a whole. In this way, professional communicators serve the greater public interest by advocating symmetrical practices to dominant coalitions in order to build or sustain long-term relationships with publics.

We conducted an exploratory analysis of top communicators and CEOs, using the 16 items that measure the preferences of the dominant coalition for different types of public relations practices. We used a statistical clustering technique to see how top communicators and CEOs would organize or

---

[7]Cutlip, Center, and Broom (1994) stated that professions "must fulfill expectations and moral obligations at the level of society," and that "right conduct takes into account the welfare of the larger society" (p. 132). In addition to the specialized knowledge required for two-way practices, professional communicators must behave in a manner that serves the greater social good as they assist clients in pursuing their own self-interests.

TABLE 7.3
Symmetrical Practices Model, as Seen by Top Communicators

Items Listed in Order of Importance

- Public relations should provide mediation for the organization—to help management and publics negotiate conflicts. [S]
- The purpose of public relations is to change the attitudes and behavior of management as much as it is to change the attitudes and behaviors of publics. [S]
- The purpose of public relations is to develop mutual understanding between the management of the organization and publics the organization affects. [S]

A = asymmetrical practices; S = symmetrical practices.

group together specific symmetrical and asymmetrical practices.[8] The results are provocative, suggesting that communicators are more discerning than are CEOs in distinguishing differences between symmetrical and asymmetrical practices.

When responses from top communicators were examined, they placed the 16 items measuring models of practices into four groups. However, these groupings differed from those originally staked out by the research team. One of the communicator groupings consisted of three items reflecting a symmetrical worldview. This grouping, which we labeled the *symmetrical practices model*, is displayed in Table 7.3. Items are listed in order of importance.[9] Note that these items address the purposes of public relations and communication management: to mediate, to change management as well as publics, and to develop mutual understanding. The actual research techniques used to accomplish these purposes are seen by top communicators as separate from the symmetrical purposes of public relations and communication management.

A second group of items, as organized by responses from top communica-

---

[8]This technique is called *exploratory factor analysis*, similar to the statistical procedures used to isolate the Excellence Factor (see chap. 1 and the appendix). When used as an exploratory tool, factor analysis examines a set of items for the most parsimonious groupings, based on how respondents answered the probes. The research team divided the 16 items into 4 groups with 4 items each, corresponding to the 4 models of practices. The appropriate items were then added together to create four indices measuring the press agentry/publicity model, the public information model, the two-way asymmetrical model, and the two-way asymmetrical model. In the exploratory phase of analysis, the same 16 items were grouped together, based on patterns in the responses of top communicators and CEOs. That is, both top communicators and CEOs were allowed to put together their own models of communication practices, based on their understanding of dominant coalition expectations.

[9]Items are listed in order of the magnitude of factor loadings. A higher factor loading means an item does a better job of measuring the concept in the model than does an item with a lower factor loading.

tors, is displayed in Table 7.4. This two-way, mixed-motive model of practices emphasizes research before and after execution of communication and public relations programs. The model describes mixed-motive purposes, because three of the items were designed to measure asymmetrical practices and one measures symmetrical practices.

When the same analysis was conducted on the responses of CEOs, symmetrical practices and asymmetrical practices were lumped together in a single model we labeled the *two-way practices model*. The two-way practices model is shown in Table 7.5. CEOs discarded the asymmetrical item that said the purpose of public relations is to persuade publics to behave as organizations want them to behave. The remaining three asymmetrical items and all four symmetrical items are grouped together by CEOs in the two-way practices model.

Differences in how CEOs and top communicators think about communication practices underscore the special role of communicators described earlier. CEOs in the Excellence Study did not perceive the profound differences in symmetrical and asymmetrical worldviews; rather, CEOs in excellent organizations said their dominant coalitions have high expectations for research-based, two-way practices. CEOs discarded the most blatantly manipulative item in the asymmetrical set, but retained the remaining asymmetrical items that emphasize research. In contrast, top communicators clearly differentiated between the symmetrical purposes of public relations and communication management from mixed-motive methods that emphasize research. In organizations with high Excellence Scores, top communicators reported high dominant coalition demand for both symmetrical purposes and research-based methods reflecting mixed motives. Communicators could subordinate mostly asymmetrical mixed-motive practices from

TABLE 7.4
Two-Way Mixed-Motive Practices Model, as Seen by Top Communicators

---

Items Listed in Order of Importance

- Before beginning a public relations program, one should do research to determine public attitudes toward the organization and how they might be changed. [A]
- Before starting a public relations program, surveys or informal research should be done to find out how much management and our publics understand each other. [S]
- Before starting a public relations program, one should look at attitude surveys to make sure the organization and its policies are described in ways its publics would be most likely to accept. [A]
- After completing a public relations program, research should be done to determine how effective this program has been in changing people's attitudes. [A]

A = asymmetrical practices; S = symmetrical practices.

TABLE 7.5

Two-Way Practices Model, as Seen by CEOs, Without Differentiating
Between Symmetrical and Asymmetrical Practices

Items Listed in Order of Importance

- Before starting a public relations program, surveys or informal research should be done to find out how much management and our publics understand each other. [S]
- Before beginning a public relations program, one should do research to determine public attitudes toward the organization and how they might be changed. [A]
- Before starting a public relations program, one should look at attitude surveys to make sure the organization and its policies are described in ways its publics would be most likely to accept. [A]
- After completing a public relations program, research should be done to determine how effective this program has been in changing people's attitudes. [A]
- The purpose of public relations is to develop mutual understanding between the management of the organization and publics the organization affects. [S]
- Public relations should provide mediation for the organization—to help management and publics negotiate conflicts. [S]
- The purpose of public relations is to change the attitudes and behavior of management as much as it is to change the attitudes and behavior of publics. [S]

A = asymmetrical practices; S = symmetrical practices.

broader symmetrical purposes of public relations and communication management. CEOs did not make such distinctions.

THE DEMAND–DELIVERY LOOP

The Excellence Survey provided the research team with a snapshot of what CEOs and top communicators said their dominant coalitions expect regarding communication and public relations practices. As detailed previously, organizations with high overall Excellence Scores have CEOs who reported a strong preference for two-way symmetrical and two-way asymmetrical practices. This is the demand for advanced, two-way practices. Top communicators in these same excellent organizations also reported high dominant coalition demand for two-way symmetrical and two-way asymmetrical practices. Further, communication departments in excellent organizations know how to deliver both two-way symmetrical and two-way asymmetrical practices.

What the Excellence Survey cannot provide is a moving picture of the interplay of the demand by the dominant coalition for advanced practices and the communication department's delivery of them. The case studies help illuminate this process, however. In the case of the blood bank, high levels of expertise in traditional practices (media relations) helped the blood bank avoid a major drop in donations at the peak of the AIDS scare.[10] This provided the top communicator with access to daily management sessions that dealt with both strategic and tactical issues. Over time, the expertise to practice two-way models was enhanced by new hires in the communication department. This, in turn, increased the ability of the communication department to contribute to strategic planning. The CEO at the blood bank expressed high confidence in both the top communicator and the staff of the department. When asked if the blood bank would revert to traditional practices if the present top communicator left, the CEO said that replacing the present top communicator would not be easy. "But the perspective [of advanced two-way practices] would not change," the CEO said firmly.

The reciprocal loop of demand and delivery is expressed succinctly by a member of the dominant coalition in a top engineering research agency, which posted an Excellence Score in the top 5% of participating organizations. As a result of slippage in the agency's national standing, the organization placed greater emphasis on public relations and communication management. "Yes, we consider public relations to be part of top management," the deputy director said, "because they have proven they can do the job. The [top communicator] gets attention quite a bit from the CEO because of the new priority mission and the fact she puts out a quality program."

CEOs and communicators mentioned crises again and again as catalysts for changes in management's views of communication; the Bhopal tragedy, the Exxon *Valdez* oil spill, the oil embargo of the 1970s, and activist opposition to nuclear power plants are examples. These events served as wake-up calls to senior managers who previously placed little importance on public relations and communication management.

Internal shakeups also played a role in management's strategic reevaluation of communication. A large manufacturing corporation scored near the bottom 10% in the 1990–1991 survey. Since then, a retirement in the communication department and the appointment of a new vice president for public affairs has radically transformed the communication function. The CEO has assumed chairmanship of the corporation since 1991, consolidating his power base and instituting numerous changes. Described as the corporation's "chief communication officer," the CEO had a keen interest in communication. The vice president of public affairs, a member of the dominant coalition, has instituted both symmetrical and asymmetrical two-way practices in programs for government, labor, and the community. These programs are supported by extensive research. The communication function

---

[10] In the early 1980s, some people feared that donating blood in some way increased their risk of contracting the AIDS virus. This unfounded fear was successfully contained, holding the drop in donations during the worst year to 3%. In other, nearby cities, donations dropped 15 to 25%.

in this organization has been transformed by a demanding CEO, a powerful vice president for public affairs, and increasing expertise in the communication department to complement traditional one-way practices. A similar restructuring at a chemical manufacturing company resulted in greater communication participation in strategic management. Strategic planning, investor relations, and public affairs were consolidated in a single portfolio under one senior vice president who supervises corporate communications.

What comes first, an enlightened dominant coalition demanding excellence or a knowledgeable communication department delivering excellence? From our case studies, we conclude that expertise typically—but not always—comes first. Dominant coalitions tend to value and support communicators who first demonstrate their worth. Certainly, excellent communication programs first require cutting-edge expertise as a prerequisite to implementation. Top communicators can parlay such expertise to reposition the communication function if they can get the attention of dominant coalitions. As dominant coalitions develop expectations for advanced practices, top communicators must be able to deliver. Over time, modest expectations for advanced, two-way practices can evolve into an ongoing expectation or demand. As our case study of the Chemical Manufacturers Association demonstrated, the delivery of excellent communication programs only whets the appetites of dominant coalitions for more of the same.

SUMMARY

Advanced practices combine two-way communication with negotiation and persuasion. Short-term asymmetrical tactics can be used to stake out more advantageous positions within the larger context of mutually beneficial relationships. Ethical communicators always subordinate asymmetrical methods to broad principles of symmetrical purpose. In doing so, communicators use both formal and informal research methods.

Advanced practices require understanding from dominant coalitions. Excellent communication is more likely to occur when dominant coalitions demand two-way practices. Of course, top communicators must understand these demands and deliver two-way practices. To do so, they must have the knowledge base in their departments to deliver.

REFERENCES

Cutlip, S. M., Center, A. H, & Broom, G. M. (1994). *Effective public relations* (7th ed.). Englewood Cliffs, NJ: Prentice-Hall.

Grunig, J. E., & Hunt, T. (1984). *Managing public relations.* New York: Holt, Rinehart & Winston.

Murphy, P. (1991). The limits of symmetry: A game theory approach to symmetric and asymmetric public relations. In L. A. Grunig & J. E. Grunig (Eds.), *Public relations research annual* (Vol. 3, pp. 115–132). Hillsdale, NJ: Lawrence Erlbaum Associates.

Raiffa, H. (1982). *The art and science of negotiation*. Cambridge, MA: Harvard University Press.

8

Building Linkages to the
Dominant Coalition

How do communicators develop linkages to CEOs and dominant coalitions to establish communication excellence? How can communicators acquire the power necessary to contribute to strategic planning and decision making? We believe that changing the roles that top communicators play provides the most direct path to excellence. Top communication departments from the Excellence Study combine knowledge of both manager and technician roles to provide the requisite foundation for excellence. To actually achieve excellence, however, top communicators must play advanced organizational roles of communication manager and senior adviser.

TOP COMMUNICATORS AS MANAGERS AND SENIOR ADVISERS

The communication manager role consists of formal authority to manage the communication function and make communication policy decisions. Top communicators in this role hold themselves accountable for the success or failure of communication programs, as do others in the organization. Through their experience and training, top communicators in this role are organizational experts in solving communication and public relations problems.

Measuring the Manager Role

Table 8.1 displays the four items used to measure communication manager role activities. Top communicators were asked how well each of the four items "describes the work *you* do." Work done by others in the communication department was excluded from these measures.

TABLE 8.1
Items Measuring the Communication Manager Role*

- I make communication policy decisions.
- I take responsibility for the success or failure of my organization's communication or public relations programs.
- Because of my experience and training, others consider me the organization's expert in solving communication or public relations problems.
- I observe that others in the organization hold me accountable for the success or failure of communication or public relations programs.

*Top communicators were asked how well each of these activities described the work that they personally did as communicators. A score of 0 for an item means the item does not describe the communicator's work at all, a score of 100 means typical or average, and a score of 200 means twice average. A communicator's manager role score is the average score given to these four items.

One CEO for an industry association explained how informal advising leads to more formal influence in strategic decision making. At first, the top communicator had the confidence of only one or two members of the organization's dominant coalition, but still made significant contributions to decision making. At the time of our case study interview, the top communicator won acceptance as one of the inner circle of top decision makers. According to the CEO, his acceptance took "a lot of knocking and arguing and cajoling and seminaring and mentoring." The top communicator said of the process, "You've got to earn your stripes."

The top communicator at a medical products company has earned a permanent place on the strategic team, according to another member of the dominant coalition. As often happens, top communicators must carve out a new managerial role for themselves among senior managers who have different views of communication. "The players [dominant coalition members] in this organization have really come to see the value that the communication department can add," he told us. "[The top communicator] has really done a good job pounding it into these guys' heads by helping them understand what role communication plays."

"You have to be comfortable working with senior management and showing them you have the necessary skills to be an asset and an expert in communication decision making," the top communicator said.

One advantage of participating in strategic decision making is that communicators can prevent conflicts with publics, rather than clean up the consequences later. "Part of the problem that public relations has had in the past," the top communicator at a public utility told us, "is that they are the people that you bring in on the tail end to make things look better, or to polish over something that's not quite right. We need to be proactive." The public utility, which ranked in the top 1% of organizations in the Excellence

Study, recognizes the need for communicators at the strategic planning table. The top communicator is a permanent fixture there.

At a financial services corporation, senior communicators report directly to the CEO as they implement communication programs in their organization, among the top 10% of those participating in the Excellence Study. Communicators are part of the top management team and interact with the CEO "frequently and directly," according to the top communicator.

At a state hospital association, the top communicator participates in meetings of the board of directors and sits as a member of the senior management staff. Her role emphasizes strategic planning at the highest level. The communication program she manages posted an overall Excellence Score in the top 5% of participating organizations.

Contact with strategic decision makers does not mean you are making or even contributing to strategic decisions. In a state lottery organization, a top-rated communication program was radically transformed after the arrival of a new CEO and the conversion of the communication department into an in-house production shop. (Under the previous CEO, these activities had been handled by an outside agency.) The new top communicator told us in a case study interview that she had frequent access to the CEO. However, other members of the dominant coalition indicated that her role was largely one of implementing decisions made by others in the dominant coalition.

Measuring the Senior Adviser Role

Unlike the formal authority of the communication manager role, the senior adviser role involves informal power. As senior counsel to the dominant coalition on matters of communication and public relations, the senior adviser exerts influence through suggestions, recommendations, and plans. Much of the senior adviser's authority comes from close contact with key publics. Senior advisers mediate the flow of two-way communication between organizations and publics.

Table 8.2 displays the four items that measure the senior adviser role. The role of manager and senior adviser can be seen in those played by two senior executives at a gas and electric utility in the Midwest. The senior vice president of customer and corporate services is a member of the dominant coalition. He describes his relations with other coalition members as "healthy and constructive." He told us, "We push each other, and we push back."

When the dominant coalition needs a communication expert, the public affairs manager also participates in strategy decisions. In that role, the public affairs manager works to "stimulate thinking" and "craft messages."

This role of senior adviser is similar to the one played by the manager of communications at an engineering research agency. Although she is not a

TABLE 8.2
Items Measuring the Senior Adviser Role*

- I am senior counsel to top decision makers when communication or public relations issues are involved.
- Although I do not make communication policy decisions, I provide decision makers with suggestions, recommendations, and plans.
- I create opportunities for management to hear the views of various internal and external publics.
- I represent the organization at events and meetings.

---

*Top communicators were asked how well each of these activities described the work that they personally did as communicators. A score of 0 for an item means the item does not describe the communicator's work at all, a score of 100 means typical or average, and a score of 200 means twice average. A communicator's senior adviser role score is the average score given to these four items.

member of the senior management team, her perspective is sought and listened to by senior managers.

Top communicators run excellent communication programs when they play either the communication manager or senior adviser roles, or both. Both formal and informal power serve excellence. Indeed, excellent organizations blur boundaries between communication issues and organizational issues. As the vice president for public affairs in a large chemical company put it, "Everything you do strategically . . . has to do with relations with the outside world." The formal authority of even the most powerful communicator must be shared with others in the dominant coalition when issues affect other areas of responsibility in organizations. The formal authority to make policy decisions specific to communication must be matched by informal influence on all issues of strategic planning and decision making.

Comparing Roles in Organizations

The extent to which top communicators play the advanced roles differs markedly in most-excellent and least-excellent organizations. When organizations with overall Excellence Scores in the top 10% were compared to organizations with overall Excellence Scores in the bottom 10%, top communicators differed substantially in their role behavior. Fig. 8.1 displays scores for the communication manager and senior adviser roles for most-excellent and least-excellent organizations.

Top communicators in least-excellent organizations reported only average levels of communication manager role playing, when compared to other role activities. Top communicators in most-excellent organizations, on the other hand, played the manager role over two-and-a-half times the average. Top communicators in least-excellent organizations reported senior adviser role playing at little better than half the average. Top communicators in

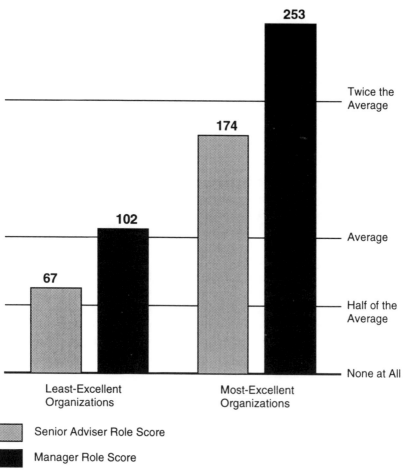

Top communicators were asked how often they perform a number of role activities. A score of 0 means the top communicator never performs that activity, a score of 100 means the top communicator performs that activity with average frequency (relative to all types of role activities), and scores greater than 100 indicate above-average performance of that activity. The scores in the table are the averages for the most-excellent and least-excellent organizations as determined by their overall score on the Excellence Factor.

FIG. 8.1.   Communication manager and senior adviser role playing in most-excellent and least-excellent organizations.

TABLE 8.3
Items Measuring the Media Relations Role*

- I maintain media contacts for my organization.
- I keep others in the organization informed of what the media report about our organization and important issues.
- I am responsible for placing news releases.
- I use my journalistic skills to figure out what the media will consider newsworthy about our organization.

*Top communicators were asked how well each of these activities described the work that they personally did as communicators. A score of 0 for an item means the item does not describe the communicator's work at all, a score of 100 means typical or average, and a score of 200 means twice average. A communicator's media relations role score is the average score given to these four items.

most-excellent organizations played this role over one-and-a-half times the average. Playing advanced organizational roles as communication managers and senior advisers helps top communicators run excellent communication departments.

PLAYING TRADITIONAL ROLES

In addition to communication manager and senior adviser roles, the research team also examined two traditional communicator roles. As detailed in chapter 4, these traditional roles are essential to executing communication programs. Indeed, even top communicators in excellent organizations play these traditional roles from time to time.

The media relations role is played by journalists-in-residence, who maintain media contacts, place news releases, and figure out what the media will find newsworthy about their organizations. In the media relations role, top communicators keep senior management posted about media coverage of

TABLE 8.4
Items Measuring the Communication Technician Role*

- I produce brochures, pamphlets, and other publications.
- I am the person who writes communication materials.
- I do photography and graphics for communication and public relations materials.
- I edit for grammar and spelling the materials written by others in the organization.

*Top communicators were asked how well each of these activities described the work that they personally did as communicators. A score of 0 for an item means the item does not describe the communicator's work at all, a score of 100 means typical or average, and a score of 200 means twice average. A communicator's technician role score is the average score given to these four items.

the organization and coverage of issues important to the organization. Table 8.3 displays the items used to measure the media relations role played by top communicators.

The communication technician role involves the mechanics of implementing communication programs. In this role, top communicators write communication materials, produce brochures and pamphlets, take photos, and produce graphics. Top communicators in this role even edit for grammar and spelling the writing of others in the organization. Table 8.4 displays the four items used to measure the extent to which top communicators play the technician role.

COMMUNICATOR CHARACTERISTICS AND ROLE PLAYING

Generally, top communicators who play the communication manager and senior adviser roles run excellent communication departments. Dominant coalitions in their organizations support the communication function and value the communication department. Communication makes substantial contributions to strategic management and planning in these organizations. What factors assist or impede top communicators in playing advanced roles in organizations?

We already know a good deal about factors that influence the roles communicators play in organizations.[1] The research team examined the relationships between role playing and several organizational and individual characteristics that prior research indicated influence role playing. Two organizational characteristics were examined: organizational size (number of employees) and communication department size (number of employees in the department). In addition, several characteristics of top communicators themselves were examined: gender, age, education, and professional activities.[2]

Organizational size, as measured by number of employees, does not affect communication manager or senior adviser role playing. Number of employees in the organization does not affect media relations or technician role playing. The number of employees in the communication department does not affect advanced role playing by top communicators. However,

---

[1]See, for example, Broom, 1982; Broom and Dozier, 1986; Broom and Smith, 1979; Creedon, 1991; Dozier, 1984, 1986, 1987, 1988, 1989, 1990; Ferguson, 1987; Grunig and Grunig, 1989; Lauzen, 1990, 1992; Lauzen and Dozier, 1992.

[2]Professional activities included the number of professional meetings attended in a typical year, how many times the top communicator was an officer in a professional association in the last 10 years, and how many times the top communicator had presented a program for a professional communication association in the last 10 years.

TABLE 8.5
Traditional and Advanced Role Playing by Male and Female Top
Communicators*

Role Scores	Gender of Top Communicator	
	Male	Female
Top communicator technician role score	62	83
Top communicator media relations role score	113	117
Top communicator senior adviser role score	111	116
Top communicator manager role score	153	148

*Top communicators were asked how often they perform a number of role activities. A score of 0 means the top communicator never performs that activity, a score of 100 means the top communicator performs that activity with average frequency (relative to all types of role activities), and scores greater than 100 indicate above-average performance of that activity.

departmental size does impact traditional role playing. Not surprisingly, top communicators play the media relations and communication technician roles more frequently in small communication departments, in which top communicators cannot easily delegate such tasks.

Regarding individual characteristics of top communicators, men and women play the communication manager and senior adviser role with equal frequency. Regarding traditional roles, women and men play the media relations role at comparable levels (see Table 8.5).

The communication technician role, however, is played more frequently by female top communicators than by male top communicators. As shown in Table 8.5, top communicators of both genders report below-average enactment of the communication technician role. Nevertheless, women's scores on the communication technician scale are substantially higher than those for men. Generally, top communicators who are women work in smaller communication departments, meaning that they must sometimes double as managers and technicians. In addition, women holding top communicator positions tend to be younger than their male counterparts. Younger communicators play the technician role more than do older communicators.

Age of top communicators makes little difference in playing the communication manager, senior adviser, or even media relations roles. (As noted earlier, younger top communicators play the communication technician role more frequently than do older communicators.) Education also does not influence playing either advanced or traditional roles. Activities such as attending professional meetings, holding office in professional associations, or making presentations to such associations do not seem to influence role enactment by the top communicator.

RESEARCH AND ADVANCED ROLE PLAYING

Many individual and organizational characteristics do not seem to influence advanced role playing by top communicators. However, one characteristic of the communication department helps top communicators play the communication manager and senior adviser roles.

Top communicators were asked the extent to which their departments contribute to strategic planning and decision making through a series of research activities. Some research activities involved formal research methods, whereas other activities gathered information through informal techniques. These research activities are discussed in chapter 3 and the items are displayed in Table 3.1.

Top communicators play the communication manager and senior adviser roles when their departments contribute to strategic planning and decision making through research, especially formal research. This seems altogether reasonable. Top communicators have something useful to contribute to dominant coalition decision making when their departments act as conduits for information about key publics. Unlike traditional roles, which focus on implementation of communication programs, the communication manager and senior adviser roles put communicators at the table before decisions are made. The Excellence Study shows that formal and informal research activities in communication departments are strongly linked to advanced role playing by top communicators. Research activities in support of strategic planning and decision making seem perfect tools to help top communicators play manager and adviser roles.

The importance of such research is illustrated in Fig. 8.2. The research contributions of the top 10% of organizations were compared to those of the bottom 10%, based on their overall communication Excellence Scores. Regarding informal research contributions to strategic planning, the most-excellent organizations posted scores nearly two-and-a-half times the average. The least-excellent organizations scored slightly below the average. Differences are even more dramatic for formal research contributions to strategic planning. In the most-excellent organizations, formal research contributions were nearly double the average contribution. In the least-excellent organizations, formal research contributions were almost nonexistent.

The web of linkages that support excellence is nearly complete. Excellent communication departments are made up of savvy communicators who know how to plan strategic programs based on information communicators collect about publics. Some communicators in excellent departments have strong expertise in traditional areas of press agentry, publicity, and public information practices, but what makes excellent departments stand out is knowledge of two-way practices to negotiate and to persuade.

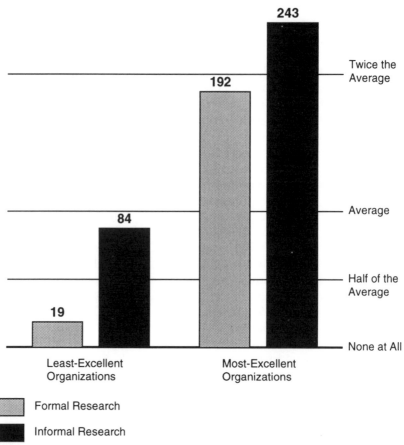

243

192

Twice the
Average

84

Average

Half of the
Average

19

None at All

Least-Excellent
Organizations

Most-Excellent
Organizations

Formal Research

Informal Research

Top communicators were asked to what extent the communication department contributes to strategic planning through research. Three items measured informal techniques; three other items measured formal research techniques. A score of 0 means the communication department makes no contribution, a score of 100 means the communication department makes an average contribution (relative to other departments in the organization), and scores greater than 100 indicate above-average contributions. The scores in the table are the averages for the most-excellent and least-excellent organizations as determined by their overall score on the Excellence Factor.

FIG. 8.2.   Informal and formal research contributions to strategic planning in most-excellent and least-excellent organizations.

In excellent organizations, dominant coalitions value and support communication. Communicators make substantial contributions to strategic planning. Dominant coalitions in these organizations demand cutting-edge, two-way communication practices. If CEOs are any indication, two-way practices mean research, without distinguishing between the conflicting symmetrical and asymmetrical worldviews that stand behind those practices.

Top communicators, on the other hand, distinguish between purely symmetrical principles that drive excellence and mixed-motive operational practices involving research. Top communicators running excellent departments clearly understand that the dominant coalition demands two-way practices. To deliver those practices, top communicators rely on strong knowledge bases in their departments.

The role behavior of top communicators is key to excellence. Top communicators exert formal power as they play the communication manager role. They exert informal influence as they play the senior adviser role. The one factor that most influences the playing of advanced roles is the contribution that communication makes to strategic planning and decision making through research.

Research provides information about relationships with key publics, a scarce and valued resource that puts top communicators at the decision-making tables of dominant coalitions. At decision-making tables, top communicators make senior managers aware of the knowledge, opinions, and behavioral predispositions of publics who influence the success or failure of organizations. Issues affect relationships with publics. Research helps top communicators identify emerging issues and track established ones, counseling senior decision makers about the implications and impact of issues on the full range of strategic decisions.

The knowledge and expertise of communicators is not enough for excellence: Communication excellence describes the understanding and behavior of CEOs and dominant coalitions, as well as communicators. Without CEOs and dominant coalitions who support and value communication and who demand two-way communication practices, the potential for excellence is diminished. In chapter 9, we consider the issues that CEOs must know and changes they must make before their organizations can achieve excellence.

SUMMARY

Top communicators are key to communication excellence. Through them, the expertise of the communication department is brought to bear on strategic issues facing organizations. The demand of dominant coalitions for advanced two-way practices is communicated to the department through top communicators. Top communicators manage the human and material resources of their departments to deliver excellence.

All of these processes occur through the organizational roles that top communicators play. Top communicators play two roles to support communication excellence. The first, the manager role, involves formal authority to make communication policy decisions. Managers hold themselves accountable for the success or failure of communication programs, as do other managers. The second role, the senior adviser role, does not have formal authority over policy; rather, senior advisers provide senior management with needed information and act as facilitators of the decisions that dominant coalitions make. Top communicators who play either role contribute to the excellence of their departments.

REFERENCES

Broom, G. M. (1982). A comparison of sex roles in public relations. *Public Relations Review, 8*(3), 17–22.

Broom, G. M., & Dozier, D. M. (1986). Advancement for public relations role models. *Public Relations Review, 12*(1), 37–56.

Broom, G. M., & Smith, G. D. (1979). Testing the practitioner's impact on clients. *Public Relations Review, 5*(3), 47–59.

Creedon, P. J. (1991). Public relations and "women's work": Toward a feminist analysis of public relations roles. In L. A. Grunig & J. E. Grunig (Eds.), *Public relations research annual* (Vol. 3, pp. 67–84). Hillsdale, NJ: Lawrence Erlbaum Associates.

Dozier, D. M. (1984). Program evaluation and roles of practitioners. *Public Relations Review, 10*(2), 13–21.

Dozier, D. M. (1986, July). *The environmental scanning function of public relations practitioners and participation in management decision making.* Paper presented at the meeting of the Public Relations Division, Association for Education in Journalism and Mass Communication, Norman, OK.

Dozier, D. M. (1987, May). *Gender, environmental scanning, and participation in management decision making.* Paper presented at the meeting of the Public Relations Interest Group, International Communication Association, Montreal.

Dozier, D. M. (1988). Breaking public relations' glass ceiling. *Public Relations Review, 14*(3), 6–14.

Dozier, D. M. (1989, May). *Importance of the concept of symmetry and its presence in public relations practice.* Paper presented at the meeting of the Public Relations Interest Group, International Communication Association, San Francisco.

Dozier, D. M. (1990). The innovation of research in public relations practice: Review of a program of studies. In L. A. Grunig & J. E. Grunig (Eds.), *Public relations research annual* (Vol. 2, pp. 3–28). Hillsdale, NJ: Lawrence Erlbaum Associates.

Ferguson, M. A. (1987, May). *Utility of roles research to corporate communications: Power, leadership and decision making.* Paper presented at the meeting of the Public Relations Interest Group, International Communication Association, Montreal.

Grunig, J. E., & Grunig, L. A. (1989). Toward a theory of public relations behavior in organizations: Review of a program of research. In J. E. Grunig & L. A. Grunig (Eds.), *Public relations research annual* (Vol. 1, pp. 27–66). Hillsdale, NJ: Lawrence Erlbaum Associates.

Lauzen, M. M. (1990, August). *Losing control: An examination of the management function in public relations.* Paper presented at the meeting of the Public Relations Division, Association for Education in Journalism and Mass Communication, Minneapolis, MN.

Lauzen, M. M. (1992). Public relations roles, intraorganizational power, and encroachment. *Journal of Public Relations Research, 4*(2), 61–80.

Lauzen, M. M., & Dozier, D. M. (1992). The missing link: The public relations manager role as mediator of organizational environments and power consequences for the function. *Journal of Public Relations Research, 4*(4), 205–220.

9

What Ceos Should Do About
Excellence

We wrote this chapter especially for chief executive officers, presidents, executive directors, and owners. You may run a corporation, a not-for-profit organization, a government agency, or an association for the professions or trades. If you read only one chapter from this book, read this one. We want to tell you about the results of a three-nation, ten-year study of public relations and communication management, the most comprehensive research ever conducted on communication in organizations.[1] CEOs like yourselves played an invaluable role in the study, telling us what they expect and what they get from their communication departments.[2]

We found a pattern in organizations with excellent communication programs, which was the same for corporations, not-for-profit organizations, government agencies, and associations. That pattern was the same for one-person communication "departments" and for large organizations with

---

[1]The Excellence Study was funded through a $400,000 grant from the International Association of Business Communicators (IABC) Research Foundation. Over 300 organizations, including corporations, not-for-profits, government agencies, and associations, provided information for the study, including questionnaires completed by CEOs in each organization. We studied organizations in Canada, the United Kingdom, and the United States. Up to 12 employees in each organization completed over 100 pages of questions about communication and public relations in their organizations.

[2]We call all of them *communication departments*, but communication goes by different names in different organizations. Department titles include *public relations, public affairs, media relations, employee relations, customer relations, investor relations*, or *member relations*. Some organizations have only one communicator on staff; others have multiple departments that deal with communication, employing scores of people.

scores of communicators. Excellent communication programs are the same in Canada, the United Kingdom, and the United States.

In this book, we have written directly to professional communicators about excellence and the role they play in delivering excellent communication programs to organizations that employ them. However, your organization cannot have excellent communication programs unless you understand what excellence is and demand it from your communicators. They may be highly creative and talented people who can help your organization become more effective, and they may have expertise you have yet to tap, but their creativity and expertise can not produce communication excellence for you and your organization without you.

WHAT YOU SHOULD KNOW ABOUT COMMUNICATION EXCELLENCE

Let us first tell you about communication excellence, distilled from the massive body of information collected in the study. Then, in the section that follows, we suggest ways you could put this knowledge to work in your organization.

As you know, people who run organizations constantly assess how different parts and components of an organization contribute to the overall mission—how they make an organization more effective. In the Excellence Study, we asked CEOs to evaluate their communication departments, to tell us the return on investment from communication expenditures.[3] In the top 10% of organizations studied (the most-excellent organizations), CEOs reported a 266% return on investment for communication expenditures. In the bottom 10% of those studied (the least-excellent organizations), CEOs reported only a 146% return on investment. When we talked to some of those same CEOs in follow-up case studies, many recalled instances in which effective communication helped avoid costly and restrictive legislation, product-liability litigation was contained, external funding was increased, and contributions from volunteers were stabilized while falling for similar organizations elsewhere. These CEOs placed specific dollar values on communication's contribution to these organizational successes. Other CEOs talked about the value of long-term relationships between the organizations they run and key constituencies or publics. What are these relationships worth to organizations? The CEO of the Chemical Manufacturers'

---

[3]We use CEO to describe all the people who run organizations. They provided us with detailed information about the communication function in their organizations through a seven-page questionnaire and, in some cases, long personal interviews.

Association put it most succinctly: "everything"—especially in times of crisis. Excellence is valued by those who run organizations with excellent communication programs.

So what do excellent communication departments have that others do not? Excellent communication departments know how to manage relations with the mass media—what to do if "60 Minutes" calls. They have creative, talented staffs that can handle the production of various communication products, from an award-winning annual report to an employee publication that people like to read. These are the traditional crafts of a communication department. Excellent departments practice these crafts better than most.

However, traditional communication crafts are not what make these departments excellent. Excellent communication departments know how to communicate in two directions, using cutting-edge expertise in public relations research. Excellent communicators know how to design appropriate messages and select appropriate media to communicate your message outward to those groups that affect your organization's survival and growth. They also know how to act as your eyes and ears, as channels of communication from the people and organizations about which you need to care. They can advise you and the rest of senior management about how these people and organizations are likely to react to the policies, procedures, and behavior of your organization. Excellent communicators help you anticipate reactions of publics before they happen, permitting you to act strategically rather than simply reacting after it "hits the fan."

Excellent communicators know how to gather information from constituents through focus group studies, surveys of publics, and systematic analysis of what the media say about your organization and issues important to you. They study opinion polls and media coverage to identify emerging issues and help manage issues already on your organization's agenda. In other words, excellent communicators help you with strategic planning and decision making. They are part of the senior management team.

Excellent communicators collect information from key constituents and help you and the rest of senior management make sense of these individuals and organizations. This information gathering can serve the purpose of persuading publics to behave the way you and the rest of senior management want them to behave. Sometimes such persuasion is the smart thing to do, and excellent communicators are good at it.

Generally, however, excellent communicators do their best work when they persuade you to change. If you agree with William Vanderbilt that the "public be damned" when they disagree with your organizational objectives, you are managing in the wrong century. Hopefully, your wake-up call will come from your top communicator, who can show you how the best long-term relationships with publics are achieved through negotiation. Disputes are best resolved by finding a common ground where organizations and people whose lives are affected by organizations each get some of what they want from the relationship.

If your top communicator can not get through, other callers will. Some CEOs get their wake-up calls when corporate headquarters is surrounded by angry protesters carrying pickets. Others get the call when consumers organize national and even international boycotts of products. Still others get it at stockholder meetings from angry investors. Government at all levels has the authority and power to call on you with new restrictive regulations that activist publics often demand.

On a small, crowded, and interdependent planet accelerating toward a single global market, you can not always get what you want. An excellent communication department does its best work when it helps senior management understand organizational constituents. Persuasion cuts two ways. Savvy CEOs let excellent communicators persuade their senior managers as well as constituents. CEOs include excellent communicators in all strategic decisions, because nobody else knows better how those decisions will affect key constituents. On that basis, senior managers come to value the communication department in a new way, and support the communication function as an important component of organizational effectiveness.

This description of excellent communicators and excellent departments differs from traditional views of public relations and communication management. According to the traditional view, communicators take the flak when hostile media take aim at an organization. Perhaps communicators can get the CEO's picture in *The Wall Street Journal*. Communicators can write speeches and crank out news releases. They can even come in after senior management has made a decision to help edit the grammar and spelling of official announcements. Communicators produce the annual report, the employee newsletter, brochures, pamphlets, and other communication products. Some CEOs think their communication departments are cutting edge because they know desktop publishing or video production.

Traditionalists do not see communicators as the organization's eyes and ears—as having something to contribute to strategic decision making. Communicators, these CEOs believe, are disseminators of information, a support function that comes into play after decisions have been made. The purpose of communication is to "get our story out there."

In organizations with less-than-excellent communication programs, CEOs hold this traditional view of communication and public relations. Senior managers in these organizations neither value nor support public relations. Communication makes little or no contributions to strategic planning and decision making. Indeed, when we looked at the talent in communication departments of these less-than-excellent organizations, we often found low levels of the knowledge required to practice two-way communication and to contribute to strategic management.

In other cases, however, we found the talent for communication excellence. The communication department had the knowledge base to deliver cutting-edge, two-way public relations practices. What was missing in these organizations was a senior management team with enough sophistication to effectively use the communication resources the organization already had.

WHAT YOU SHOULD DO

No organization in the Excellence Study had a perfect communication department or program. Every organization can improve on its communication practices. Whether the organization you run has an excellent or less-than-excellent communication program, we modestly suggest the following strategies for improving communication in your organization.[4]

Your Top Communicator Is Key

The top communicator in your organization is key to building and maintaining an excellent communication program. In organizations with excellent communication programs, top communicators counsel their CEOs and other members of the senior management team about relationships with key constituents. Perhaps downsizing has left employees nervous about their personal futures, uncertain about the organization's direction, and less productive. The relationship between the senior management team and employees requires attention. What can be done to improve this relationship? What are employees thinking and feeling? Of course, personnel and human resource managers play an important role in this diagnosis, but top communicators in excellent organizations also make important contributions to the diagnosis and solution of such problems.

What do current customers and members know and how do they feel about your organization? How does that affect future purchases or membership renewal? Who are your potential customers or members? What do they know and how do they feel about your organization? Why aren't they customers or members? Managers of marketing or membership departments are key decision makers. In organizations with excellent communica-

---

[4]We are college professors who study public relations and communication management and teach what we know about it to our students. In short, we are not CEOs and we do not run organizations like yours. However, we have listened carefully to what CEOs with excellent communication departments and programs have to say about their successes. In the spirit of their enthusiasm, we pass these suggestions from them along to you.

tion, top communicators also bring important information to the table about current and potential customers or members.

How will the issues of environmentalism, sexual harassment, and cultural diversity affect your organization and its key relationships with regulators, employees, and activist organizations? When the senior management team plans ahead, anticipating the impact of these and other issues, top communicators in excellent organizations make substantial contributions to such strategic planning and decision making.

Whenever senior management considers entering a new market, building or expanding a factory, downsizing or reorganizing personnel, acquiring or merging with another corporation, or developing a new product line, top communicators in excellent organizations participate. These communicators are expert at anticipating how these changes will affect key relationships.

In many organizations we studied, top communicators are ready and eager for such strategic responsibilities. They are blocked by CEOs and senior management teams that think the public relations function should become involved only after decisions are made to disseminate messages. Potentially, these organizations have excellent communication departments, but that full potential will never be achieved until CEOs make their communicators part of the senior management team.

In a few organizations we studied, top communicators lacked both the vision and expertise to contribute to strategic planning and decision making. They saw themselves as support staff, disseminating messages to implement policies made by others on the senior management team. If they want communication excellence, CEOs in these organizations need new top communicators.

Begin with a long meeting with your top communicator. Discuss your expectations for communication excellence at length. Evaluate whether your top communicator sees your expectations for excellence as a threat or an opportunity. Ask your top communicator for an impromptu evaluation of each communicator on staff. What knowledge or expertise does the department now possess? What is missing? Top communicators need to think strategically about how relationships are affected by what the organization does and what key constituents do. Assess whether your top communicator can play this role.

Conduct an Excellence Audit

The foundation of excellence is the knowledge base of your communication department. Work with your top communicator to conduct a formal audit of the knowledge base in the communication department. You and your top communicator may decide to enlist the help of an outside consultant.

Chapters 1 though 5 of this book provide a broad-brush picture of what to look for in an excellent knowledge base. Key elements of that expertise include the capacity to conduct research on key constituents, using both formal and informal methods. Does anyone in your communication department know how to conduct focus group studies? If not, does someone know what to look for in a consultant who provides such services? Does anyone in your communication department know how to design a face-to-face, telephone, group-administered, or mail survey? If not, does someone know where to go for expert help? Does anyone in your communication department know how to make sense of focus group or survey results? Can someone there advise you on the implications of focus group and survey findings for decision making?

Does anyone in your communication department know how to track in the media the issues important your organization? Can someone in the department look at public opinion polls available in the public domain to track these same issues? Does he or she know how to spot emerging issues that may lead to conflict between your organization and key constituents later on? Does anyone in your communication department understand dispute resolution and the tools negotiators use to resolve disputes?

Note that such an audit is focused on knowledge or expertise, not actual practices. To conduct research, communicators with the requisite expertise need budgets. Among communicators with the expertise just outlined, the biggest problem is convincing senior management that excellence in public relations and communication management requires research. Research requires budgets that recognize this need and incorporate the necessary support for it.

Note also that top communicators in larger organizations cannot be expected to hold all the expertise for communication excellence. Departments possess the expertise, not individuals alone. In smaller organizations with a single communicator, communication excellence is achieved through expertise in some of the areas outlined earlier, supplemented with the help of an occasional outside consultant.

Build in Excellence Through Training and Hiring

If an excellence audit identifies areas in which your communication department is weak, use on-site training to develop the knowledge base of the communication department. Provide support so that individual communicators can attend special workshops and seminars at off-site locations, or can pursue college-level studies directly relevant to excellence expertise. Incorporate your demand for communication excellence into the promotion policies for your communication department; that is, create a need to know. Identify the gaps in departmental expertise so that when personnel turnover or expansion occurs, new communicators are hired to bring the expertise for excellence with them.

Bring Senior Management up to Speed

Key to communication excellence is the support of the senior management team, one that values the work of the communication department. The work of an excellent communication department differs fundamentally from the work of less-than-excellent departments. Top communicators in excellent organizations are key members of the senior management team, even if the organizational chart does not say so. Top communicators, with the support of the expertise in their departments, make substantial contributions to strategic planning and decision making. Using formal and informal research techniques, they help with diagnosis and problem solving, then execute effective communication programs to build lasting, long-term relationships with key constituents.

Such excellent practices cannot happen in a vacuum; excellent communication programs occur in organizations in which senior managements understand excellence. Senior management teams demand excellence, then provide the necessary support to communication to make excellence happen. In many organizations with the potential for communication excellence, senior managers need to rethink public relations and communication management.

Potentially, key relationships are affected by every strategic decision made. Every senior manager can play a role in establishing mutually beneficial relationships with key constituents. Every senior manager can do great damage to those same relationships by making decisions in ignorance, without considering how a decision affects the organization's various strategic relationships.

Every senior manager cannot be expert on the knowledge, opinions, and behavioral predispositions of all the publics affected by an organization. In excellent organizations, top communicators and their staffs provide such expertise. Senior managers in excellent organizations value this expertise and call on it frequently when strategic decisions are made. They value and support communication precisely because communicators help other managers make better decisions. This, in turn, makes organizations more effective.

An off-site retreat provides a useful setting for beginning to reorient senior management teams. An outside consultant can assist in organizing such an event. The key objective is buy-in. An excellence retreat for senior management is successful if senior managers leave the retreat knowing that they practice public relations and communication management with every strategic decision they make. Strategic decisions affect relationships. When relationships are factored into decision making, senior managers practice proactive public relations and communication management. When relationships are ignored in decision making, organizations often must practice reactive public relations.

Communicators provide specialized expertise in helping senior management teams make better decisions. That is why we say excellent organizations when we describe organizations with excellent communication programs. Communication excellence comes from the quality of strategic decisions made by senior management that anticipate the impact of decisions on relationships, modifying those decisions appropriately to build or maintain long-term, mutually beneficial relationships.

Organizations change slowly. Senior managers can begin to change their thinking about public relations and communication management at such a retreat. The process continues on a daily basis as top communicators prove themselves through meaningful contributions to strategic decision making. In some organizations, strategic decision making is controlled by a few top managers. The idea of including others may not please some managers who are used to an organizational culture in which only a few people monopolize authority. However, a shift toward greater participation in decision making and greater emphasis on teamwork provides a better environment for communication excellence.

In our case studies of excellent organizations, we learned that including communicators in strategic decision making yields benefits for senior management. Having a sophisticated and informed communicator at the table helps everyone do his or her job better. Excellent communicators can provide that ounce of prevention that keeps all of senior management out from under pounds of hostile press clippings, off "60 Minutes," out of court, and free of activist protests.

Part III

The Character of Organizations

The qualities of communication excellence consist of an inner sphere—the knowledge base of the communication department—and a middle sphere—expectations about communication shared by top communicators and senior management. Both of these spheres rest within the third sphere, the character of organizational culture. The chapters of Part III consider the role that culture plays in excellence.

Fig. III.1 provides a graphic representation of this outer sphere. Two attributes of culture affect the quality of communication in organizations. These can be thought of as general and specific characteristics of organizational culture.

Generally, organizations differ in the participative and authoritarian character of their cultures. Participative cultures infuse employees with a sense of teamwork, cooperation, and a shared mission. Organizations with participative cultures involve a wide range of employees in decision making. Employees regard managers in participative cultures as caring about their subordinates as people as well as employees. Authoritarian cultures, on the other hand, stress centralized decision making and authority. Employees in organizations with authoritarian cultures see different and even competing agendas in different departments, rather than a common mission, and such employees feel that they are not trusted to make decisions. Every organization has elements of both authoritarian and participative cultures.

Specifically, organizations differ in how they treat employees who are women or are from culturally diverse backgrounds. This specific aspect of culture affects excellence for two reasons.

FIG. III.1.   Components of the outer sphere of organizational culture.

First, public relations and communication management became a female majority occupation in the United States in 1982. Today, women constitute about 60% of the public relations labor force in the United States. In Canada, women make up over 62% of working communicators. A similar gender shift has occurred in the United Kingdom as well. The role and status of communication and public relations in organizations is closely linked to the role and status of women.

Second, organizations generally—and communication departments in particular—will have more effective communication programs if employees come from culturally diverse backgrounds. The reason is simple: For organizations to build mutually beneficial long-term relationships with publics, people inside the organization must have the capacity to see issues or conflicts through the eyes of their publics. Communicators from culturally diverse backgrounds tend to make better boundary spanners. How organizations support, neglect, or mistreat employees from culturally diverse backgrounds affects the overall quality of communication excellence.

Beyond the boundaries of organizations, do larger cultural influences affect excellence? Specifically, does the type of organization affect excellence? Are excellent communication programs more common in for-profit corporations, not-for-profit organizations, government agencies, or professional-trade associations? Are excellent communication programs more common in Canada, the United Kingdom, or the United States? These questions are addressed in Chapter 12.

Part III concludes with findings from the Excellence Study that suggest how changes occur in the cultures of organizations. The case study portion of the Excellence Study suggests that communicators have played key roles in helping to transform organizational cultures.

10

Participation and Authority in the Culture of Organizations

The research team for the Excellence Study wanted to learn about organizational culture and the role that it plays in communication excellence. Many scholars have studied organizational culture.[1] We define *organizational culture* as the sum total of shared values, symbols, meanings, beliefs, assumptions, and expectations that organize and integrate a group of people who work together. A brief explanation of organizational culture is provided in Exhibit 10.1.

Our case study interviews provided rich insights into the values and beliefs that serve to integrate employees in organizations, and how those values and beliefs affect communication. At several organizations with excellent communication programs, we found exactly what we expected.

At a public utility with an overall Excellence Score in the top 1% of participating organizations, the top communicator told us, "We have one focus; our goals are all the same; everybody's working toward those goals."

A not-for-profit organization that promotes behavior leading to reduced risk of heart disease also posted an overall excellence score in the top 1% of participating organizations. The chief executive officer (CEO) described his organization as tightly integrated. Decision making in that organization involves all those who will be affected. "No one is left out," he declared.

In other organizations, we found the organization's core values undergo-

---

[1]In chapter 21 of *Excellence in Public Relations and Communication Management* (Grunig, 1992), we provided a detailed review of the literature on organizational culture, paying special attention to the role that organizational culture plays in communication and public relations.

EXHIBIT 10.1
About Organizational Culture

The concept of organizational culture has its roots in anthropology, where various anthropologists have sought to define culture. Some define *culture* as a system of values that help people in a culture interact with each other by making social settings less ambiguous. Regarding the cultures of organizations, some scholars define *organizational culture* as core values of organizations that unify the social dimensions of organizations. Others have described organizational culture as the rules of the game for getting along in organizations, the ropes or how things get done in a particular organization. Still others regard an organization's culture as a system of meaning that can be analyzed through signs and symbols. Employees tell each other stories about their organization and the people in it. These stories are artifacts that investigators can study to learn about an organization's culture.

The Excellence research team considered organizational culture important to communication excellence. The culture of an organization affects the way employees communicate with each other. If an organization's culture favors communication as a one-way flow of commands from superiors to subordinates, then communication is less than excellent. If senior management makes strategic decisions in a highly centralized manner, seeking input from only those with formal authority, then public relations is less than excellent.

ing profound changes. A chemical manufacturing corporation posted overall Excellence Scores in the top 25%. We asked the top communicator to describe the core values of his organization. "We've made tremendous strides with senior management," he told us. "Senior managers still have a fundamentally conservative mind set [but] we deal with senior management as a public." When asked if he saw the change in the worldviews of senior management as incremental, he replied, "Yes, it's a slow process."

At the chemical manufacturing corporation, communicators actively assisted in shifting core values. In a state arts organization, a newly hired top communicator received much of the credit for introducing the value of teamwork. "Much of the in-fighting has quieted down because we have more money to work with and a sense of direction, a 'work-together' approach as our bottom line," the CEO told us, crediting the top communicator for much of the organization's recent success in fund raising.

In other organizations, the core values of organizations affect communication excellence in subtle and interesting ways. In one organization with an overall Excellence Score in the top 5% of participating organizations, conflicting values were discovered through case study interviews. The survey of employees at a disabled services organization indicated that teamwork, shared decision making, and participation were generally high, in the top

10%.[2] Yet the top communicator described the CEO as a "benevolent dictator" who favored highly centralized decision making. Strong participative values exist side by side with the strong authoritarian values of a "benevolent dictator" in an organization with an excellent communication program.

A gas and electric company posted an overall Excellence Score in the top 10% of participating organizations. When it merged with another company, top communicators from both organizations worked closely with senior management to guide the merger process. This process included a strategic shift in core values of the new organization. Senior management is trying to transform the organizational culture from an "old-line bureaucracy managed in an autocratic way to an organization that is nimble and flexible," a senior vice president told us. The new company is changing its old core values so that it "is positioned to be successful in a competitive environment," he said, "and is managed in a participative way." In the 1990–1991 survey of employees, the "participative way" of this company was ranked in the bottom third. How participative is the utility's organizational culture today? In our 1994 case study, we concluded that the culture at the utility was in transition, with its old autocratic ways locked in an intense struggle with its new participative values. Interestingly, organizations in transition from autocratic to participative cultures, what we call *culturally intense* organizations, generally post high overall communication Excellence Scores.

On the other hand, high levels of teamwork and shared decision making do not make up for shortfalls in the communication department. For example, an insurance company posted an overall Excellence Score in the bottom 10%. Yet, a sampling of employees told us that their organization was among the top 5% of organizations when it came to teamwork, shared decision making, and participation. The barriers to excellence were found in the communication department and in senior management's expectations of the department. Communicators did not have the expertise for manager role playing or for advanced, two-way practices, nor did the CEO expect such communication practices. "We're pretty much one-way," the top communicator said, describing her department as "technical support to marketing."

A member of the dominant coalition, the vice president that supervises the communication department, agreed. "[The communication department] in this organization is basically one way," she said.

---

[2]By taking the averages for all employees in an organization, we were able to combine these measures with other measures of the organizations we studied. For example, the average employee scores on the participative culture scale placed an organization in the top 10% because—on average—this average was higher than the employee averages in 90% of the other organizations.

Participative organizational values emphasizing teamwork and shared decision making cannot make up for knowledge deficiencies in the communication department, nor can they compensate for the "communicator-as-technician" mindset in senior management. These case study interviews and others helped us interpret findings from the 1990–1991 survey of employees in participating organizations.

PARTICIPATIVE AND AUTHORITARIAN CULTURES

We asked regular employees—people other than top communicators and CEOs—about the values that drive their organizations. Over 4,600 employees in Canada, the United Kingdom, and the United States filled out questionnaires to participate in this portion of the study. In the questionnaires, employees responded to 45 items that measure different aspects of organizational culture. We then analyzed the data, looking for ways to group the items together that were similar to how employees grouped such items.[3] As we had theorized, employees recognized two basic patterns of values, symbols, meanings, or beliefs in the organizations where they worked. We call one of these sets of values *participative organizational culture*. The 10 items that best measure participative organizational culture are shown in Table 10.1.

Teamwork runs strong through participative organizational cultures. Feeling part of the team, working together, fostering interdepartmental coordination, and maintaining team-level responsibility for getting the job done are values and beliefs central to participative organizational cultures. Participative organizational cultures also share decision-making authority, fostering a sense of equality, because decisions are made with the involvement of those most affected by the decision. Participative organizational cultures emphasize employees caring for each other, both up, down, and sideways in the organization. Such organizations are also open to ideas from the outside.

Participative values, assumptions, beliefs, and expectations differ markedly from authoritarian organizational cultures. The 10 items that provide the best measures of authoritarian organizational culture are shown in Table 10.2. Centralized control and authority mark these organizational cultures.

---

[3]Factor analysis was used to group items together, based on responses of the employees themselves. If employees give high scores to the statement that "everyone is treated as an equal in this organization," those same employees might give high scores to the statement that "this organization is open to ideas from the outside." Similarly, employees giving low scores to the first statement may give low scores to the second statement. When this pattern occurs for a set of items, they make up a factor or cluster of items measuring a similar idea or value.

TABLE 10.1
Participative Organizational Culture

Over 4,600 employees in the organizations participating in the Excellent Study described the organizations where they work using a series of evaluative statements. In order of importance,* these 10 evaluative statements describe participative organizational cultures.

- Nearly everyone feels he or she is part of a team in this organization.
- Everyone works together here to make the organization effective.
- The departments in this organization seem to work together like a well-oiled machine.
- Senior managers in this organization care deeply about other employees.
- Everyone is treated as an equal in this organization.
- Most decisions in this organization are made after thorough discussion between all the people who will be affected in a major way.
- This organization is open to new ideas from the outside.
- Senior managers here believe in the sharing of power and responsibility with lower-level employees.
- People take an interest in each other in this organization. It is common to find supervisors who feel that it is part of their job to know about the personal problems that may be bothering their subordinates.
- Most projects are done through teamwork. Each individual is expected to contribute to the team effort, but the team as a whole is ultimately held accountable and rewarded or punished for its efforts.

*Factor analysis was used to isolate two types of organizational culture. The 10 items included in this table provide the best measures of participative organizational cultures, based on the size of the factor loadings. These items were then added together to create an index of participative organizational culture.

TABLE 10.2
Authoritarian Organizational Culture

Employees in organizations participating in the Excellent Study described the organizations where they work using a series of evaluative statements. In order of importance,* these 10 evaluative statements describe authoritarian organizational cultures.

- Advancement in this organization is based more on *who* you know than on *how well* you perform.
- Rigid control by management often makes it difficult for me to be innovative in this organization.
- Senior management in this organization believes that it must have nearly total control over the behavior of subordinates.
- Most departments in this organization do not share a common mission; each has different priorities that conflict with the priorities of other departments.
- This organization usually is closed to new ideas from outside.
- Managers in this organization seem to believe that employees lack initiative and must constantly be given instructions.
- Decisions are usually based on authority here—the way the CEO and the people close to him or her want things done.
- Most people who work here seem to be afraid of senior managers.
- Senior administrators in this organization believe that they know best because they have more knowledge than lower-level employees.
- Decisions are usually based on tradition here—the way things always have been done.

*Factor analysis was used to isolate two types of organizational culture. The 10 items included in this table provide the best measures of authoritarian organizational cultures, based on the size of the factor loadings. These items were added together to create an index of authoritarian organizational culture.

Decision making is highly centralized, based on tradition and generally closed to new ideas from outside the organization. Distinctions between senior managers and other, lower-level employees are pronounced, with employees reporting that top managers act like they always know best. The various departments in authoritarian organizational cultures do not share a common mission. Employees say managers act as if the employees they supervise don't have initiative and require constant direction.

In addition to questions about organizational culture, employees were asked to assess their satisfaction with their jobs. We also asked employees to evaluate the nature of communication within their organizations, because such patterns are linked to excellence through the role that communication departments play in internal communication.

ORGANIZATIONAL CULTURE AND JOB SATISFACTION

Employees who describe their organizational cultures as participative exhibit higher levels of individual and organizational job satisfaction when compared with employees who see their organizations as less participative. *Individual job satisfaction* means the inherent satisfaction employees derive from the work content itself, when they regard their work as interesting and challenging rather than boring or a dead end. Individually satisfying work gives employees a sense of accomplishment and most days they look forward to coming to work. The five items that measure individual job satisfaction are displayed in Table 10.3.

Organizational job satisfaction, on the other hand, comes from the external rewards or recognition that organizations give employees for the work they do, whether or not such work is inherently satisfying. Organizational job satisfaction increases when employers treat their employees well through

TABLE 10.3
Individual Job Satisfaction

Employees in organizations participating in the Excellent Study described their individual satisfaction with their jobs using the five evaluative statements listed here.*

- On the whole, my job is interesting and challenging.
- I look forward to coming to work almost every day.
- My work gives me a sense of accomplishment.
- My work is a dead-end job.**
- My work is boring.**

---

*The scores given to each item were added together to create an index of individual job satisfaction. The average score was then computed for each organization, based on responses from all participating employees within that organization.

** The scores on these items were reversed to make them consistent with the direction of the other items in the set.

TABLE 10.4
Organizational Job Satisfaction

Employees in organizations participating in the Excellence Study described organizational-level satisfaction with their jobs using the 13 evaluative statements listed here.*

- In general, this organization has treated me well.
- I feel as though I have a real chance to get ahead in this organization.
- The best-qualified people usually are chosen for promotion in this organization.
- I am satisfied with my pay and benefits.
- This organization has a genuine concern for the welfare of its employees.
- I am satisfied with my day-to-day working conditions.
- I am satisfied with the recognition I receive for good performance in my job.
- I have found this organization to be a good place to work.
- Both men and women are treated well in this organization.
- My immediate supervisor is hard to please.**
- It is easy to work with my coworkers.
- There is a good opportunity of advancement in my job.
- Minorities are treated well in this organization.

*The scores given to each item were added together to create an index of organizational job satisfaction. The average score was then computed for each organization, based on responses from all participating employees within that organization.

** The score on this item was reversed to make it consistent with the direction of the other items in the set.

pay, benefits, and work conditions, and when opportunities for advancement are fair and nondiscriminatory, based on merit rather than connections. Organizational job satisfaction increases when it's easy to work with both supervisors and coworkers, and when good work is recognized and factored into advancement opportunities. The 13 items measuring organizational job satisfaction are displayed in Table 10.4.

Individual and organizational job satisfaction were first examined as characteristics of individuals. Scores were then averaged for all participating employees in each organization, creating measures of satisfaction for the organization itself. We found that individual and organizational job satisfaction tended to increase with increases in participative values of organizational culture.[4] On the other hand, as authoritarian organizational cultural values increased, individual and organizational job satisfaction tended to go down.[5]

---

[4]These relationships were tested using correlation coefficients, which allowed the research team to examine all participating organizations. This technique is more powerful than comparing the top 10% of participative organizational cultures to the bottom 10% of participative organizational cultures. Unfortunately, such data analysis cannot be displayed in bar graphs, such as Fig. 10.1.

[5]As with measures of participative values, the relationships between job satisfaction and authoritarian values in organizations were tested using correlation coefficients.

ORGANIZATIONAL CULTURE AND COMMUNICATION
WITHIN ORGANIZATIONS

The research team expected that employees in organizations with highly participative organizational cultures would report highly symmetrical patterns of internal communication. We developed a set of items to measure the symmetrical qualities of internal communication. Table 10.5 displays the seven items used.

When patterns of internal communication are symmetrical, employees are comfortable talking to superiors about work performance and things that have gone wrong. Discussions of difference of opinion are encouraged by both the employee's immediate supervisor and the organization as a whole. Communication is seen as a way for superiors to help subordinates with problems. Communication is described as two way.

We expected that organizations with highly authoritarian cultures would have highly asymmetrical patterns of internal communication. Table 10.6 displays the three items used to measure asymmetrical internal communication.

Asymmetrical patterns of internal communication show when employees say the purpose of communication in their organizations is to get employees to behave as management wants them to behave. Internal communication is asymmetrical when employees say communication flows one way, from managers to employees. Such employees maintain that they receive little feedback from superiors.

Employee reports of symmetrical and asymmetrical communication in their organizations supported our expectations. Employees reported high

TABLE 10.5
Symmetrical Communication Inside Organizations

Employees in organizations participating in the Excellence Study described the degree of symmetrical communication within the organization using the seven evaluative statements listed here.*

- I am comfortable talking to administrators about my performance.
- Most communication between administrators and other employees in this organization can be said to be two-way communication.
- This organization encourages differences of opinion.
- The purpose of communication in this organization is to help administrators to be responsive to the problems of other employees.
- My supervisor encourages differences of opinion.
- I am usually informed about major changes in policy that affect my job before they take place.
- I am comfortable talking to my supervisor when things are going wrong.

---

*The scores given to each item were added together to create an index of symmetrical communication within the organization. The average score was then computed for each organization, based on responses from all participating employees within that organization.

TABLE 10.6
Asymmetrical Communication Inside Organizations

Employees in organizations participating in the Excellence Study described the degree of asymmetrical communication within the organization using the three evaluative statements listed here.*

- The purpose of communication in this organization is to get employees to behave in the way administrators want them to behave.
- Most communication in this organization is one-way: from administrators to other employees.
- I seldom get feedback when I communicate to administrators.

*The scores given to each item were added together to create an index of asymmetrical communication within the organization. The average score was then computed for each organization, based on responses from all participating employees within that organization.

levels of symmetry in patterns of internal communication in those organizations that placed high value on teamwork, shared decision making, and participation. These same employees reported low levels of asymmetrical practices. On the other hand, employees reported strong patterns of asymmetry in those organizations with highly authoritarian cultures. Any symmetrical patterns of internal communication were weak in these authoritarian organizations.

LINKING ORGANIZATIONAL CULTURE TO COMMUNICATION EXCELLENCE

Originally, we viewed participative cultural values as essential to communication excellence, and believed that authoritarian values necessarily impeded excellence. Indeed, our case studies provided instances, such as the public utility and heart health organization mentioned earlier, in which highly participative organizations posted top overall communication Excellence Scores. However, the insurance company case study showed that a highly participative organizational culture cannot make a communication department excellent without the expertise for advanced practices and senior managers who want them. Further, we discovered several instances in which highly conservative and autocratic organizational cultures were changing into more participative cultures. Organizations such as the gas and electric company and the chemical manufacturing corporation had very strong communication departments playing key roles in bringing about these transformations. Yet, these excellent communication departments operated in culturally intense environments, where strong authoritarian and participative values vied for cultural dominance.

These case study findings helped us to reformulate the contribution of organizational culture to communication excellence. That thinking is reflected in the three spheres of communication excellence. The outer sphere of participative organizational cultures is not so essential to communication excellence as are the two inner spheres. Further, the participative and authoritarian values within the same organization affect each other and communication excellence in unexpected ways.

Indeed, employees in organizations with high overall communication Excellence Scores described strong participative values in the cultures of their organizations. At the same time, these same employees also reported slightly higher than average levels of authoritarian values. The participative and authoritarian scores for the most-excellent and least-excellent organizations in the study are displayed in Fig. 10.1. Apparently, some organizations with excellent communication programs are both more participative and

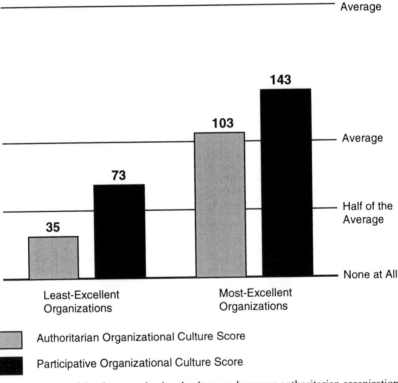

The average participative organizational culture and average authoritarian organizational culture scores were computed for the organizations posting overall Excellence Scores in the top 10% (most-excellent organizations) and bottom 10% (least-excellent organizations) of those participating in the study.

FIG. 10.1.   Levels of participative and authoritarian culture in most-excellent and least-excellent organizations.

more authoritarian than organizations with less-than-excellent communication.

We didn't expect these findings, so we put on our thinking caps and revved up the computer. Fortunately, we had our case study reports to give us clues. Our thinking took a wrong turn when we conceived of organizational cultures as static. In fact, several case studies showed that the cultures of some of the most-excellent organizations were in transition. Old values clashed with new values as senior managers reengineered their organizations to be more flexible and responsive, to make better use of the contributions of all employees. We began to think of the cultures of these organizations as intense, with strong authoritarian and participative values butting against each other.

This new thinking helped us to unravel the intriguing interaction of authoritarian and participative values. On average, the most-excellent organizations in the survey posted authoritarian scores at slightly above average, and participative scores at about one-and-a-half times average. Least-excellent organizations, on the other hand, posted below-average scores for both participative and authoritarian cultures. Participative cultural values are stronger than authoritarian values among both the most-excellent and least-excellent organizations. The difference is that least-excellent organizations have lower levels of both sets of values, when compared to most-excellent organizations.

When we computed the dominant culture of organizations,[6] predominantly participative organizations were only slightly more frequent among the most-excellent organizations. Among those most-excellent organizations, 52% reported predominantly participative cultures. Among least-excellent organizations, 47% reported predominantly participative cultures.[7] The five-percentage-point difference is of no significance, either practical or statistical.

This prompted the research team to examine authoritarian and participative values of each organization together. One might think that authoritarian cultural values would go down as participative values go up, and vice

---

[6]We compared each organization's participative culture score with its own authoritarian culture score. If its participative culture score was higher than its authoritarian score, the organization was classified as having a predominantly participative culture. If the authoritarian culture score was higher, then the organization was classified as predominantly authoritarian.

[7]The scales used to measure participative and authoritarian cultures were generated by the factor analysis that first clustered similar items together. Because of the nature of these scales (normalized), roughly half of the organizations were classified as predominantly participative and half authoritarian. We expected the vast majority of most-excellent organizations to be predominantly participative and the vast majority of the least-excellent organizations to be predominantly authoritarian. When the findings differed from our expectation, we began further investigation, which resulted in the findings reported in this section.

versa. However, that's not always the case. On a hunch, we took all organizations in the survey and placed them into one of four categories. If organizations had above-average participative scores and below-average authoritarian scores, we classified them as *culturally participative*. If organizations had above-average authoritarian scores and below-average participative scores, we classified them as *culturally authoritarian*. We reasoned that culturally participative organizations would have higher overall communication excellence scores than culturally authoritarian organizations would.

Other combinations are possible, however. Some organizations had below-average scores on both the participative and authoritarian culture scales. We called these organizations culturally indifferent, because these organizations did not exhibit strong characteristics of either culture. Some organizations had above-average scores on both the participative and authoritarian culture scales. We classified these organizations as culturally intense, and thought of these organizations as driven by two strong but competing sets of values.

Fig. 10.2 displays the four different types of organizational cultures, based on this classifying scheme. Average overall communication Excellence Scores are shown for each of the four types in percentile form.[8] As we had originally thought, culturally participative organizations posted higher overall communication excellence scores than did culturally authoritarian organizations. However, the highest communication excellence scores were posted by culturally intense organizations, where strong authoritarian and strong participative values struggled with each other. The chemical manufacturing corporation and the gas and electric company described earlier are among these culturally intense organizations. Culturally indifferent organizations—where neither participative nor authoritarian values were strong—fare only marginally better than authoritarian organizations with regard to overall communication excellence (see Fig. 10.3).

It's difficult to change an organization's culture and its presuppositions about communication. On the other hand, the research team thought that communication departments are given windows of opportunity to advance toward excellence when their organizations undergo fundamental changes due to mergers, new leadership, new competition, new markets, new products, and the like. As with the gas and electric company, a merger created the opportunity to overhaul an old-line autocratic bureaucracy into a participative and responsive organizational culture. Communicators carved out new

---

[8] The most understandable way to present overall Excellence Scores is in percentile form. A percentile score represents an individual organization or group of organizations in relation to the Excellence Scores of a representative group of 100 organizations. A score of 50 is average, meaning that about 50 organizations posted higher scores and 50 posted lower scores. A 90th percentile score means an organization posted scores better than 90 of 100 organizations or in the top 10%.

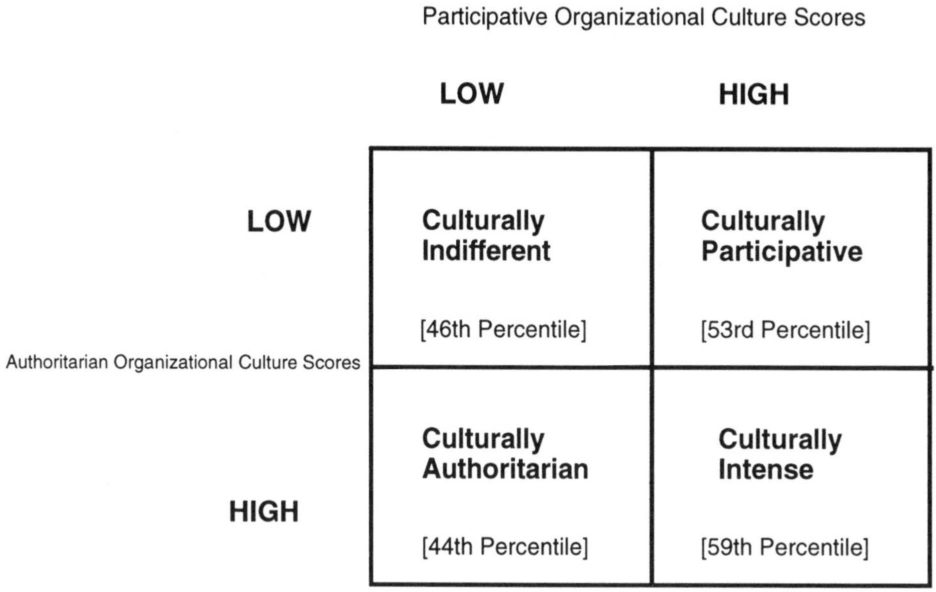

Participative Organizational Culture Scores

	LOW	HIGH
LOW	Culturally Indifferent [46th Percentile]	Culturally Participative [53rd Percentile]
HIGH	Culturally Authoritarian [44th Percentile]	Culturally Intense [59th Percentile]

Authoritarian Organizational Culture Scores

FIG. 10.2.   Overall communication excellence scores for four types of organizational culture.

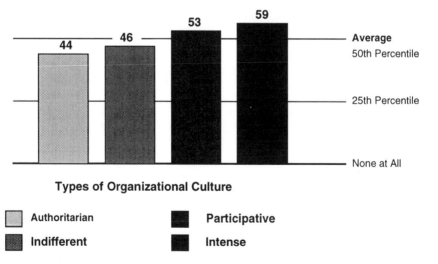

FIG. 10.3.   Levels of communication excellence for authoritarian, indifferent, participative, and intense cultures.

positions of leadership by helping senior managers guide that change. Cultural presuppositions can be redefined through the push and pull of two strong, opposing sets of cultural values. This creates opportunities for communicators with expertise to redefine the communication function.

SUMMARY

Participative organizational cultures that value teamwork and broadly share decision making provide a nurturing environment for communication excellence. Authoritarian organizational cultures, with centralized decision making based on authority and competing agendas among departments, are not generally conducive to excellence. However, the cultures of organizations are dynamic. Sometimes communication excellence springs from the intense competition of strong participative and authoritarian values in the same organizations. Such intense cultural conflicts in organizations emerge when radical changes such as mergers or industrywide crises occur. Such culturally intense organizations also provide windows of opportunity for communication excellence.

The culture of organizations can do little to nurture excellence if the other components of excellence are missing. The departmental knowledge base to play the manager role and engage in two-way communication practices is prerequisite to excellence. Senior managers must understand and expect excellence from their communication departments. Without the expertise and shared expectations from senior management to practice excellence, the organization's culture does not matter.

REFERENCES

Grunig, J. E. (Ed.). (1992). *Excellence in public relations and communication management.* Hillsdale, NJ: Lawrence Erlbaum and Associates.

11

Empowering Women and Culturally Diverse Employees

How organizations address diversity—how they support employees from diverse backgrounds—reflects an important aspect of *culture*, the values that bring employees together to accomplish a common mission. When values provide support to women employees and those from culturally diverse backgrounds, communication is more likely to be excellent.

"It's very important to have a diverse work force, because the population out of which you hire the best and brightest people is diverse," a vice president at a large chemical manufacturing company told us. "If we don't have a diverse work force, then we are only going to effectively hire out of some fraction of the population and, gradually, the quality of our work force—relative to our competitors—is going to diminish."

The vice president had summarized for us the most pragmatic reason for gender and ethnic diversity among employees: Diversity is simply smart business. "This [chemical company] has been a male-dominated corporation," he continued. "It still is. There is really no diversity in senior management; it's all White males."

Despite the logic of gender and ethnic diversity, he had also described a situation that prevailed in many organizations we studied: dominant coalitions made up exclusively of White males. For example, an organization that provides services to the disabled posted overall excellence scores in the top 5% of participating organizations. The majority of departments in that organization are headed by women. The most senior positions, however, are held by men. An invisible glass ceiling in that organization prevents women from advancing to the most senior positions.

Sometimes glass ceilings shatter from major changes in the organization. The merger of a Midwest gas and electric company with another put cracks in the glass ceiling there. The top communicator, who managed an excellent communication program, sees opportunities for women to advance to top positions. "The merger will make some of this happen," she told us. The company is in the forefront of the business community, so visible that inequitable treatment of women would be noticeable. "It's politically correct to do these things," she explained, "and you are in the spotlight if you don't."

At another utility that posted an overall Excellence Score in the top 1%, corporate restructuring has created similar opportunities for women to advance. The CEO told us that mentoring plays a critical role in the advancement of women and individuals from culturally diverse backgrounds. That sentiment was echoed in other interviews. "To get into top management, it takes a mentor to help women break in," the communication manager at an engineering research agency said. The agency where she works posted an overall Excellence Score in the top 5%. "It takes talent, hard work, personality, being at the right place at the right time," she said, explaining the route to senior management positions at this university-based research organization. "This is true for everybody, but it's harder for women." What about employees from culturally diverse backgrounds who are not women? "This state is still part of the South," she replied. "When the door opened at the university for one group, it opened for the other."

At a not-for-profit organization that promotes heart health, the CEO has established a Women and Minorities Leadership Committee to develop professional growth opportunities for current employees. "We are far from where we need to be," the CEO told us. Women make up 60 percent of the organization's staff but only 25% of the 16 vice presidents are women. Employees from culturally diverse backgrounds make up 19% of the organization's staff, but only 1 of the 16 vice presidents is from a culturally diverse background. Organizations with excellent communication programs such as this one have not resolved all the issues related to gender and cultural diversity. These organizations are trying hard to do something about it.

An oil company with overall Excellence Scores in the top 5% pursues diversity by providing training for women and minorities. "We actively recruit and actively look when there's promotional opportunities [by] having women and minorities on the slate of candidates," the support services manager with the oil company said in a case study interview. "There's equal opportunity [so] that it's not just a slam dunk for the White male to get the job."

THE LINK BETWEEN EXCELLENCE AND DIVERSITY

In our case study interviews, we found many organizations with excellent communication programs actively tackling issues important to employees who are women and/or from ethnically diverse backgrounds. This is no coincidence. Organizations that value gender and ethnic diversity among their employees hold values that foster communication excellence as well.

Cultural diversity among all employees—and especially among boundary spanners in communication departments—helps organizations to stay in touch with what's going on outside the organization. Senior managers in organizations tend to become isolated from outside changes. They are surrounded by people just like themselves (i.e., White males). Such dominant coalitions develop their own systems of codes to make sense of the world outside, a private language that further insulates them from reality. That is, dominant coalitions make up their own reality, consistent with the perceptions of senior managers who construct it.

The concept of requisite variety suggests that an organization needs to have as much diversity inside the organization as exists beyond the boundaries of the organization. The variety within provides a basis for building mutually beneficial relationships with diverse peoples and groups outside the organization. Without such requisite variety, senior managers of organizations interact awkwardly with constituents different from themselves. Communication is difficult; misunderstandings are common. Misunderstandings become downright dangerous when they lead to boycotts, lawsuits, and labor disputes.

Communicators play a critical role in strategic planning, precisely because they know what's going on outside the organization and in relationships with key publics. Communicators cannot play this role if they suffer from the same blind spots as do other members of senior management. Communicators from culturally diverse backgrounds can play critical roles as go-betweens, the boundary spanners who can translate what management says to publics and what publics say to management.

Trends in the public relations labor force indicate that some progress has been made in attracting individuals from culturally diverse backgrounds. Fig. 11.1 tracks the sometimes erratic increase in the number of African Americans and Hispanics in the public relations labor force in the United States.[1]

---

[1]The Bureau of Labor Statistics conducts monthly surveys of employed persons for the U.S. Department of Labor. In its listing of detailed occupational categories, communicators are labeled as "Public Relations Specialists." In January of each year, the survey findings for the

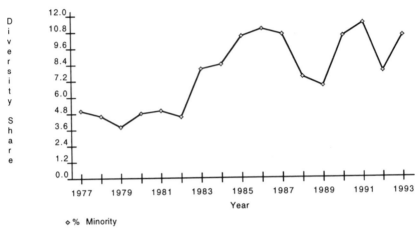

FIG. 11.1.   African-American and Hispanic share of the public relations work force in the United States, 1977–1993.

Such diversity is critical to excellence in public relations and communication management, but communicators from culturally diverse backgrounds cannot provide needed requisite variety to senior management if they are not part of strategic management and planning. In part, that's why organizations with excellent communication programs actively seek to prepare and promote employees from culturally diverse backgrounds to senior management positions. Some of those employees are communicators who cannot provide the tools for excellence without access to management decision making.

WOMEN AND COMMUNICATION

The Excellence team paid special attention to the role and status of women in organizations. The role and status of communication in organizations is inexorably linked to the support and opportunities that organizations provide employees who are women.

Fig. 11.2 shows why the status and role of women in organizations is so critical to communication excellence. In short, most professional communi-

previous calendar year are summarized. Currently, the gender and ethnic status of the labor force is broken down for each detailed occupational category. This research provides the best estimates of characteristics of the communication and public relations labor force. See the January issues of the U.S. Department of Labor publication, *Employment and Earnings*, for annual summaries of U.S. labor force characteristics.

cators in the United States today are women. In the 1960s, women made up roughly only 25% of the public relations labor force in the United States (Smith, 1968). In 1982, women reached numeric parity with men in the public relations labor force, only to drop slightly below 50% in 1984–1985. Since then, the female majority in public relations has continued to increase. In 1994, women constituted nearly 60% of the public relations labor force in the United States (U.S. Department of Labor, 1995).

A similar transformation of the public relations labor force is occurring in Canada. Under the category "Professional Occupations in Public Relations and Communication," the 1991 Canadian national census showed that 62% of the 24,565 communication and public relations professionals working in Canada were women. Although changes in Canadian occupational coding strategies preclude comparisons over time, Canadian communication professionals indicate that much of the gender shift has occurred in the last several decades.[2]

The research team examined a wide range of policies and practices that organizations can enact to hire, support, and encourage the advancement of female employees, including communicators. These included steps that helped women become employees, such as flex time, opportunities for women who must relocate, child-care services, and multiple employment centers. We examined policies that discourage or forbid gender discrimina-

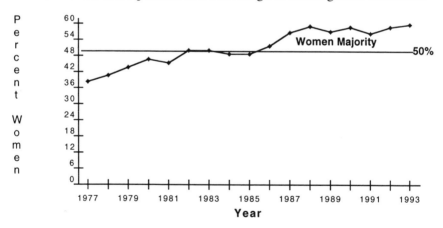

FIG. 11.2.   Women's share of the public relations work force in the United States, 1977–1993.

---

[2]Statistics on the Canadian labor force were provided to the Excellence team courtesy of the Labour Market Information Unit, Metro Vancouver, Canada Employment Centre, Vancouver, B.C. We thank Robert Mattiole, Labour Market Information Analyst, for his assistance.

tion, for example policies regarding sexual discrimination, guidelines for handling sexual harassment, and equal pay for equal work. In addition, organizations can encourage female employees to advance to the highest ranks through mentoring programs, informal assistantships, and paid memberships in professional associations. In all, 22 items were included on the top communicator and CEO questionnaires to measure organizational support of female employees.

Fig. 11.3 displays overall organizational support for women employees in the most-excellent and least-excellent organizations. Among the most-excellent organizations, both CEOs and top communicators reported above-average support. In the least-excellent organizations, both CEOs and top communicators reported below-average support. Generally, CEOs tended to report higher levels of support for women employees than did top communicators. Samples of employees in the most-excellent organizations

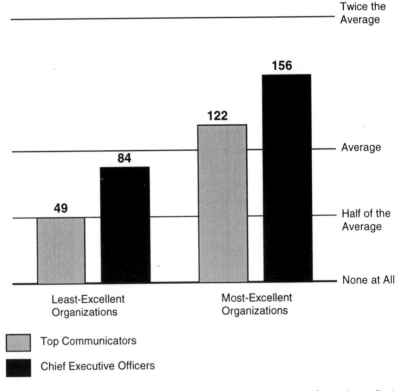

FIG. 11.3.   Overall level of support provided to women employees in most-excellent and least-excellent organizations, as reported by top communicators and CEOs.

TABLE 11.1
Nondiscrimination Policies Enacted to Protect Women Employees

- Developed specific guidelines for handling problems of sexual harassment.
- Established effective policies to deal with sexual discrimination.
- Avoided "perks" that divide employees on the basis of their gender and tenure, such as all-male clubs or executive dining rooms.
- Allowed flex time for employees.
- Funded or reimbursed employees for work-related travel.
- Set up a system of maternity and paternity leave.

reported higher levels of support for women than did samples of employees in least-excellent organizations.[3]

We wanted to break down support for women employees into components. How do people in organizations group or cluster these policies, procedures, and activities? Do organizations with excellent communication programs do more in each component area than did less-than-excellent organizations? To find out, we took the responses from top communicators and subjected them to the same clustering technique we had used to isolate the Excellence Factor.[4] Three groups of support activities emerged, reflecting distinct clusters of policies and procedures used to support women employees.

The first group of items reflects policies and procedures to protect female employees from the most blatant forms of discrimination, while providing such benefits as flex time and reimbursement for work-related travel. These items are displayed in Table 11.1, and can be roughly interpreted as the basics of any support system. In many instances, these organizational policies and procedures implement protections already mandated by law. We labeled this set of items the *non-discrimination policies* of organizations.[5]

A second set of items goes beyond the minimalist policies and procedures

---

[3]The employee questionnaire also included a set of measures of support for women. The scores were averaged for all employees in an organization. Averages were converted into percentile scores, with 50th percentile equal to average. Among employees in most-excellent organizations, the average percentile score was 63. Among employees in least-excellent organizations, the average percentile score was 39.

[4]We used factor analysis to isolate three distinct sets of policies and procedures that support employees who are women. Factor analysis is a technique that groups items together, based on patterns in the responses of subjects in the study. For a more complete explanation of factor analysis, see Exhibit 1.1.

[5]The items that allow flex time for employees and fund employee's work-related travels seem to more logically fit with items measuring supportive environments for women. However, these items were more closely associated with the nondiscrimination items in the answers provided by top communicators.

TABLE 11.2

Steps Taken to Provide a Supportive Work Environment for Women

- Fostered women's leadership abilities.
- Provided a supportive climate for women at work.
- Monitored the use of sexist language in all realms of the organization's communication.
- Included women in the informal informational network.
- Provided opportunities for women to take risks.
- Paid men and women equally for equal or comparable work.

shown in Table 11.1 to provide a supportive work environment; these items are displayed in Table 11.2. Roughly interpreted, these items describe policies, procedures, and activities that encourage women to take risks, network with others, and develop their leadership potential. In addition, activities include eliminating sexist language from organizational communication and providing equal pay for equal or comparable work. We labeled these items the *supportive climate* activities of organizations.[6]

The third set of items seek the advancement of women in organizations through more active, affirmative steps. These items are displayed in Table 11.3. Roughly interpreted, these actions seek to promote women through mentoring programs and a related technique involving informal assistants. This set includes activities to promote understanding of the concerns of women employees. In addition, these policies both assist women who must relocate and provide for multiple employment centers. We labeled these the *mentoring-advancement* activities of organizations.[7]

How do organizations with excellent communication programs compare to less-than-excellent organizations with regard to each of these areas? We compared most-excellent organizations to least-excellent organizations in the areas of nondiscrimination policies, supportive climate, and mentoring/advancement. The results are displayed in Fig. 11.4.

Generally speaking, most-excellent organizations outperform the least-excellent organizations in each category of support for women employees. The least-excellent organizations are below average in all three areas. The most-excellent organizations are above average in two of three areas. Most-excellent and least-excellent organizations all perform better with regard to

---

[6]The equal pay item in this set seems to logically belong with the nondiscrimination items in Table 11.1. However, this item was more closely associated with the other supportive-environment items in the responses of top communicators.

[7]As with the other measures, one of the items in the mentoring-advancement group logically belongs with another group. The item measuring policies to promote understanding of women's concerns logically belongs with the "supportive environment" items in Table 11.2. However, this item was more closely associated with the mentoring-advancement items in the responses of top communicators.

TABLE 11.3
Mentoring and Advancement Programs Established for Women

- Provided opportunities for women who must relocate or have relocated.
- Furthered the talents of women through mentoring programs.
- Built a system of multiple employment centers that allow mobility for employees.
- Groomed women for management by selecting them as "informal assistants" to those in the next-higher position.
- Enacted specific policies, procedures, or programs designed to promote an understanding of the concerns of female employees.

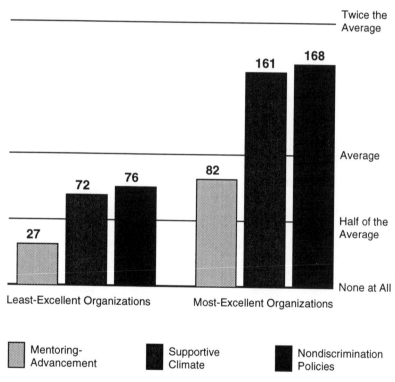

FIG. 11.4 Types of support systems for women employees in most-excellent and least-excellent organizations.*

*Average scores on each set of items were computed for those organizations with overall Excellence Scores in the top 10% of participating organizations, as well as for organizations in the bottom 10% of organizations. These average scores are displayed in the graph for each of the nondiscrimination policies, the supportive climate, and the advancement-mentoring activities of organizations.

nondiscrimination policies and providing supportive climates for women employees. Mentoring and advancement activities are less frequent in both types of organizations, although most-excellent organizations are three times more likely to support these advancement activities than are least-excellent organizations.

Clearly, communication excellence is linked to activities of organizations to protect women employees from discrimination, provide a supportive climate, and help them in their professional advancement. Such organizational conduct reflects a set of cultural values that—like participative values—provide fertile soil for communicators and senior managers to construct excellent communication programs. These values regarding women are especially important, because women constitute the majority of working communication and public relations professionals. Indeed, 51% of top communicators in the Excellence Study are women. How do top communicators in the Excellence Study who are women compare to those who are men?

COMPARING MEN AND WOMEN COMMUNICATORS

In the study, men and women who completed the top communicator questionnaire showed few demographic differences. The men were somewhat older than the women (45 years vs. 39 years). Men and women had roughly equal levels of education, both generally and in public relations. Women were more likely than men to be members of the International Association of Business Communicators (52% vs. 26%). Women supervised smaller communication departments than did their male counterparts. On average, women supervised departments with 8 staff members; men supervised departments with 19 employees.

We chose not to ask top communicators about salaries. In part, we chose to stay focused largely on organizational characteristics, rather than focus on individual communicators. Members of the research team have studied salary differences in a number of prior studies.[8] We know that women are paid less than men. Because women are generally younger than men, we take this factor into account. Men generally still earn higher salaries than women do, even when comparing communicators of equal professional experience. In the past, women have tended to play the technician role predominantly and have been excluded from participation in management decision making. The gender salary gap appears to be closing, however.[9]

---

[8]See, for example, our discussion in chapter 15 of *Excellence in Public Relations and Communication Management* (Grunig, 1992). Other studies include Broom (1982); Dozier (1987, 1989); and Dozier, Chapo, and Sullivan (1983).

[9]In comparable samples of PRSA members in 1979 and 1991, women communicators earned 58 cents for every dollar earned by their male counterparts. In 1991, women were earning 74 cents

Regarding overall communication excellence, male and female department heads in the Excellence Study were virtually identical. Converting overall Excellence Scores to percentile scores (where the 50th percentile is average), communication programs supervised by men placed at the 52nd percentile, and communication programs supervised by women placed at the 49th percentile. The difference is of no practical significance.

Top communicators provided information on their own manager and technician role playing. Manager and technician role playing for both men and women in the study are shown in Fig. 11.5. Not surprisingly, these department heads play the manager role much more frequently than the technician role. Male and female department heads are roughly equal in playing the manager role, doing so about one-and-a-half times the average. Technician role playing is below average for both men and women. However, women play the technician role much more frequently than men: Whereas 80% of women play the manager role more frequently than the technician role, 94% of the men play the manager role predominantly.

We thought playing the technician role might be due to the smaller departments women supervise, requiring all hands to pitch in with technical duties. Indeed, our analysis showed that top communicators in smaller department generally do play the technician role more frequently than department heads with larger technical support staff. However, even when we controlled for the influence of department size, women still did much more technical work than men.[10] This finding meshes with the observation of a top communicator in an engineering research agency, who told us everyone works hard to advance—but women work harder. We concluded that others in the organization may download technical work on department heads who are women, whereas they would not do the same if the department head were a man.

Of the most-excellent organizations, women head 59% of those communication departments. On the other hand, women head 67% of the communication departments in least-excellent organizations. [Men tend to cluster toward the center.]

---

for every dollar earned by men. Some of the salary difference is due to differences in professional experience, manager role playing, and contributions to management decision making. When these influences are controlled, women in 1979 earned 79 cents for every male dollar earned. In 1991, women earned 95 cents for every dollar earned by men. Women with sufficient professional experience seemed to play the manager role with greater frequency in 1991, compared to 1979. Women with sufficient professional experience also played an expanded role in managerial decision making in 1991, compared to 1979 (see Dozier & Broom, 1995).

[10]We conducted analysis of variance on the technical role activities of men and women, introducing the number of employees in departments as a covariate or control variable. After equalizing men and women with regard to departmental staff size, women still posted higher technician role scores than men did.

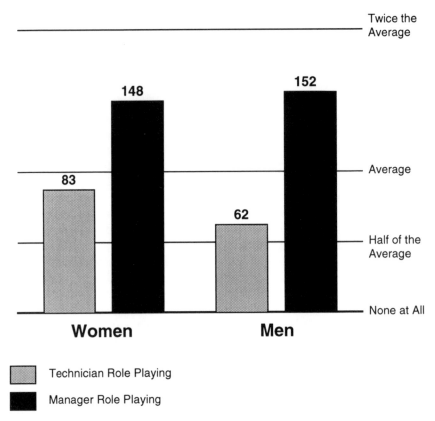

FIG. 11.5. Levels of manager and technician role playing by men and women who are top communicators (all organizations).

Male and female department heads do not differ in terms of the overall excellence of the communication programs they manage. Female department heads do, however, carry an extra burden of technical duties such as writing, editing, and production tasks, when compared to their male counterparts. Nevertheless, women engage in manager role activities just as often as men. For this reason, only 8% of male department heads described their dominant role as communication technician.[11] Among women who head communication departments fully, 22% described their dominant role as technician.

---

[11]We compared each top communicator's manager role score to his or her technician role score. If the manager role score is higher, the top communicator's dominant role is manager. If the technical role score is higher, the top communicator's dominant role is technician.

SUMMARY

An important quality of organizational culture is the treatment of female employees and employees from culturally diverse backgrounds. In fact, this quality of organizational culture is an important part of overall communication excellence. Employees from diverse backgrounds provide organizations with the requisite variety to construct pictures of reality inside the organizations that more closely match the reality as others outside the organization understand it. The principle of requisite variety is especially important in a communication department, which must act as a go-between in the relationship of senior management with key publics. Besides, as the vice president for a chemical manufacturer told us, diversity simply makes good business sense, as organizations can hire the most talented employees from the largest possible pool.

In addition to the principle of requisite variety, the policies, procedures, and actions regarding women employees are also important to communication excellence. That's because women make up the majority of working professionals in public relations and communication management. At the most basic level, organizations support women through clear-cut nondiscrimination policies. In addition, organizations work to provide a supportive work climate for women. Finally, organizations can take affirmative steps to ensure the advancement of women into top management positions, through mentoring and informal assistants programs. Organizations with excellent communication programs provide more support to women in all three areas than do less-than-excellent organizations.

Regarding top communicators in the Excellence Study, male and female department heads were equally successful in running excellent communication programs. Data suggest, however, that women work harder to achieve that excellence, by taking on a larger share of technical work in the department as well.

REFERENCES

Broom, G. M. (1982). A comparison of sex roles in public relations. *Public Relations Review, 8*(3), 17–22.

Dozier, D. M. (1987, May). *Gender, environmental scanning, and participation in management decision making.* Paper presented at the meeting of the Public Relations Interest Group, International Communication Association, Montreal.

Dozier, D. M. (1989). Breaking the "glass ceiling." *Public Relations Review, 14*(4), 6–14.

Dozier, D. M., & Broom, G. M. (1995). Evolution of the manager role in public relations practices. *Journal of Public Relations Research, 7*(1), pp. 3–26.

Dozier, D. M., Chapo, S., & Sullivan, B. (1983, August). *Sex and the bottom line: Income differences between men and women in public relations.* Paper presented at the meeting of the

Public Relations Division, Association for Education in Journalism and Mass Communication, Corvallis, OR.

Grunig, J. E. (Ed.). (1992). *Excellence in public relations and communication management.* Hillsdale, NJ: Lawrence Erlbaum and Associates.

Smith, R. W. (1968). Women in public relations. *Public Relations Journal, 36*(10), 26–27.

U.S. Department of Labor. (1995). *Employment and earnings,* Table 22, *41*(1), 206.

12

The Global Qualities of Excellence

The culture of organizations provides the soil in which communication excellence can either flourish or struggle to survive. What about the culture of the larger society? Are organizations in Canada imbued with cultural values of the larger society that either encourage or discourage excellence? Do organizations in the United Kingdom carry the cultural imprint of that society, making them systematically more excellent or less excellent than their North American counterparts?

Between the culture of individual organizations and the values of the larger society are cultural differences that mark for-profit corporations, not-for-profit organizations, government agencies, and professional-trade associations. Does the corporate environment, for example, systematically favor communication excellence over not-for-profit organizations, government agencies, and associations?

IS EXCELLENCE GLOBAL?

The research team was interested in a larger issue behind these questions about nations and types of organizations: Is communication excellence global? The team wanted to know if basic principles of excellence applied broadly across national and cultural borders.

An alternative view suggests that the principles of excellence are ethnocentric products of the American researchers and communicators that designed and participated in the study, along with our close cultural cousins in Canada and the United Kingdom. According to this view, principles of excellence are substantially different in other cultures that do not share our common English heritage.

To help resolve these questions, differences in excellence across national boundaries are examined. The three nations in the Excellence Study—Canada, the United Kingdom, and the United States—are analyzed first. Because of cultural similarities of these three nations, preliminary research in Slovenia is also reported. This former communist republic provides a strong cultural contrast to the three nations in the Excellence Study. Differences also exist among corporations, not-for-profit organizations, government agencies, and professional-trade associations. The impact of these differences on excellence is explored at the end of the chapter.

⌀ EXAMINING DIFFERENCES IN NATIONS AND ORGANIZATIONAL TYPES

The research team looked at the overall Excellence Scores of organizations in Canada, the United Kingdom, and the United States. Each of the organizations studied was placed in one of three national groups, based on the location of the organization's headquarters. Average overall Excellence Scores for the three national groupings were first computed, and then converted to percentile scores. These scores allowed meaningful interpretations of differences between groups. Percentile scores are explained in Exhibit 12.1. In addition, differences were examined between nations for each of the 20 qualities that contribute to the overall Excellence Score.

All of the organizations in the study were assigned to four groups, based on type of organization. In selecting organizations, the team made sure to include an adequate number of corporations, not-for-profit organizations, government agencies, and professional-trade associations.[1] Now the team had the opportunity to see if these differences between types of organizations made a difference in overall excellence, as well as various qualities that contribute to overall excellence.

△ ORGANIZATIONAL CULTURE, NATION, AND TYPES OF ORGANIZATIONS

The first step in the analysis was to check differences in organizational culture across nations and across types of organizations. In our study of over 4,600 employees, we isolated two basic types of organizational culture. Organizations with authoritarian cultures favor centralized decision making, based on formal authority and tradition. Departments in such organizations pursue their own agendas, rather than a common, unified mission. Employees feel their supervisors don't trust them, because they are super-

---

[1] See the appendix for more details on how we sampled organizations by type and nation for the study.

EXHIBIT 12.1
About Percentile Scores

Throughout this chapter, we use percentile scores. Percentile scores show an organization's position in a group of 100 representative or typical organizations in the Excellence Study. When an organization has a percentile score of 50 on a measure, it means that the organization is "average" with regard to that characteristic. Half the organizations posted higher scores on that measure and half posted lower scores. The 50th percentile score, then, is the average score for any characteristic that's expressed as a percentile score. Organizations with percentile scores below the 50th percentile are below average, based on the standard set by all organizations in the study. Organizations with scores greater than the 50th percentile are above average.

Percentile scores can be computed for groups of organizations. In this chapter, we examine differences among organizations located in Canada, the United Kingdom, and the United States. We also look at differences among corporations, not-for-profit organizations, government agencies, and professional-trade associations. We average the percentile scores for all organizations in a group. If this average is greater than the 50th percentile, then the group is above average. Some members of the group may score below average, but they are more than compensated for by other organizations above the average. If the group average is below the 50th percentile, then organizations in that group generally posted lower-than-average scores.

Small differences between groups are not of any practical importance. Such differences may be caused by inaccuracies that creep into measurement from a number of sources.* When differences between group percentile scores become large, they represent a systematic difference between the groups that are worth interpreting. Statistical tests (not reported here) helped us determine when differences between groups were large enough to be meaningful.**

---

*These errors occur when individuals in organizations report information that either overestimate or underestimate characteristics to some degree. Error is also introduced from the process of selecting organizations to study that may not be perfectly "representative" of all organizations in a particular group.

**A technique called analysis of variance allows researchers to determine if differences between groups are large enough to represent a systematic difference, rather than a difference that can be accounted for as error.

---

vised closely. Organizations with participative cultures, on the other hand, favor teamwork. Decision-making authority is broadly shared by those affected by decisions. A common mission brings various departments together like parts of a well-oiled machine.

Authoritarian and participative culture scores for organizations in Canada, the United Kingdom, and the United States were compared. Regarding participative culture, no meaningful differences were found. American and Canadian organizations posted averages for participative culture slightly above the total average. Organizations in the United Kingdom reported participative culture scores slightly below the total average. These differences were slight, however. Regarding authoritarian culture, Canadian organizations posted averages slightly below those of organizations in the United Kingdom and the United States. However, differences were negligible.

Meaningful differences were found, however, when the team examined the cultural values of corporations, not-for-profit organizations, government agencies, and professional-trade associations. Generally, corporations posted above-average scores for both authoritarian and participative cultures; such corporations are culturally intense.[2] Not-for-profit organizations posted participative culture scores slightly below average and authoritarian culture scores substantially below the total average. Not-for-profit organizations are noteworthy for their rejection of authoritarian cultural values, rather than for their acceptance of participative values. Government agencies posted average participative and authoritarian culture scores slightly below average. Professional-trade associations posted below-average scores for both participative and authoritarian culture—many professional-trade associations are culturally indifferent.[3]

From this analysis, the team concluded that any influence of national cultures did not come into organizations through the organization's cultural values. If national cultures affect excellence in the organizations studied, the route of that influence tends to bypass organizational culture. Regarding types of organizations, corporations seem to be culturally intense, with strong participative and authoritarian values competing for the soul of the organization. Professional-trade associations seem culturally indifferent, with weak participative and authoritarian values. Regarding communication excellence, this analysis led the team to expect no differences among nations but to expect some differences among corporations, not-for-profit organizations, government agencies, and professional-trade associations.

NATIONAL DIFFERENCES IN COMMUNICATOR CHARACTERISTICS

Table 12.1 provides a breakdown of key communicator and organizational characteristics for Canada, the United Kingdom, and the United States. Women head the vast majority of departments we studied in Canada. In the United Kingdom, however, men headed communication departments by an

---

[2] As detailed in chapter 10, culturally intense organizations have strong attributes of both participative and authoritarian cultures. The conflicting values of these two cultures in such organizations permit opportunities for excellence. In fact, culturally intense organizations post the highest overall Excellence Scores.

[3] As detailed in chapter 10, culturally indifferent organizations have weak participative and weak authoritarian cultural values. Neither cultural imperative is particularly strong in such organizations. Culturally indifferent organizations, along with culturally authoritarian organizations, post low overall Excellence Scores.

TABLE 12.1
Demographic Characteristics of Top Communicators and Departments in
Canada, the United Kingdom, and the United States

Characteristics	Canada	United Kingdom	United States
Gender			
Women	61%	40%	51%
Men	39%	60%	49%
Age (in years)	42	44	42
Education			
Less than college degree	29%	44%	4%
Bachelor's degree	39%	23%	34%
Some graduate school	18%	14%	26%
Master's or doctorate degree	14%	19%	36%
Public relations training			
None	9%	31%	21%
Some continuing education classes	36%	40%	21%
Some college course work	39%	17%	29%
Bachelor's or master's degree in public relations	16%	12%	29%
Average number of employees in communication department	12	11	14

equally large margin over women. Women headed slightly more departments than did men in the United States.

Ages of top communicators in the three nations were virtually identical.
Top communicators with American organizations were generally better
educated, with 96% holding at least a bachelor's degree and 36% holding
advanced degrees. Top communicators with the Canadian organizations
studied also posted high levels of education, with 71% holding bachelor's
degrees and 14% holding advanced degrees. Top communicators in the
United Kingdom reported lower levels of education, with 44% reporting no
college degree at all.

About 91% of the top communicators in the Canadian organizations
reported some formal training in public relations, but only 16% said they
held college degrees in public relations.[4] American top communicators were
the most likely to have college degrees in public relations (29%), but 21%

---

[4] Regarding education, we distinguished between general education in communication or
speech communication and specific professional training in public relations. Whereas public
relations and communication management are somewhat interchangeable in the professional
setting, the terms *communication* and *public relations* have distinctly different meanings in
higher education. Communication courses tend to study communication in organizations from
a liberal studies perspective, to provide students with a well-rounded education about communication. Public relations courses, on the other hand, tend to favor professional training, geared
to showing students how to do public relations and communication management.

said they had no formal training at all. In the United Kingdom, the majority of top communicators had either completed only some continuing education (41%) or had no formal training at all (31%). Communication departments in Canada, the United Kingdom, and the United States employed roughly equal numbers of employees.[5]

NATIONAL DIFFERENCES IN COMMUNICATION EXCELLENCE

When overall Excellence Scores for the three nations were compared, no meaningful differences were found. Organizations in Canada, the United Kingdom, and the United States were remarkably similar in overall excellence. Communicators in Canadian organizations may derive some symbolic satisfaction from the fact that the Canadian organizations studied posted higher overall Excellence Scores than those in the United Kingdom or the United States. Organizations in the United Kingdom that we studied posted the lowest average. However, the spread over all three nations is only three percentile points. After studying the statistical analysis that helps tell whether differences between groups are meaningful, the team declared this contest a three-way tie for first! (See Fig. 12.1.)

When the specific qualities that contribute to excellence were compared, however, some national differences were rather strong. Recall that departmental knowledge is core to communication excellence. Communication departments in Canada, the United Kingdom, and the United States were examined for differences in their expertise to play the manager role and implement advanced, two-way symmetrical and asymmetrical practices. Overall, the organizations studied in the United Kingdom reported slightly higher-than-average levels of expertise regarding the manager role and two-way practices. The Canadian organizations studied were above average in manager role expertise, slightly above average in the expertise needed for two-way asymmetrical practices, and about average in two-way symmetrical expertise. Organizations in the United States were about average in all three areas (see Fig. 12.2).

Another important quality of excellence is the communication department's contributions to organizational strategic planning. Such contributions depend, in part, on manager role expertise and the knowledge to

---

[5]Differences in education and public relations training may reflect national differences in the availability of education in public relations specifically and college education generally. As explained in the appendix, the goal of the Excellence Study was to gather information in great depth from each of the organizations we studied. Therefore, a nonprobability sampling strategy was used. For this reason, characteristics of top communicators we studied do not predict the characteristics of all top communicators in those nations.

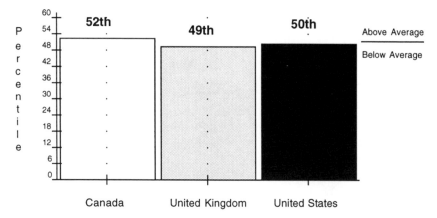

FIG. 12.1.   Overall communication excellence of organizations in Canada, the United Kingdom, and the United States.

engage in two-way practices. Top communicators and CEOs in each organization described communication's strategic contribution, and strong national differences were found. Communication departments in Canadian organizations made larger contributions to strategic planning, when compared to departments in the United States and the United Kingdom. Canadian top communicators and CEOs agreed that communication's contribution was large. In fact, Canadian CEOs rated that contribution higher than did top communicators (see Fig. 12.3).

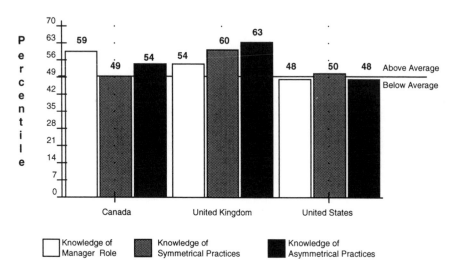

FIG. 12.2.   Knowledge of manager role and two-way practices in communication departments in Canada, the United Kingdom, and the United States.

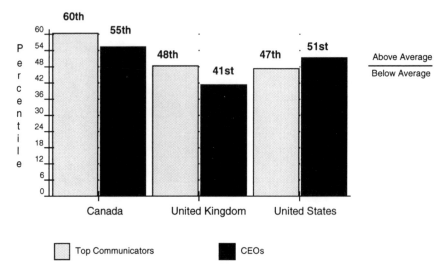

FIG. 12.3.   Contribution of communication departments to strategic planning in Canada, the United Kingdom, and the United States, as reported by top communicators and CEOs.

The contribution of communication departments in the United States was about average. Top communicators in the United States reported higher strategic planning contributions than did their CEOs. In the United Kingdom, communication's contribution to strategic planning was below average. CEOs in the United Kingdom reported that this contribution was greater than that reported by their top communicators.

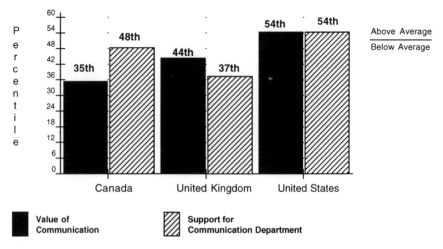

FIG. 12.4.   Value and support for communication in Canada, the United Kingdom, and the United States, as Reported by CEOs.

CEOs were asked how much communication was valued and supported by dominant coalitions in their organizations. CEOs in the United States reported the highest levels of such communicator clout among dominant coalitions, although this clout was only somewhat above average (see Fig. 12.4). Among Canadian organizations, CEOs reported that support for the communication department was slightly below average (48th percentile). However, dominant coalitions in these Canadian organizations do not generally value the communication function. In the United Kingdom, CEOs reported that the value and support of communication by their dominant coalitions was generally below average.

Interesting national patterns emerged from the responses of top communicators and CEOs about the expectations of dominant coalitions for advanced two-way practices. The top of Fig. 12.5 displays information from each nation about senior management's demand for two-way symmetrical practices. In Canada and the United States, both top communicators and CEOs report similar levels of demand. In Canada, top communicators put such demand at slightly above average, whereas their CEOs placed such demand at slightly below average. A similar pattern prevailed for demand for two-way asymmetrical practices as well.

In the United States, top communicators reported below-average demand for symmetrical practices, whereas their CEOs reported above-average demand. A similar pattern prevailed for two-way asymmetrical practices.

In the United Kingdom, however, CEOs and top communicators provided extremely different estimates of demand from the dominant coalition for both symmetrical and asymmetrical practices. Regarding symmetrical practices, top communicators placed demand at the 88th percentile whereas their CEOs placed such demand at the 41st percentile. The difference is not so pronounced for asymmetrical practices. Nevertheless, top communicators placed demand from the dominant coalition at the 64th percentile whereas their CEOs placed it at the 41st percentile.[6]

In summary, no systematic differences exist in overall communication excellence in the organizations studied in Canada, the United Kingdom, and the United States. Certain differences do exist regarding some of the qualities that contribute to excellence. However, the sampling strategy used in the Excellence Study emphasized the intensive study of organizations. Statistically speaking, the team is not comfortable generalizing about all organizations in Canada, the United Kingdom, and the United States based on those in the Excellence Study. However, extrapolating results from those

---

[6]Because the sample in the United Kingdom was smaller than samples for Canada and the United States, these differences may be due to the larger effects of sampling error that occur in smaller samples.

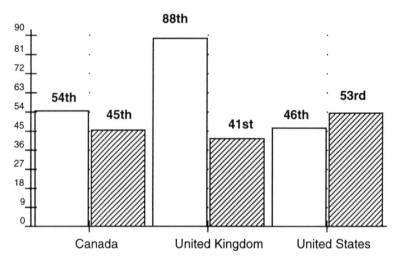

Symmetrical Practices Expected by Dominant Coalitions

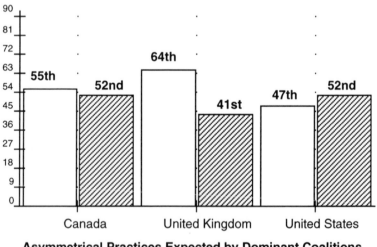

Asymmetrical Practices Expected by Dominant Coalitions

☐ Reported by
Top Communicators

▨ Reported by
CEOs

FIG. 12.5.   Demand from dominant coalition for two-way practices in Canada, the United Kingdom, and the United States, as reported by top communicators and CEOs.

organizations studied suggests that the general qualities of communication excellence can be found in all three nations. On average, organizations in Canada, the United Kingdom, and the United States showed remarkably similar levels of excellence.

The HERMES Study

Findings about Canada, the United Kingdom, and the United States alone do not support the general declaration that communication excellence is truly global. These three predominantly English-speaking nations prepare communicators for their careers in very similar ways.[7] Hofstede (1980) compiled a 39-nation study, conducting surveys with employees in each nation who were employed by the same transnational corporation. Called the HERMES study (a fictitious name for the corporation, used to mask its identity), Hofstede found that his samples of employees in Canada, the United Kingdom, and the United States showed similar cultural values regarding several issues important to excellence.

The three nations placed high value on individualism. Personal achievements and individual welfare define self-worth. Individualistic Canada, the United Kingdom, and the United States stood in sharp contrast to other cultures, in which people defined their worth in relationships with larger groups. HERMES employees in Venezuela, Columbia, and Pakistan were most collectivist. Note the parallels between collectivist cultures and the emphasis on teamwork in participative organizational cultures. Authoritarian organizational cultures, on the other hand, emphasize agendas of individuals and departments separate from those of the organization. Collectivist cultures seem conducive to participative organizational cultures in which excellent communication tends to flourish.

In a similar vein, cultures can be described in terms of how well they fit traditional (stereotypic) notions of masculinity and femininity. Cultures that value assertiveness, competition, and acquiring possessions have masculine cultures, using the word in its traditional sense. HERMES employees in Japan and Austria posted the highest masculine scores, whereas employees in Sweden and Norway posted the lowest scores. Those in the United Kingdom and the United States posted above-average masculinity scores, whereas Canada's masculinity score was about average. Traditional femininity embraces nurturing, placing greater value on relationships with people and quality of life over job advancements and earnings. Excellence incorporates feminine values by placing great importance on establishing and maintaining long-term relationships through negotiation and compromise.

---

[7]Studies of practitioner groups in the three nations suggest few differences in the preparation of communicators for the practice (White, 1987; White, Hammonds, & Kalupa, 1987; White & Trask, 1982).

In some cultures, power is concentrated among a powerful, privileged few. In the HERMES study, such class-oriented cultures included the Philippines, Mexico, and Venezuela. These cultures favor hierarchical organizational structures like those found in authoritarian organizations. Other cultures place less emphasis on social class; power is spread broadly among people. These societies seem more conducive to the shared power of participative organizational cultures. HERMES employees in Austria, Israel, and Denmark scored the lowest in terms of such concentration of power based on social class. Canada, the United Kingdom, and the United States scored toward the middle, slightly below the average.

Some cultures tolerate uncertainty better than others. HERMES employees in Sweden and Denmark tolerated uncertainty best, whereas employees in Greece and Portugal reported a strong desire to avoid uncertainty. Canada, the United Kingdom, and the United States scored close together in the lower quarter of employees in the 39 nations studied. Cultures that avoid uncertainty reduce ambiguity by enforcing many formal rules, and do not tolerate deviant views. Regarding excellence, tolerating uncertainty helps symmetrical internal communication. Cultures that tolerate deviant views will foster organizations that negotiate more successfully with external publics, seeking long-term relationships with those whose views differ from those in dominant coalitions.

In short, Canada, the United Kingdom, and the United States are too culturally similar to put communication excellence—as explained in this book—to a tough cross-cultural test. We needed an opportunity to try out our understanding of communication excellence in a country very different from Canada, the United Kingdom, and the United States. We received big assistance in our endeavor from an unlikely source: the decline of communism.

Excellence in Slovenia

With the decline and collapse of the former Soviet Union, the nations of eastern Europe began to spin free of 50 years of authoritarianism under the Stalinist model. In 1990, a public relations firm named Pristop was established in Slovenia to help organizations cope with publics that previously were not allowed to organize under the old regime. In 1991, Slovenia declared its independence from the former Yugoslavian Federation. Owners of the new firm began a long-term collaboration with several members of the Excellence team. Pristop has become an experiment in the use of generic principles of communication excellence in a nation and culture profoundly dissimilar to those that gave birth to the Excellence Study.

Pristop has translated the top communicator, CEO, and employee questionnaires from the Excellence Study and administered them to 30 organizations in Slovenia that possessed some type of organized public relations function. Initial analysis of the data, as indicated by mean scores on each of the measures on the Excellence Factor, show striking similarities between Slovenian organizations and those studied in Canada, the United Kingdom, and the United States. Other aspects of communication and public relations in Slovenia show differences as well.

In interviews with three principles of the Slovenian public relations firm, we found that several key attributes of excellence have been successfully applied:

• Knowledge of the manager role and advanced two-way practices have been successfully applied. The firm has mastered these advanced skills and provides training to communicators in client organizations. Such communicators are largely communication technicians. They typically lack visibility among senior managers. To build a strong national foundation for communication excellence, Pristop is working closely with the University of Ljubljana to offer short professional development seminars, as well as to build a public relations curriculum into the university's degree offerings.

• The firm has experienced success only with those client organizations in which Pristop has direct access to the CEO. Pristop seeks to position communicators on the organization's management team. This often proves challenging, because most client organizations are highly authoritarian. Many organizational managers in Slovenia are not versed in strategic management, so Pristop helps them develop such expertise.

At the same time, the team found several factors in Slovenia that impede communication excellence:

• Female communicators in Slovenia are not as respected by senior managers as are male communicators. Clients have asked Pristop "not to send a female but send someone who is more serious." Sometimes, Pristop must have older men present proposals that women have developed, in order to circumvent such widespread gender discrimination.

• Most Slovenian organizations have not experienced activist pressure. Sometimes, Pristop helps publics to organize and elect leaders so that the client organization can have somebody with whom to negotiate.

The Slovenian experiences suggest that the general principles of excellence can be applied globally. Clearly, other tests are needed in other diverse cultures before a sweeping generalization can be made. At the same time, principles of excellence must be introduced incrementally, in accordance with prevailing cultural values.

For example, internal communication in most Slovenian organizations is top down, reflecting the authoritarian cultural values that dominated all public life only a few years ago. Symmetrical communication, in which employees talk back to senior managers, must be introduced in small increments, permitting the organizational culture to adapt to change. Using research to scan for potential conflicts with strategic publics must also occur in small, incremental steps. Most Pristop clients are unwilling to budget research expenses.

In summary, the broad generic principles of excellence apply to any culture in which organizations make strategic choices and the people affected by those choices can respond. Until recently, organizations in Slovenia were highly constrained and could exercise only a narrow range of strategic choices. Likewise, the people of Slovenia were constrained from acting against organizations that adversely affected them. Once organizations and publics were given choices, the generic principles of excellence became applicable.

The attributes of the larger social culture may foster some qualities of excellence, while impeding others. The rapid political, economic, and social changes in Slovenia foster a strong need for senior managers to think strategically about long-term relationships. At the same time, rigid authoritarian values block the symmetrical communication practices necessary for organizations to adapt to change.

EXCELLENCE IN DIFFERENT TYPES OF ORGANIZATIONS

Examination of national differences in excellence tentatively suggests that generic principles of excellence can be applied globally. At the same time, specific applications of excellence differ across cultures, based on local conditions. This same logic suggests that generic principles of excellence apply to for-profit corporations, not-for-profit organizations, government agencies, and professional-trade associations. At the same time, these types of organizations are likely to differ in the specific applications of excellence.

COMMUNICATOR CHARACTERISTICS IN ORGANIZATIONAL TYPES

Table 12.2 provides a breakdown of communicator characteristics for corporations, not-for-profit organizations, government agencies, and professional-trade associations. Communicators and communication departments differ across the types of organizations. In corporations, men are much more likely than women to head communication departments. In government agencies, men and women head communication departments in roughly equal numbers. In not-for-profit organizations and professional-trade associations,

TABLE 12.2
Demographic Characteristics of Top Communicators and Departments in
Corporations, Not-For-Profit Organizations, Government Agencies, and
Professional-Trade Associations

Characteristics	Corporations	Not-For Profits	Gov't Agencies	Associations
Gender				
Women	44%	61%	51%	60%
Men	56%	39%	49%	40%
Age (in years)	42	43	43	41
Education				
Less than college degree	17%	7%	14%	7%
Bachelor's degree	35%	28%	38%	30%
Some graduate studies	21%	29%	15%	33%
Master's or doctorate degree	27%	36%	33%	30%
Public relations training				
None	23%	20%	12%	29%
Some continuing education	25%	31%	29%	22%
Some college course work	29%	18%	33%	31%
Bachelor's or master's degree	23%	31%.	26%	18%
Average number of employees in communication department	15	8	18	9

women head roughly 60% of communication departments. The average age of top communicators is about 42 with only slight differences across different types of organizations.

Top communicators in corporations are less likely to hold a college degree. Top communicators in not-for-profit organizations and professional-trade associations are more likely to have attended graduate school and to hold advanced degrees. Top communicators differ little across types of organizations with regard to specialized training in public relations. Corporations and government agencies have significantly larger communication departments, based on number of employees. In contrast, not-for-profit organizations and associations have roughly half as many employees in their communication departments.

TYPES OF ORGANIZATIONS AND DIFFERENCES IN EXCELLENCE

Corporations, not-for-profit organizations, government agencies, and professional-trade associations differ little in overall communication excellence (see Fig. 12.6). Professional-trade associations posted the highest average overall Excellence Scores. Corporations and not-for-profit organizations

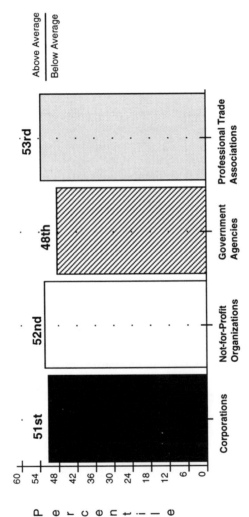

FIG. 12.6.   Overall communication excellence scores for corporations, not-for-profit organizations, government agencies, and professional-trade associations.

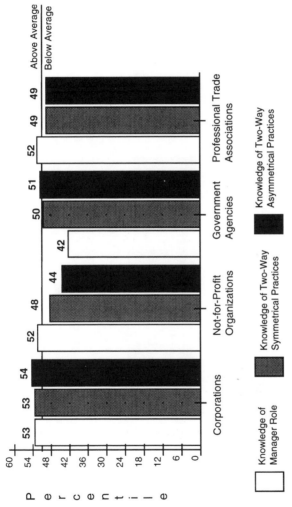

FIG. 12.7. Level of knowledge to play the manager role in communication departments in corporations, not-for-profit organizations, government agencies, and professional-trade associations.

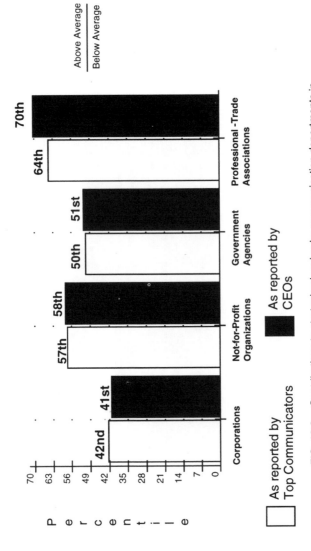

FIG. 12.8. Contributions to strategic planning by communication departments in corporations, not-for-profit organizations, government agencies, and professional-trade associations, as reported by top communicators and CEOs.

also posted averages slightly above average. Government agencies, on the other hand, were slightly below average. The range of differences, however, is slight and of no practical importance. As with overall excellence among nations, we declare this contest a four-way tie for first place.

Types of organizations differed only slightly regarding core knowledge (see Fig. 12.7). Corporations posted slightly above-average scores for manager role expertise and knowledge of two-way practices. Not-for-profit organizations posted average scores for manager role knowledge and two-way symmetrical practices, but below-average scores for two-way asymmetrical practices. Government agencies posted below-average expertise for the manager role but average levels of expertise for two-way practices. Professional-trade associations posted average scores for manager role knowledge and expertise for two-way practices.

Regarding contributions of the communication department to strategic planning, considerable differences exist across types of organizations (see Fig. 12.8). Communication departments in professional and trade associations made large contributions to strategic planning. This view was reflected in information provided by both top communicators and CEOs. Communication departments in not-for-profit organizations also made above-average contributions to strategic planning, a perception shared by both top communicators and CEOs. Communication departments in government agencies made average contributions. In corporations, however, both CEOs and top communicators agreed that contributions to strategic planning from communication departments were below average. Regarding the value and support given to communication by dominant coalitions, such clout differed little across the types of organizations.

SUMMARY

The culture of the larger society in the three nations we studied does not seem to affect the overall excellence of communication in the organizations of those countries. The values and beliefs that differ across corporations, not-for-profit organizations, government agencies, and professional-trade associations also do not seem to affect overall communication excellence. An organization's culture provides values, beliefs, and expectations that either enhance or restrict excellence. An organization's culture, in turn, may reflect values and beliefs from larger cultural systems. However, this linkage is weak. Some qualities that contribute to excellence do differ among nations and types of organizations. These variations reflect cultural differences that nourish some qualities of excellence while retarding others.

This chapter completes the explanation of the spheres of excellence first introduced in chapter 1. At core, excellence requires a knowledge base in the communication department to play the manager role and enact advanced two-way practices. Such expertise, however, requires shared expectations with senior management. Specifically, senior managers must value communication and its contribution to strategic planning. Such contributions come from departments that practice two-way communication, acting as eyes and ears of organizations, as well as spokespersons. Senior managers expect top communicators to run their departments strategically.

Core expertise and shared expectations are nurtured in participative organizational cultures that enhance excellence. Culturally intense organizations also favor communication excellence. Larger cultural values, represented by national cultures and the different types of organizations, may enhance or retard different qualities of excellence. Arguably, generic principles of excellence, represented by the three spheres in Fig. 1.1, are global in scope.[8]

REFERENCES

Hofstede, G. (1980). *Culture's consequences.* Beverly Hills, CA: Sage.

White, J. (1987). *Professional development needs of UK public relations practitioners.* Institute of Public Relations: London.

White, J., Hammonds, L., & Kalupa, F. (1987, August). *Professional development needs of U.S. public relations practitioners.* Paper presented at the meeting of the Association for Education in Journalism and Mass Communication, San Antonio, TX.

White, J., & Trask, G. (1982). *Professional development needs of Canadian public relations practitioners.* Halifax, Nova Scotia: Dalhousie University, Canadian Public Relations Society and Advanced Management Centre.

---

[8]This finding may be due to the close cultural similarities of the three nations studied. Perhaps cultural differences are not sufficiently pronounced in the Excellence Study to permit the impact of national culture on communication excellence to be detected. Further research is needed. Among others, Excellence team member K. Sriramesh at Purdue University is currently pursuing such a research agenda.

13

Changing the Character of Organizations

When conducting the survey portion of the Excellence Study in 1990–1991, a large company in the United States that manufactures metal posted an overall Excellence Score near the bottom 10% of participating organizations. Employees reported through their questionnaires that the company culture wasn't particularly participative, ranking it in the bottom quarter of organizations studied.

When the research team talked to the top communicator in 1994, the character of the corporation was changing. The public relations manager who filled out the top communicator questionnaire in 1990–1991 had since retired. In 1992, the CEO consolidated his power by assuming chairmanship of the board of directors. Among his first acts, he appointed a vice president for public affairs, who now supervises public relations. As a member of the dominant coalition, the new vice president participates actively in strategic management and planning through the corporate management committee.

The team learned that the CEO had developed an understanding of communication as he moved up through corporate ranks. As CEO, he travels between corporate divisions regularly, frequently making "floor visits" and meeting with professional employees to listen to their concerns. He writes his own speeches. Externally, he exhorts the heavy industries to take responsibility for their collective corporate image. By image, he means "a reflection of reality—a mirror of an industry's strengths and importance."

The old, "rigid" decision-making hierarchy, the public relations manager told us, is giving way to more decentralized autonomy within corporate divisions. Participative cultural values now compete with traditional authoritarian values that used to drive all decision making. Excellence of the communication function and the participative quality of the organization's culture are changing simultaneously.

What factors are driving these ongoing changes in communication and the organizational character of this large manufacturing company? Hard times—over the last 10 years, this company has seen its market share and its profits decline. All divisions and departments have felt the squeeze of downsizing. Communication has taken some hits, but communication plays a much more strategic role today than it did with a larger staff in 1990–1991. Based on the case study, the research team concluded that the communication function is lean, muscular, and able to hold its own in the company's strategic management.

This case illustrates how new leadership can play an important role in changing communication and the character of organizations. In this chapter, the role of communication is explored as an active agent to change the character of organizations to enhance communication excellence.[1] To do so, consider what top communicators and CEOs told the team about changing the character of organizations.

CAN YOU MANAGE CHANGE IN ORGANIZATIONAL CULTURE?

Some people who study organizations—call them purists—say you cannot manage change in organizational culture. If by *cultural change* one means the unconscious evolution of unspoken assumptions and beliefs among most members of organizations, then our definition makes notions of managing cultural change seem fanciful at best. Pragmatists, on the other hand, regard organizational culture as the core values that are reflected in the rules of the game, the "way we do things" in an organization. Peters and Waterman (1982), in their study of excellence in organizations, assigned a pivotal role to shared values, one part of an organization's culture that managers can help change.

The research team describes its members as humble pragmatists. Communicators and others can play a role in changing aspects of an organization's

---

[1]We use the term character to describe those tangible aspects of organizational culture that managers can identify and seek to influence. We take the democratic view that the character of organizations is found in the assumptions and values of most members of an organization at all ranks in the hierarchy. We take the pragmatic view that how senior managers behave and the values implicit in such behavior models those values for others in the organization. Members of organizations tell stories about the exemplary behavior of leaders that take on qualities of organizational myths. The voluntary retelling of these myths by organizational members at all levels of an organization provides a mechanism for transferring assumptions and values among old members and to new members.

culture. However, such change occurs slowly. In the Excellence Study, the team found powerful forces at play whenever major changes occurred in the character of organizations. These powerful forces are generally—but not always—necessary to bring about change in organizations. According to the power-control perspective,[2] organizations are made up of people who form coalitions. The most powerful of these—the dominant coalition—seeks first and foremost to maintain its power (Robbins, 1990). Those among that elite with the power to run an organization tend to favor the status quo. Dominant coalitions make decisions that satisfice—that are good enough for organizational purposes but also maintain coalition power. As organizational scholar Jeffrey Pfeffer (1978) put it, big structural changes in organizations amount to quasi-revolutions that shake up power relationships in dominant coalitions. These big shakeups represent both opportunities and dangers for communication departments with the expertise to play new roles in organizations.

COMMUNICATION DEPARTMENT PREREQUISITES FOR CHANGES IN EXCELLENCE

Participative organizational cultures provide a nurturing organizational setting for communicators and dominant coalitions to manage excellent communication programs.[3] However, many organizations with strong participative cultural values do not have excellent communication programs. Likewise, several excellent communication programs operate in very inhospitable authoritarian organizations. Clearly, a nurturing organizational setting imbued with participative cultural values is not sufficient to cause excellence to happen, nor is a participative culture even necessary for excellence. Before organizational culture can matter to excellence, communication departments must meet certain prerequisites. Communication departments that are preparing for excellence fall into two categories: internally challenged departments and perceptually challenged departments.

---

[2] The power-control perspective describes the thinking of some scholars of organizations who question the notion that organizations are rational machines that try to optimize responses to their environments.

[3] We consider organizations we labeled culturally intense in chapter 10 as providing favorable settings for communication excellence. These organizations have both strong participative and strong authoritarian values. Among those we examined as case studies, such organizations were actively shifting from an authoritarian organizational culture to a more participative organizational culture. Competing cultural values exist in these transitional organizations. These transitional organizations posted high overall Excellence Scores. Organizations with strong participative values and weak authoritarian values also posted high overall Excellence Scores. In both cases, participative cultural values—either ascending or established—provide a nurturing setting for excellence.

Internally Challenged Departments

Top communicators of internally challenged departments need go no further than a departmental staff meeting to identify the most significant barrier to excellence. The members of their departments lack the knowledge base for excellence; such departments are internally challenged. In chapter 5, steps were suggested that individual communicators and communication departments can take to build the knowledge base for excellence.

Internally challenged departments are unlikely to participate in changing the character of their organizations, except perhaps as disseminators of communication in support of programs designed by others. The powerful forces that precipitate changes in organizational character represent a threat to these departments. Regarded as largely functionary, such departments are among the excess baggage tossed overboard when the organizational ship takes on water.

Perceptually Challenged Departments

Perceptually challenged departments have the knowledge to enact advanced two-way practices. They have the expertise to play the communication manager role and to use advanced, two-way practices. However, such departments must respond to the demands of unsophisticated dominant coalitions. These dominant coalitions regard public relations and communication management as a technical support function, standing by to "get the word out" once the dominant coalition has made all the strategic decisions. Perceptions of communication by such dominant coalitions stand in the way of communication excellence, regardless of the participative nature of their organizations.

Because dominant coalitions hold these misperceptions, perceptually challenged departments are also at risk in times of crisis and turmoil. Metaphorically, such departments may be mistaken for excess baggage in sinking times, rather than the life preservers they actually are. Nevertheless, these same powerful forces create opportunities to change the character of organizations—and alter the function of communication.

CRISES THAT CHANGE COMMUNICATION AND
ORGANIZATIONAL CHARACTER

Our survey of organizations in 1990–1991 helped identify the qualities of communication departments, dominant coalitions, and organizational cultures that contribute to overall excellence. However, the survey could not tell us how excellent communication programs—and the participative organizational cultures that support excellence—came to be. The case studies in 1994, however, provided important insights. The team found that crises and upheavals simultaneously create opportunities for excellence to flourish and organizational cultures to become more participative.[4] The cases that follow help to show why.

A large oil company posted an overall Excellence Score in the top 5% of participating organizations. The vice president of public affairs manages four separate communication and public relations units with a combined staff of 120. He sits on both the public affairs and public policy committees, and is an active member of the dominant coalition. A large internal research unit allows public affairs to act as eyes and ears for the organization.

How did communication excellence come about at this oil company? Two events were key in the redefinition of the company's communication function: the oil embargo of the 1970s and the Exxon *Valdez* tanker spill in the 1980s.

During the oil embargo, public regard for the oil industry plummeted. "It kind of hit the industry by surprise," the director of research told us. The oil industry believed that public anger should be directed at the oil exporting nations imposing the embargo, not the oil companies. The embargo made clear the need for a sophisticated environmental scanning and issues management system—the eyes and ears of the corporation—to keep the company's finger on the pulse of public opinion.

The Exxon *Valdez* tanker spill provided another reminder to senior management how events in the world can affect the company's position among millions of its customers. These same events—which generate rapid shifts in public opinion—can affect legislative and policy issues radically.

These issues are no small potatoes for this Fortune 500 company. In 1993, public affairs initiatives by the company resulted in favorable tax legislation, saving the company $20 million. Three separate pieces of unfavorable environmental legislation were deflected, saving the company roughly $1 billion.

Consider another crisis that affected a not-for-profit organization. In the early 1980s, the AIDS threat propelled the top communicator at a community blood bank into a leadership position. Some people thought that donating blood might increase their risk of contracting the HIV virus. In other large cities in the same state, blood donations dropped 15 to 25%. Effective media relations in this community held the drop in blood donations to only

---

[4] Of course, organizations with strong authoritarian cultures become even more rigid and authoritarian in times of conflict, turbulence, and crisis. However, powerful external forces sometimes can cause shakeups in dominant coalitions—a reordering of the power relationships among those who run the organization. Under these circumstances, communicators can help transform organizational character and the communication function.

3%. The communication department at the blood bank posted an overall Excellence Score in the top 10% of participating organizations.

Upheavals and a change in leadership combined to bring about character shifts in another organization. The top communicator at a chemical manufacturing company described to us the slow process of getting the dominant coalition to develop a more sophisticated understanding of communication and a less rigid, less conservative mind set. "It starts with a chairman and a president who recognize the criticality of communication in the broadest sense," he said. Excellence means "understanding the importance of old-fashion, one-way communication being done right, as well as the two-way part of it being done right." What event helped trigger this rethinking of communication? The tragedy in Bhopal, India, sent shudders through the entire chemical industry. Like the oil industry, chemical companies needed sophisticated communication systems to deal with a rapidly changing environment, a good set of eyes and ears to find out what's going on, and the expertise to advise senior managers about what to do next.

Consider the organizational impact of changes in the health care sector. A state hospital association posted an overall Excellence Score in the top 5% of participating organizations. The top communicator participates in board meetings of the association and serves on the senior management team. She regards communication as the art and science of being proactive. "You really need to be able to watch the outside world," she told us, "and be able to anticipate what it is going to do."

Proactive public relations today is a far cry from the communication function 13 years ago, when the CEO joined the association. In those days, the communication function was limited to writing newsletters. The rapid growth of competition in the health care industries changed all that. "Our whole mission changed," the CEO said. "I realized the importance of communication with the public. I insisted on hiring new people with strong skills, both in writing and speaking and in management."

Two upheavals brought about changes in communication and corporate culture in a Midwestern utility. A gas and electric company posted an overall Excellence Score in the top 10% of participating organizations. The senior vice president that supervises communication and public relations reports directly to the president and is a member of the company's dominant coalition.

Communication was not always excellent at this company. Before the late 1970s, the company was run by managers who came up through the ranks from engineering. The dominant coalition maintained a narrow focus on technological and engineering issues. Then the engineers tried to build a nuclear power plant and learned about the importance of public relations the hard way. A senior vice president described the nuclear power plant ordeal as a "rude" and expensive awakening for the organization. The dominant coalition realized that it needed a sophisticated communication department to make sure the company was "attending to perceptions of the people," making sure that those perceptions were "aligned with reality." Communication now plays an important role in "not letting large differences occur" between the versions of reality held by the dominant coalition and those of key publics.

At the time of our interview, the senior vice president was helping to manage the merger of his company with another utility. During the transition, he told us, the dominant coalition sought to change the character of the merged organization from an "old-line bureaucracy managed in an autocratic way to an organization that is nimble and flexible and is positioned to . . . be successful in a competitive environment and is managed in a participative way."

Note the sequential impact of the two major upheavals at this utility. First, the crisis over construction of a nuclear power plant in the 1970s forced the old dominant coalition to rethink communication and senior management's narrow approach to business issues. The second upheaval, a merger two decades later, found a more powerful communication department prepared to play a leadership role in transforming organizational character from authoritarian to participative values. Communication in the merged company likely will become even more excellent as participative cultural values become stronger than the traditional authoritarian values. The communication department would not have played a leadership role in transforming organizational character if it had been internally or perceptually challenged. Only powerful communication departments can hope to transform organizational character in times of crisis and upheaval.

Even excellent communication departments are not guaranteed safe passage in times of upheaval. A final case provides a cautionary example to close our discussion of transformations of communication and organizational character. In 1990–1991, a state lottery posted an overall Excellence Score in the top 1% of participating organizations. In 1994, when the team revisited this organization, much of a once-excellent communication function was gone. The top communicator had been transferred to a middle-management position in marketing. The new top communicator meets with the CEO frequently—to take orders. The communication department has been restructured as a technical support unit. Production work, which the department used to farm out to an agency, has been brought back inside. These changes in the communication function are due to the appointment of a new CEO since the 1990–1991 survey. "There is a new CEO who has a different concept of the public relations role in an organization," the former top communicator told us.

WHAT COMES FIRST, EXPERTISE FOR EXCELLENCE OR THE DEMAND FOR IT?

As indicated by the case studies, crises and upheavals contribute to changes in organizational character that create opportunities for—and threats to—communication excellence. Does the crisis or upheaval create opportunities for communication departments to use their advanced expertise, or do crises or upheavals cause dominant coalitions to go out and hire new communicators with the expertise to build excellent communication departments? Put another way, do powerful forces create opportunities for perceptually challenged departments to demonstrate their potential, or do dominant coalitions confront the limitations of their internally challenged communication departments in times of crisis and move to replace key communicators? Apparently, both of these scenarios apply.

At the chemical company, a perceptually challenged department made slow progress with its dominant coalition until an astute vice president realized that communicators could do more. "[Excellence] started with fact we had some good people," the vice president told us. "If I hadn't had a couple of talented communication managers, I couldn't have done anything."

At the state hospital association, the move toward excellence began with the CEO hiring a new top communicator to cope with an increasingly complex health care environment. With the association's changing mission, the CEO insisted on hiring new people with the expertise to enact two-way practices and play the communication manager role. An internally challenged department was upgraded through a change in communication personnel.

CHANGING ORGANIZATIONAL CHARACTER WITHOUT UPHEAVAL

The character of organizations changes slowly. Major crises and upheavals—a new CEO, a merger, corporate restructuring, public outrage and backlash, new competition, activist publics—can accelerate change for a brief period. Changes in the power alignments of dominant coalitions create opportunities for the simultaneous rethinking of communication and organizational character.

What can communicators do to instill participative values in an organization's character when there's no crisis or upheaval? One recommended tactic is to work for symmetrical internal communication. Table

10.5 in chapter 10 provides a list of seven qualities of symmetrical internal communication. These qualities include comfort in talking to supervisors about work performance or when things go wrong. Symmetrical internal communication means two-way communication that encourages differences of opinion and management's responsiveness to problems of employees.

The total quality management (TQM) programs in many of the organizations studied provide an overt rationale for trying to instill symmetrical values in superior–subordinate communication. Arguably, successful TQM programs need symmetrical internal communication. In this way, TQM becomes the stealth vehicle for bringing two-way symmetrical communication inside organizations. The communication department can play an active role in this change, working in alliance with human resources. Communication workshops and formal channels for bottom up communication are ways that symmetrical internal communication can be enhanced. As internal communication becomes more symmetrical, an organization's character evolves toward a more participative culture.

SUMMARY

The character of organizations changes slowly. For organizations to change toward participative values, often a crisis or an upheaval is needed. These upheavals—a new CEO, a merger, corporate restructuring, new competition, activist publics, declining profits, an epidemic or disaster—represent both an opportunity and a threat for communicators. On the one hand, these powerful forces can accelerate positive changes in organizations by restructuring power relationships in dominant coalitions. There's no guarantee, however, that these changes will lead to communication excellence or participative values; sometimes, new leadership in the dominant coalition may decide to disassemble an excellent communication department and replace it with a mediocre one.

To take advantage of powerful forces that change organizations, communication departments must have the expertise for excellence. Dominant coalitions must understand communication excellence and demand the same from their departments. Weak communication departments are not in a position to help manage changes in organizational character.

Short of an upheaval, communicators can enhance participative cultural values by working to build symmetrical internal communication. This can be done, in part, by conducting workshops and developing formal channels of bottom-up communication. Human resources departments may be powerful allies in this effort.

REFERENCES

Peters, T. J., & Waterman, R. H., Jr. (1982). *In search of excellence*. New York: Harper and Row.

Pfeffer, J. (1978). *Organizational design*. Arlington Heights, IL: AHM Publishing.

Robbins, S. P. (1990). *Organization theory: Structure, design, and applications* (3rd ed.). Englewood Cliffs, NJ: Prentice-Hall.

Part IV

Putting Excellence to Work

In this final part of the book, the research team examines how communicators put excellence to work managing communication programs. In Parts I through III, a detailed picture was sketched of what excellence *is*. In the chapters that follow, we consider what excellent organizations *do* to manage programs that build and maintain beneficial relationships with key publics. The top communicator questionnaire listed and collected basic information on 17 publics and asked for detailed information on each organization's 3 top publics. With over 300 organizations in the study, the goal was to identify broad patterns in programs that apply across national boundaries and types of organizations. How do excellent organizations run communication programs for specific publics? How do they differ from less-than-excellent organizations? The information discussed in Part IV was not used to construct the Excellence Factor; rather, these data put to test the broad model of communication excellence in specific communication programs.

Chapter 14 examines the origins of communication programs designed for particular publics. Both traditional and strategic approaches to launching communication programs are examined. Because excellent communication departments act as eyes and ears for their organizations—because they serve as early warning systems of emerging turbulence and conflict—the role of scanning was examined in the planning of and decision making for communication programs.

In chapter 15, traditional and advanced practices in the execution of communication programs are examined. Top communicators were asked to describe each of their top three communication programs in terms of traditional, one-way models, as well as in terms of advanced, two-way models.

The purpose was to determine if advanced departmental expertise and support from senior management translated into two-way practices in running communication programs.

In chapter 16, a key question of the Excellence Study is examined: What is communication excellence worth to an organization? The analysis begins with individual programs and examines how communicators evaluate the effectiveness of those programs. Then the analysis shifts to a broad view of excellence and effectiveness. The research shows that communicators and senior managers in excellent organizations answer the question of value in a number of ways. These findings provide the framework for all communicators to develop measures of worth for excellent communication programs.

14

Origins of Communication Programs

To study the implementation of communication programs for specific publics, top communicators were asked to indicate how much time and money (of the overall department budget) they spent with each of 17 publics we listed for them. Then they were asked to indicate the three publics that absorbed the highest percentage of their department's budget. For these top publics, detailed questions were asked about origins, practices, and program evaluation.

To analyze these data, the top seven publics were identified that had programs dedicated to them among the largest number of organizations. Fig. 14.1 displays the percentage of organizations with communication programs that involve these publics.

Nearly every organization studied (93%) managed communication programs that involved the mass media. About two thirds of organizations had employee communication programs. Slightly more than half ran community relations programs. Over a third managed consumer or customer relations programs. The remaining communication programs—member relations, governmental relations, and investor relations—were operated by one-fifth of the organizations studied.

THE ROOTS OF EXCELLENT PROGRAMS

From where do excellent communication programs come? Is the genesis of a communication program linked to excellence? Do excellent organizations launch new communication programs in ways that distinguish them from less-than-excellent organizations?

The research team had suspicions, of course. Public relations scholar Glen Broom once speculated that communication programs often become routinized, carried on year after year like "perpetual motion machines . . . with the original causes and motivations lost in history" (1986, p. 7). Broom must have had less-than-excellent organizations in mind when he described communication programs trapped or frozen in routine. In designing the questionnaire for top communicators, items were included that tapped historical and traditional approaches to initiating new communication programs. The team used its understanding of roles research and previous studies of the four models of communication practices to come up with a theory.

The team speculated that less-than-excellent organizations established communication programs at some point in their histories. Perhaps management launched an employee communication program after a strike or the threat of one. Maybe the CEO decided the organization needed a media relations program after an investigative reporter raked him or her over the coals. Senior managers might have once decided to initiate a community relations program when local activists delayed the approval by a planning commission of a plant expansion. All of these are good reasons to start a communication program to build better relationships with key constituents.

In less-than-excellent organizations, communication departments would be set up to run these programs. Hired largely for their technical skills to get the organization's side of the story told, communicators in such departments would use one-way models to disseminate information to their targeted publics. Serving largely in a support role to the dominant coalition, such communicators would not be in the loop when senior managers made strategic decisions about communication programs. The top communicator,

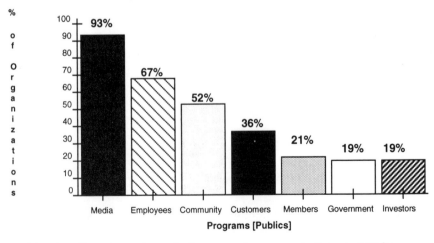

FIG. 14.1.   Percentage of organizations managing communication programs for each of seven major publics.

TABLE 14.1
Traditional and Strategic Origins of Communication Programs

Top communicators were asked how communication programs were initiated for each public identified. They were asked to use the items listed here to indicate how that decision was made for each public. (Items are listed in order of importance.*)

Traditional Origins
- For this program, public relations produces publications, news releases, videotapes, and the like, but did not participate in the decision to begin the program.
- Senior management made the decision with little input from the public relations head and instructed the public relations department to implement the program.
- We continue the program because we have had it for many years.
- Although the public relations head is not a part of senior management, senior management asked for input from public relations before making the decision to begin the program.

Strategic Origins
- We started the program after strategic planning showed the public could hurt or help the organization.
- The public relations head was a part of senior management and participated fully in the decision to conduct the program.

*Factor analysis was used to determine which items in the set provide better measures of the underlying concept. Items are arranged here based on the strength of their relationship with the two concepts measured. See Exhibit 1.1 for a detailed explanation of this clustering technique.

we speculated, would be brought in after decisions had been made to implement the program. Over time, these programs would have less and less to do with actual problems or threats facing organizations. They would continue from year to year through routine decision making, based on what was done last year. Such programs would become functionary, simply window dressing for organizations with pockets deep enough to sustain a largely symbolic activity.[1] That thinking led to the creation of the items in the traditional origins section of Table 14.1.

Do excellent organizations differ from less-than-excellent organizations in the ways that top communicators describe the traditional or historical origins of communication programs? Fig. 14.2 provides the answer. We compared the organizations with overall Excellence Scores in the top 10% of organizations studied to organizations in the bottom 10%. We looked at the origins of programs for the media, employees, the community, customers, members, the government, and investors.[2]

---

[1]For a detailed discussion of functional and functionary public relations, see Bell and Bell (1976).

[2]Because of the small number of communication programs for customers, members, the government, and investors, the top 10% and bottom 10% of organizations included too few such programs to make comparisons meaningful. To correct for this, the overall Excellence Score was lowered for the top organizations and the qualifying score was raised for the bottom organizations. This provided roughly 30 organizations in both the top and bottom categories.

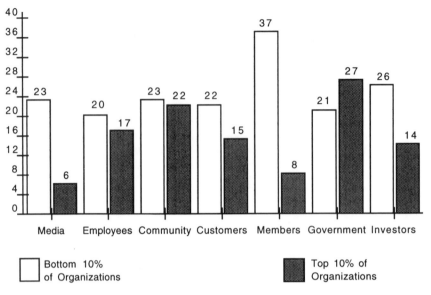

FIG. 14.2. Traditional or historicist origins of communication programs.

Fig. 14.2 displays the average scores on the scale measuring traditional or historicist origins of communication programs. A score of 100 on the scale is average. All scores for both the most-excellent and least-excellent organizations are well below average, meaning that neither group believed that their communication programs were particularly driven by tradition or history.[3] Note, however, that least-excellent organizations posted higher averages for six of the seven publics. Only in governmental relations did the most-excellent organizations describe their programs as more traditional or historically driven than did the least-excellent organizations. In subsequent analysis, governmental relations programs generally tended to be exceptions to rules of communication excellence. (This issue is considered in the section on *exception of government relations,* later in this chapter.)

When all organizations in the study were examined, extremely weak links were found between the historical origins of communication programs and overall excellence of organizations.[4] Coupled with the generally low scores given to traditional origins of programs, the team concluded that the historical origins of programs have little to do with overall communication excellence.

---

[3]In general, top communicators in all organizations studied indicated that traditional origins did not describe their communication programs very well.

[4]Only member relations programs showed a strong link between historical origins and overall excellence. Overall Excellence Scores were lower for those organizations, indicating strong traditional origins for their member relations programs.

Strategic Origins

We thought excellent organizations would design communication programs strategically, to cope with emerging or present problems in relationships with publics. Top communicators managing excellent departments would be involved integrally in decisions to initiate new communication programs. Top communicators earn a place at the decision-making table because they control a scarce resource: intelligence about the awareness, knowledge, attitudes, and behaviors of strategic publics.

As explained in Exhibit 14.1, this intelligence is gained through information-gathering practices called *environmental scanning*. Through environmental scanning, communicators would identify emerging or existing publics that could either help or hurt their organizations. Because they possess needed intelligence about these publics, top communicators would be involved intimately in planning strategic responses to these publics. Measures

---

EXHIBIT 14.1
About Environmental Scanning

Environmental scanning means collecting information about the world outside the organization in order to construct a good enough map of that world for strategic decision making. Like all maps, those that organizations construct for decision making include essentials while leaving out unimportant details. These maps need updating, but only as often as changing conditions require. Environmental scanning is an important part of issues management.

Different departments in organizations pay attention to parts of the organization's environment. Marketing pays attention to customers and what's going on with them. Human resources pays attention to what's going on with employees. Often, however, organizational policies, procedures, and actions affect many individuals, groups, and organizations outside the organization. Often, nobody inside the organization is tracking those outside the organization who are affected—"It's not my department!"

Organizations create publics by virtue of the things organizations do. In excellent organizations, those in public relations and communication management constantly scan the organization's environment, looking for those affected by organizational behaviors. Who is affected by the organization's actions? Are those affected aware of this? What do they know? How do they feel? How might they behave? To answer these questions, excellent communicators use a wide range of information-gathering techniques, ranging from formal scientific surveys to informal swapping of information from key informants, such as reporters. Communicators scan media content, including articles in alternative media, using formal and informal analytic tools.

Acting strategically, an organization devotes resources to communication programs to build relationships with a public that can help or hurt the organization. The strategic decision to establish such programs is based on information gleaned from environmental scanning.

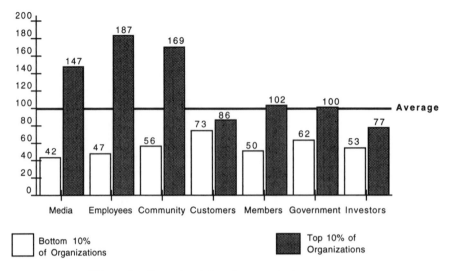

FIG. 14. 3.   Strategic origins of communication programs.

of such origins of communication programs are displayed in the strategic origins section of Table 14.1.

How do the communication programs for most-excellent and least-excellent organizations compare with regard to strategic origins of these programs? Fig. 14.3 displays average scores given each public for the strategic origins of those communication programs by most-excellent and least-excellent organizations. Each program can have both traditional and strategic roots. In every instance, top communicators in most-excellent organizations described the origins of their programs as more strategic than did communicators in least-excellent organizations. The differences are most dramatic for communication programs involving the media, employees, and the community. For the most-excellent organizations, the strategic origins of these programs are substantially above average. For least-excellent organizations, strategic origins of these programs are about half of the average. Only communication programs with customers show small differences between most-excellent and least-excellent organizations.

When all organizations were examined, the linkages between overall excellence and the strategic origins of communication programs were strong.[5] We conclude from these findings that excellent organizations are much

---

[5]The linkage was weaker for customer relations, however. In examining all organizations, correlation coefficients were computed between strategic origin scores for each public and overall Excellence Scores. The coefficients, in descending order, were: employee relations ($r = .44$), investor relations ($r = .44$), media relations ($r = .37$), community relations ($r = .37$), government relations ($r = .35$), member relations ($r = .31$), and customer relations ($r = .25$). These coefficients were then squared to provide an estimate of explained variance that overall Excellence Scores provide for the strategic origins of each program. Explained

more likely than less-than-excellent organizations to initiate communication programs strategically, with the full involvement of the top communicator.

THE ROLE OF SCANNING IN STRATEGIC ORIGINS OF PROGRAMS

As indicated in Exhibit 14.1, a strong role for environmental scanning was expected in organizations with excellent communication programs. The logic was straightforward: To build communication programs in response to publics that can either help or hurt organizations, and to involve top communicators in those strategic decisions, communicators had to bring to the table something that senior management needed. The top communicator's ticket was the intelligence gleaned from environmental scanning; so top communicators were asked about a series of activities that could be used to plan and implement communication programs. They were asked the extent to which

---

TABLE 14.2
Formal and Informal Scanning of Publics

Top communicators were asked how communication programs were planned and carried out for each public over the last three years. The items listed here measure how information was gathered to detect potential problems between publics and the organization. (Items are listed in order of importance.*)

Formal Scanning
- Formal research studies are used to track public reactions to the organization.
- The program subscribes to or uses the services of public opinion research agencies.
- Surveys are conducted of key publics.
- Demographic data are used to help make decisions concerning publics.
- Communication or public relations audits are conducted to find out about publics.

Informal Scanning
- Complaints are reviewed to find out how publics feel about the organization.
- Program managers talk with field personnel to find out about key publics.
- After the organizations conducts special events, people are called back to get their reaction.
- Depth interviews are conducted with members of the organization's publics.
- Phone calls are made to members of target publics to keep in touch.

---

*Factor analysis was used to determine which items in the set provide better measures of the underlying concept. Items are arranged here based on the strength of their relationship with the two concepts measured. See Exhibit 1.1 for a detailed explanation of this clustering technique.

---

variance exceeded 10% for all relationships, except customer relations, with overall Excellence Scores accounting for 6% of the variance in the strategic origins of these programs. In the behavioral sciences, a variable that account for 10% or more of the variance in another variable has moderate to strong predictive power (see Cohen, 1988). Although the explained variance is smaller for customer relations, the relationship is positive. This weaker relationship may be an artifact of measurement and of no practical significance.

each activity characterized each of their three top communication programs. Among those activities were measures of both formal and informal environmental scanning activities. These activities are shown in Table 14.2. An open-ended scale was used for each activity; a score of 100 was average. Five activities were used to measure formal environmental scanning, and five additional activities were used to measure informal scanning.

Formal Scanning Activities

Formal scanning activities included sophisticated (and expensive!) techniques for keeping track of what was going on with each public. These included services of public opinion research agencies and communication or public relations audits. Decision makers used demographic data as well as surveys of key publics and public reactions to organizations.

We compared the most-excellent organizations to the least-excellent organizations regarding their use of formal scanning techniques. For every program, most-excellent organizations posted higher scores regarding formal or scientific scanning. Regarding community relations, the most-excellent organizations posted an average score of 119, which is above average. The least-excellent organizations posted an average of one, meaning that formal scanning was virtually nonexistent among these organizations for this public.

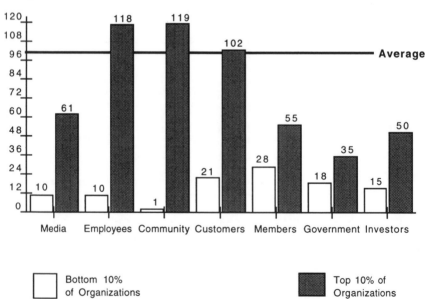

FIG. 14.4.   Formal or scientific scanning among most-excellent and least-excellent organizations.

In general, the findings in Fig. 14.4 are dramatic. When all the organizations in the study were examined, the same pattern prevailed. For six of the seven publics, the level of overall communication excellence was a strong predictor that organizations would use formal scanning techniques. Only governmental relations showed a weaker linkage than the others. (This issue is considered in the section on *the exception of government relations* later in the chapter.) Even in this case, however, higher levels of overall communication excellence tended to indicate somewhat higher levels of formal scanning.[6]

Informal Scanning Activities

Informal scanning activities are quicker and cheaper than are formal scanning activities. Although they may not provide the level of quantification that senior management needs for many strategic decisions, informal techniques often provide the first detection of emergent problems. Informal techniques provide communicators with sensitive antennae they need to get their first tingle of turbulence or problems on the horizon. Paying attention to complaints from publics, talking with field personnel, checking on reactions to special events, conducting depth interviews, and calling members of publics just to stay in touch give communicators early access to critical shifts among publics. When senior management screws up, communicators are likely to hear about it first through informal scanning techniques. We thought that excellent organizations would use informal scanning to detect problems or conflict. These organizations would then follow up with more formal techniques to explore further and finally describe problems or conflicts with key publics.

How do most-excellent organizations compare to least-excellent organizations in using informal scanning techniques? Comparisons are shown in Fig. 14.5. The least-excellent organizations use informal techniques much more frequently than formal techniques. However, so do the most-excellent organizations. For each public, the most-excellent organizations use these informal techniques more than do least-excellent organizations. Regarding government and investor relations, however, the differences are small.

---

[6]As with strategic origin scores, correlation coefficients were computed between overall Excellence Scores and the level of formal scanning methods used with each public. These coefficients, in descending order, were: customer relations ($r = .62$), investor relations ($r = .60$), community relations ($r = .58$), employee relations ($r = .54$), media relations ($r = .42$), member relations ($r = .33$), and government relations ($r = .19$). These correlation coefficients were then squared to provide an estimate of the variance in formal scanning techniques that could be predicted from overall Excellence Scores. All estimates were above 10%, except governmental relations, with overall Excellence Scores accounting for 4% of the variance in formal scanning scores.

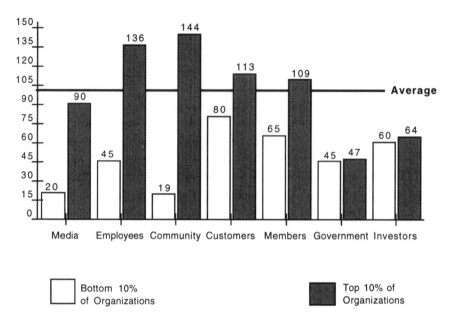

FIG. 14.5.   Informal scanning among most-excellent and least-excellent organizations

When all organizations in the study were examined, the same linkage between overall excellence and informal scanning techniques prevailed for six of the seven publics. Only in communication programs for governmental relations did we detect a weak link between overall excellence and informal scanning.[7]

THE EXCEPTION OF GOVERNMENTAL RELATIONS

Governmental relations programs seem to operate independent of the principles of excellence detailed in Parts I though III of this book. Among the most-excellent organizations, governmental relations programs seem more historically rooted than those in the least-excellent organizations. The link between overall excellence and formal and informal scanning techniques is weak for governmental relations programs. Why?

---

[7]Correlation coefficients were computed between overall Excellence Scores and informal scanning scores for each public. The coefficients, in descending order, were: community relations ($r = .57$), employee relations ($r = .45$), investor relations ($r = .42$), media relations ($r = .41$), customer relations ($r = .40$), member relations ($r = .34$), and government relations ($r = .17$). The coefficients were then squared. All resulting estimates of explained variance in informal scanning techniques exceeded 10%, except governmental relations, with overall Excellence Scores accounting of about 3% of the variance in informal scanning scores.

Fortunately, the Excellence team includes Fred C. Repper, retired vice president of public relations for Gulf States Utilities. He worked for several years in governmental relations for the company in Washington, D.C. Repper and other members of the team identified several reasons why governmental relations would tend to be an exception to the general principles of excellence:

- Governmental relations and especially lobbying tend to be run by lawyers and CEOs in many organizations, rather than by communication departments. For this reason, governmental relations programs tend to run independent of both the strengths and weaknesses in communication and public relations departments.
- Lobbyists tend to draw heavily on their personal contacts in legislative and regulatory bodies, rather than on formal training in communication and public relations. Because a major component of overall excellence is communication expertise, quasi-autonomous governmental relations programs may march to a different drum than do other communication programs.

As Repper said, excellent communication programs support each other through an integrated approach to communication. Media relations programs, for example, may successfully place editorial commentary on the Op-Ed page of a newspaper. That commentary, in turn, can support efforts of lobbyists in communicating with legislators or regulators. Normatively speaking, governmental relations programs should be linked to overall excellence, just like communication programs for the other six publics studied. Practically speaking, however, governmental relations programs tend to run independent of the overall excellence—or lack of excellence—in the organizations studied.

As is reported in chapter 16, governmental relations programs continue to be exceptions to the general principles of excellence. The reasons outlined previously provide good explanations for the anomaly of governmental relations programs and overall excellence.

SUMMARY

This chapter reports the first test of our model of communication excellence, graphically depicted in Fig. 1.1. Does overall excellence in an organization translate into communication programs that are implemented according to principles of excellence? Our answer is a resounding *Yes!* When we looked at the origins of communication programs for seven key publics, we found that excellent organizations tend to launch new communication programs strategically. Such programs focus on publics that senior managers have decided can either help or hurt their organizations. Top communicators are very much a part of such decision making. Scanning, we conclude, provides senior managers in excellent organizations with the ticket they need to make an impact at the decision-making table. They provide important intelligence about what's going on with key publics. This intelligence is extracted from information gathered through both formal and informal techniques that detect, explore, and finally describe emerging problems and conflicts with publics.

REFERENCES

Bell, S. H., & Bell, E. C. (1976). Public relations: Functional or functionary? *Public relations review, 2*(2), 47-57.

Broom, G. M. (1986, August). *Public relations roles and systems theory: Functional and historicist causal models.* Paper presented at the meeting of the Public Relations Interest Group, International Communication Association Annual Convention, Chicago.

Cohen, J. (1988). *Statistical power analysis for the behavioral sciences* (2nd ed.). Hillsdale, NJ: Lawrence Erlbaum Associates.

15

Using Traditional and Advanced Practices

Excellent communication departments know how to implement communication programs based on two-way practices. They know how to act as conduits for information from publics into their organizations, informing decision making at the highest levels. Senior managers in organizations with excellent communication understand that communication should flow two ways between dominant coalitions and key publics. The Excellence Factor includes measures of advanced, two-way practices. At the core, knowledge of advanced, two-way practices provides a foundation for communication excellence. In the middle sphere, favorable attitudes toward such practices among senior managers set up a demand–delivery loop for excellence.

What's missing from this picture, however, is behavior of organizations as they implement communication programs with specific publics. Do excellent organizations actually use two-way practices? Do these excellent organizations use two-way practices more than do less-than-excellent organizations? The answer to both questions is *Yes!* But this tells only part of the story. Case studies indicated that excellent organizations have strong craft expertise as well. Interviews showed that traditional one-way practices are strong in excellent communication departments. Regarding communication programs with specific publics, what does the survey of top communicators show? In planning and implementing communication programs, how are traditional, one-way practices and advanced, two-way practices brought together? Do excellent organizations differ from less-than-excellent organizations in uses of one-way and two-way practices?

TRADITIONAL, ONE-WAY PRACTICES

Traditional, one-way practices predominate in communication programs whose work is mostly done to support other departments and activities in organizations. For example, a hotel chain posted an overall Excellence Score in the bottom 20% of organizations studied—communicators there provided support services to the marketing department. An insurance company scored in the bottom six percent. "The communication department and its employees weigh very much toward the technical aspects of communication," the vice president who supervises communication told us.

Often, CEOs call the shots—for better or worse. A state lottery organization, which posted an overall Excellence Score in the top 1% in 1991, disassembled its cutting-edge communication program when a new CEO took over in 1993. "Some feel the [top communicator] should play a policy, decision-making role," the former top communicator told us. "Others feel that the director, as well as the department as a whole, should strictly disseminate information, acting as a service."

How do excellent and less-than-excellent organizations use traditional, one-way practices to plan and implement communication programs with specific publics? To find out, top communicators were asked to describe in their questionnaires the different ways they conducted their top three communication programs. They were asked to respond to a series of items, indicating how well each item described each program. They used a scale on which a score of 100 was average, a score of 50 was half of the average, a score of 200 twice the average, and so forth.

Table 15.1 shows the items used to measure press agentry practices and public information practices for each program. Press agentry practices equate communication with publicity, as communicators try to get favorable publicity in the media and keep unfavorable coverage out. Public information practices, on the other hand, treat communicators as journalists in residence, disseminators of information from their organizations to publics, not as advocates or mediators. Such journalists-in-residence are too busy pounding out copy to do research; they measure success by the mass of news clips they placed. Unlike press agents, these journalists-in-residence place a premium on disseminating accurate information. Like press agents, they don't volunteer information that generates negative publicity.

Both press agentry and public information practices reflect traditional orientations in communication and public relations. Communicators view themselves—and are viewed by others—as disseminators of information, primarily through public media. They play communication support roles, brought in after decisions are made by senior management to get the word out, to get the organization's story told. Implicitly, information flows one

TABLE 15.1
Traditional, One-Way Approaches to Program Execution

For each public, top communicators were asked to describe the different ways that public relations programs were conducted. The items listed here describe traditional practices.

Press Agentry Practices
- The purpose of this program was, quite simply, to get publicity for the organization.
- In this program, we mostly attempted to get favorable publicity into the media and keep unfavorable publicity out.
- For this program, public relations and publicity meant essentially the same thing.
- We determined how successful this program was from the number of people who attended an event or used our products or services.

Public Information Practices
- For this program, public relations was more of a neutral disseminator of information than an advocate for the organization or a mediator between management and publics.
- In this program, we disseminated accurate information but did not volunteer unfavorable information.
- For this program, nearly everyone was so busy writing news stories or producing publications that there was no time to do research.
- Keeping a clipping file was about the only way we had to determine the success of the program.

way, from senior management outward to employees, the media, the community, and other publics. The craft of such communicators is wrapped up in journalistic skills to tell the organization's story. In these models, communicators play no role as conduits of information from publics to senior management. Logically enough, such communicators play no significant role in management decision making.

Press Agentry Practices

Fig. 15.1 shows the level of press agentry practices for most-excellent and least-excellent organizations. Overall, press agentry practices do not tend to describe the programs of most-excellent or least-excellent organizations. All scores are below average for most types of organizations. With the exception of employee communication, the least-excellent organizations tended to use press agentry practices to a greater degree than did most-excellent organizations. When all organizations in the study were analyzed, overall excellence had little to do with the infrequent use of press agentry practices in running communication programs.[1]

---

[1]Overall Excellence Scores were correlated with press agentry scores for each of the seven publics. Correlation coefficients were positive and negative for different publics. This means that overall Excellence Scores were associated with higher levels of press agentry practices for some

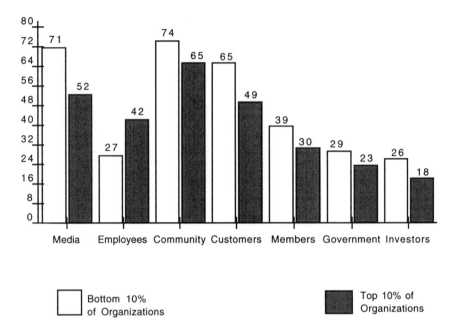

FIG. 15.1. Use of press agentry practices in communication programs among most-excellent and least-excellent organizations.

Public Information Practices

Most-excellent organizations were compared to the least-excellent organizations regarding public information practices. The results are displayed in Fig. 15.2. As with press agentry practices, most organizations tended to downplay public information practices. With the exception of employee communication, the least-excellent organizations showed greater use of public information practices than did most-excellent organizations. However, these differences were small. When all organizations were examined, overall excellence had little to do with the infrequent use of public information practices in running communication programs.[2]

practices for some publics (employees, community, and investors) and lower levels of public information practices for other publics (media, customers, the government, and members). The coefficients, in descending order, were: investor relations (r = .10), employee relations (r = .07), community relations (r = .03), community relations (r = -.01), member relations (r = -.10), media relations (r = -.12), and government relations (r = .-14). When these coefficients were squared, overall Excellence Scores predicted about 2% (or less) of the variance in public information practices for the seven publics.

[2]Overall Excellence Scores were correlated with public information scores for each of the seven publics. Correlation coefficients were positive and negative for different publics. This means that overall Excellence Scores were associated with higher levels of public information

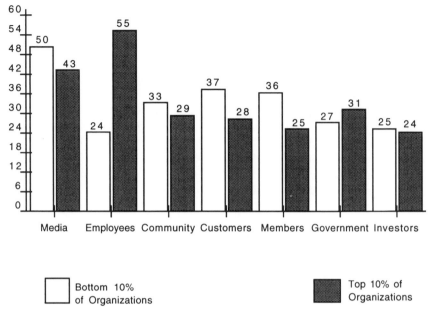

FIG. 15.2.   Use of public information practices in communication programs among most-excellent and least-excellent organizations.

ADVANCED, TWO-WAY PRACTICES

Two-way practices showed up over and over again in our case studies. For example, an organization that promotes healthy heart behavior and supports research on the heart posted an overall Excellence Score in the top 1% of organizations. The top communicator there told us that "talking to people" was a major organizational priority. She spends much of her time working with field staff and volunteers with the local chapters, "doing what they do." This provides an important pipeline of information back to senior managers, helping them stay "in touch with the real world."

The new top communicator at a state arts organizations, which seeks to fund an array of community arts projects, described an important role for communicators as mediators. "One of my roles is to bridge the gap between

practices for some publics (employees and investors) and lower levels of public information practices for other publics (media, community, customers, the government, and members). The coefficients, in descending order, were: investor relations ($r = .09$), employee relations ($r = .02$), customer relations ($r = -.02$), government relations ($r = -.03$), community relations ($r = -.08$), member relations ($r = -.08$), and media relations ($r = -.11$). When these coefficients were squared, overall Excellence Scores predicted about 1% (or less) of the variance in public information practices for the seven publics.

different mentalities," he told us, People in the arts organization and the state and federal legislators that fund arts projects "definitely have a different perspective of things." He also serves as a conduit for information from publics back to senior managers of the arts organization. "We can *listen* to people about what *we* can do better," he said tersely, summarizing the symmetrical philosophy of communication.

Another communicator works for a medical equipment manufacturer that markets its products globally. The company posted an overall Excellence Score in the top 5%. "I have to keep on top of what's brewing internally and externally," he explained, "so I can plan on how to address the issues with publics around the world."

Because publics often involve large numbers of people, social science research tools are needed to gather intelligence about what publics know, how they feel, and how they may behave. "We do a lot of surveying, a lot of focus group analysis, to stay on top of where the customer is," the top communicator with a private utility told us. His company had posted an overall Excellence Score in the top 1%. "Last year, I probably went to 50 focus groups in 20 cities across our system."

Top communicators were asked whether two-way practices described their approaches to publics. Table 15.2 shows the items used to measure two-way asymmetrical and two-way symmetrical practices. Two-way asymmetrical practices emphasize the use of research to change publics. The goal is to use persuasion to make publics behave in ways consistent with organizational objectives. Attitude surveys are used to plan communication programs that describe organizations in ways most acceptable to publics. Public attitudes are studied in order to change them more effectively. Program effectiveness is measured by how much public attitudes change. Symmetrical practices, on the other hand, place greater emphasis on mutual understanding and negotiation of conflict. Whereas asymmetrical practices emphasize changing publics to behave as management wants them to behave, symmetrical practices emphasize changing senior management as much as publics.

Both two-way practices are research-based activities that involve communicators in the two-way flow of information back and forth between senior management and publics. As a mixed-motive game, such advanced practice sometimes seeks to persuade publics, to help organizations press for an advantageous position. However, such short-term competitive tactics must be subordinate to strategies that seek long-term, mutually beneficial relationships between organizations and publics. Asymmetrical practices emphasize short-term gain. Symmetrical practices emphasize a philosophy of mutually beneficial relationships over the long term. These seemingly

TABLE 15.2
Advanced, Two-Way Approaches to Program Execution

For each public, top communicators were asked to describe the different ways that public relations programs were conducted. The items listed here describe advanced practices.

Two-Way Asymmetrical Practices
- Before starting this program, we looked at attitude surveys to make sure we described the organization and its policies in ways our publics would most likely accept.
- Before beginning this program, we did research to determine public attitudes toward the organization and how they might be changed.
- In this program, our broad goal was to persuade publics to behave as the organization wants them to behave.
- After completing this program, we did research to determine how effective it had been in changing people's attitudes.

Two-Way Symmetrical Practices
- Before starting this program, we did surveys or informal research to find out how much management and our publics understood each other.
- The purpose of this program was to change the attitudes and behavior of management as much as it was to change the attitudes and behaviors of publics.
- The purpose of this program was to develop mutual understanding between the management of the organization and publics the organization affects.
- For this program, the organization believed public relations should provide mediation for the organization, to help management and publics negotiate conflict.

opposite organizational worldviews can go hand in hand in the implementation of communication programs.

Two-Way Asymmetrical Practices

Two-way asymmetrical practices were compared for most-excellent and least-excellent organizations. Fig. 15.3 shows the results. Most-excellent organizations described higher levels of two-way asymmetrical practices than did least-excellent organizations for each of the top seven publics. The top publics most frequently addressed by organizations in the Excellence Study include media relations, employee relations, community relations, customer relations, member relations, government relations, and investor relations. Differences between most-excellent and least-excellent organizations are quite dramatic. For example, most-excellent organizations indicated near-average levels of asymmetrical practices in their community relations programs. Least-excellent organizations, on the other hand, reported asymmetrical practices at near-zero levels. When all organizations were analyzed, overall communication excellence is strongly linked to the use of asymmetrical practices with each of the seven publics. This linkage with overall excellence and asymmetrical practices is strongest for customer

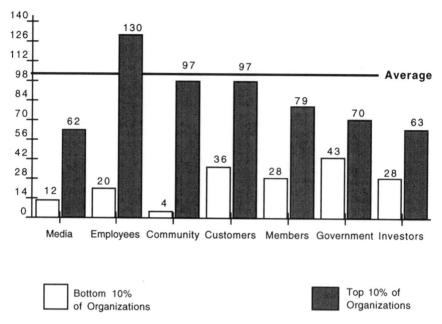

FIG. 15.3.   Use of two-way asymmetrical practices in communication programs among most-excellent and least-excellent organizations.

and employee relations. The greater the overall excellence of organizations, the more likely they are to use two-way asymmetrical practices in running communication programs.[3]

Two-Way Symmetrical Practices

Two-way symmetrical practices in running communication programs were compared for most-excellent and least-excellent organizations. The results for the seven publics are shown in Fig. 15.4. For all publics, most-excellent organizations reported higher levels of two-way symmetrical practices than

---

[3]Overall Excellence Scores were correlated with two-way asymmetrical scores for each of the seven publics. Correlation coefficients were positive and substantial for each public, ranging from a low of .23 (government communication) to .55 (customer and investor communication). This means that overall Excellence Scores were associated with higher levels of two-way asymmetrical practices for all publics . The coefficients, in descending order, were: customer relations ($r = .55$), investor relations ($r = .55$), employee relations ($r = .51$), member relations ($r = .43$), media relations ($r = .40$), community relations ($r = .39$), and government relations ($r = .23$). When these coefficients were squared, overall Excellence Scores predicted from about 5% of the variance (government communication) to 30% of the variance (customer and investor communication) in asymmetrical practices for the seven publics.

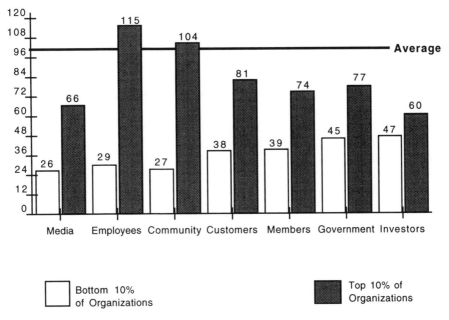

FIG. 15.4.   Use of two-way symmetrical practices in communication programs among most-excellent and least-excellent organizations.

did least-excellent organizations. The differences again are dramatic, especially for employee and community communication. When all organizations were examined, strong linkages were found between overall excellence and symmetrical practices for each of seven publics. The greater the overall excellence of organizations, the more likely they were to use two-way symmetrical practices in running their communication programs.[4]

SUMMARY

Organizations use both traditional, one-way practices and advanced, two-way practices to run communication programs with specific publics. Traditional practices include the press agentry model, in which communication is

---

[4]Overall Excellence Scores were correlated with two-way symmetrical scores for each of the seven publics. Correlation coefficients were positive and substantial for each public, ranging from a low of .29 (government communication) to .48 (employee communication). This means that overall Excellence Scores were associated with higher levels of two-way symmetrical practices for all publics. The coefficients, in descending order, were: employee relations ($r = .48$), investor relations ($r = .47$), member relations ($r = .47$), customer relations ($r = .45$), media relations ($r = .35$), community relations ($r = .34$), and government relations

equated with publicity, and the public information model, in which communication is equated with dissemination of information, rather than advocacy or mediation. These traditional practices do not describe the running of communication programs for most organizations. Further, such traditional practices, whether frequent or infrequent, have little to do with the overall excellence of organizations. Advanced practices include the two-way asymmetrical model, which emphasizes persuasion, and the two-way symmetrical model, which emphasizes mutual understanding and dispute resolution. Both types of advanced, two-way practices describe the way excellent organizations run their communication programs. Differences between excellent and less-than-excellent organizations are dramatic.

Excellent organizations and less-than-excellent organizations are distinguished by communication departments that act as eyes and ears for senior management—as conduits for information from publics to senior decision makers. Although both excellent and less-than-excellent communication departments sometimes follow traditional practices in running communication programs, one-way practices have nothing to do with overall excellence.

Regarding symmetry and asymmetry, the findings here support the conclusion reached in chapter 7 that symmetrical and asymmetrical practices are most usefully viewed as parts of a mixed-motive game. The seemingly contradictory philosophies of symmetrical and asymmetrical worldviews are fused. Asymmetrical practices describe short-term tactics for seeking organizational advantages, driven by extensive use of research. In the mixed-motive games they play, both organizations and publics seek to negotiate outcomes that are most advantageous.

However, seeking advantage is constrained by the need to maintain the integrity of the game. Symmetry provides the underlying strategic philosophy for advanced practices. Short-term tactical advantage (asymmetrical practices) cannot jeopardize long-term strategy (symmetrical practices). Immediate gains must be subordinated to long-term, mutually beneficial relationships with publics, which is the goal of two-way symmetrical practices.

$(r = .29)$. When these coefficients were squared, overall Excellence Scores predicted from about 8% of the variance (government communication) to 23% of the variance (employee communication) in symmetrical practices for the seven publics.

16

Communication Excellence
Makes a Difference

Ask top communicators and CEOs to place a monetary value on excellent communication and they may tell you what they told us. "I could talk about the subject in general," said the top communicator at a hotel chain. "But to say how much money is saved is quite hypothetical, I think."

The senior vice president of public affairs for a large chemical manufacturer said he "could not begin to dollarize the function. In some respects, it's an infinite value. In some respects, it's like throwing money in a hole."

"Some things can't be easily quantified," the top communicator at a hospital association said about communication's worth to her organization. "Some things are impossible to quantify."

Despite these oft-repeated protests, communicators and CEOs do place a value on excellent communication. With effort, many communicators and senior managers we talked to placed a monetary value on excellence.

In this chapter, we consider the big question that motivated the Excellence Study: Is excellent communication worth anything to organizations? Put another way, does communication excellence help organizations achieve their objectives? The short answer to both questions is *yes!* If that answer satisfies, close the book. If not, the rest of this chapter provides more detailed answers. In fact, the Excellence Study provides four basic answers to the question of communication's worth.

First, excellent organizations set measurable goals and objectives for their communication programs, then evaluate how successfully those programs achieved their goals. Through these evaluations, senior management can assess the value of communication programs in terms of outcomes achieved.

Second, excellent organizations can identify several mushy consequences of excellent communication. These include such things as employee productivity, stock prices, a hospitable climate, an organization's national standing, and even corporate "image." By mushy, we mean that the outcome may be quantifiable (e.g., stock prices), but excellent communication can claim only partial (and nonquantifiable) credit for that outcome. By mushy, we also mean that some outcomes have no direct monetary value, but they are highly valued nevertheless. The national standing of an engineering research agency, for example, is enhanced through excellent communication programs. How much is national standing worth? The CEO cannot tell you its monetary value, but he can tell you that the national standing of his agency is extremely important to him and other senior managers.

Third, excellent organizations avoid mistakes that create conflict with key publics. Excellent organizations avoid regulation or litigation that could cost them money. How much money do you save by avoiding restrictive regulation and litigation? In some cases, the savings are highly speculative. In other cases, reasonably precise estimates of savings can be made.

Fourth, job satisfaction of employees is higher among employees working for organizations with excellent internal communication. Symmetrical internal communication helps support a positive climate among workers in organizations. This increases both individual and organizational job satisfaction. This satisfaction, in turn, affects other relationships important to organizations (e.g., customer relations).

SETTING IMPACT OBJECTIVES FOR COMMUNICATION PROGRAMS

Let's first consider the worth of communication in its most narrow and precise sense. One of the qualities that separates excellent from less-than-excellent organizations is the impact evaluation of communication programs. Top communicators were asked how they planned and carried out communication programs over the last three years. Among the items were measures of goal setting and program evaluation.

How do communicators go about measuring the effect of communication programs? Before a program can be evaluated, communicators first must specify exactly what the program seeks to achieve. Program objectives can be divided into two general categories: process objectives and impact objectives. Process objectives are communication activities that some communicators establish as program outcomes. They confuse process (communicating) with the outcomes (impact on relationships) those processes are suppose to effect. Was the program successful in actually implementing the communication activities in the plan? If so, the program was a "success." For example, a communicator might decide that the objective of the employee relations program is to publish four employee magazines over the next 12 months. The process of communicating becomes an end in itself.

Impact objectives seek to maintain or change what publics and senior management know, how they feel, and even how they behave. Action and communication strategies are simply means to achieve an end, the process of building relationships. Consider the same employee relations program in the previous paragraph. Program impact objectives for the program might include increased awareness and knowledge of the organization's mission among employees. Other impact objectives might include increased individual and organizational job satisfaction. Planning symmetrically, communicators might seek to increase senior management's understanding of employee frustrations and concerns through a series of small group discussions. Publishing the employee magazine is an integral part of the implementation strategy, but such publishing activities are not an outcome.

Measures of both process and impact objectives were included in the list of outcomes for programs. Table 16.1 shows the four items that cluster to form an index of impact objectives for communication programs. These descriptions of program objectives emphasize outcomes such as knowledge, attitude, and behavior of target publics.

Top communicators evaluated their communication programs in terms of these measures of impact objectives. Fig. 16.1 shows how the most-excellent organizations compare to the least-excellent organizations in terms of impact objectives for communication programs of seven publics. With the exception of the virtual tie for governmental relations programs, most-excellent organizations were substantially more likely to set impact objectives for each of their programs, when compared to least-excellent organizations. When all organizations were analyzed, communication excellence was strongly linked to setting impact objectives for six of seven publics. The linkage between excellence and the use of impact objectives was weaker for

TABLE 16.1
Setting Objectives that Measure Program Impact

Top communicators were asked to indicate the extent to which each of the items listed here described the objectives they chose for each of their communication programs. Items are listed in order of importance.*

- Getting the target public to believe the message.
- Changing or maintaining the behavior of the target public.
- Creating or maintaining a favorable attitude by the target public.
- Getting the public to remember the message.

---

*Factor analysis was used to determine which of these measures did the better job of measuring the underlying construct (impact objectives), based on how top communicators answered the questions. See Exhibit 1.1 for a more detailed explanation of factor analysis.

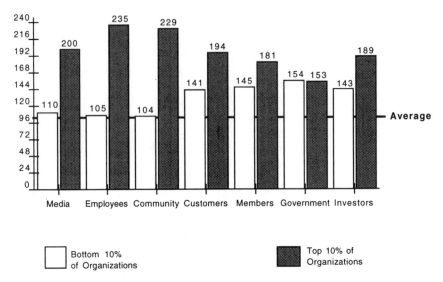

FIG. 16.1.   Choice of impact objectives in planning communication programs among most-excellent and least-excellent organizations.

governmental relations programs.[1] As noted in chapter 15, governmental relations programs tend to be managed by lawyers and CEOs somewhat independent of communication and public relations departments.

EVALUATING COMMUNICATION PROGRAMS

After objectives are set for communication programs, how do communicators evaluate the success of those programs in achieving those objectives? We asked top communicators to tell us how they measured the effect of each communication program. Based on previous studies, we knew that communicators use three basic strategies for measuring the effects of programs.[2]

---

[1]Overall Excellence Scores were correlated with impact objectives scores for each of the seven publics. All relationships were positive, meaning that the use of impact program objectives generally increases with increases in overall excellence. The coefficients, in descending order, were: employee relations ($r = .48$), investor relations ($r = .48$), member relations ($r = .46$), customer relations ($r = .39$), media relations ($r = .36$), community relations ($r = .35$), and governmental relations ($r = .16$). These coefficients then were squared to provide estimates of the explained variance that overall excellence predicts in terms of setting impact objectives for programs. Explained variances exceeded 10% for six of seven programs, ranging from a low of 12% for community relations programs to a high of 23% for employee and investor relations programs. Governmental relations programs, on the other hand, showed a weaker correlation. Overall Excellence Scores accounted for about 3% of the variance in the use of impact objectives for governmental relations programs.

[2]For a more detailed discussion of program evaluation, see chapter 7 of *Excellence in Public Relations and Communication Management* (Grunig, 1992); see also Dozier (1990).

Media Placement Evaluation

Table 16.2 displays items used to measure the degree to which communicators use media placement or clip file evaluation to measure the effects of programs. For each public, top communicators were asked the extent to which the dissemination of messages, the tracking of placements, and media contacts are used to measure accomplishments of communication programs. Such program evaluation focuses on program processes (communication activities) rather than true outcomes (maintenance or change in relationships). Nevertheless, such media placement evaluation is useful when combined with other techniques. By analyzing program effectiveness in terms of necessary processes, communicators can make sense of other evaluations of impact. For example, an impact evaluation might show that a program failed to achieve desired objectives, in terms of what publics know, how they feel, or the way they behave. Why? Evaluation of media placements can help answer this question. Perhaps the program was ineffective at placing messages necessary to communicate with target publics; placement evaluation helps communicators find out.

We compared uses of media placement evaluation among most-excellent and least-excellent organizations. The results are shown in Fig. 16.2. For six of seven publics, most-excellent organizations used media placement evaluation to a greater degree than did least-excellent organizations. Logically, media placement evaluation was emphasized most in the evaluation of media relations programs. Whereas most-excellent organizations reported above-average use of media placement evaluation for this public, least-excellent organizations used this evaluation strategy less than half of the average. Even most-excellent organizations placed little emphasis on media placement evaluation for member relations and governmental relations programs. Regarding governmental relations, least-excellent organizations reported greater emphasis on media placement evaluation than did most-excellent organizations. When all organizations were examined, overall excellence was strongly linked to the use of media placement evaluation for

TABLE 16.2
Media Placement (Clip File) Evaluation of Communication Programs

Top communicators were asked to indicate how well each item listed here characterized the way each communication program was planned and carried out.

- This program monitors the dissemination of messages (news stories, editorials, letters to editors) through a formal, ongoing content analysis of items in a clip file.
- This program tracks news releases and other placements through a comprehensive clip file.
- In this program the number of inches placed, reach, and other vital statistics are logged for clip files.
- Personnel in this program monitor dissemination of messages through close personal contacts among mass-media professionals.

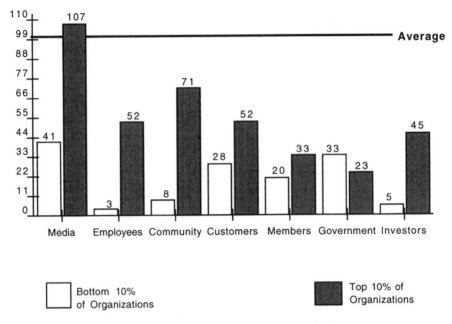

FIG. 16.2.   Media placement (clip file) evaluation of communication programs among most-excellent and least-excellent organizations.

media, employee, community, customer, and investor relations programs. For member relations programs, the linkage was much weaker. For governmental relations programs, the relationship was negative. The greater the overall excellence of an organization, the lower the use of media placement evaluation for governmental relations programs.[3] This result was unexpected. Governmental relations programs generally show weak relationships between overall excellence and various measures of program process and outcomes. However, this finding implies that the greater an organization's overall excellence is, the less its use of placement evaluation with its governmental relations program is. The relationship is not strong, however.

---

[3]Overall Excellence Scores were correlated with media placement evaluation scores for each of the seven publics. Positive coefficients emerged for overall excellence with media placement evaluation for media, employee, community, customer, member, and investor relations programs. A negative coefficient emerged for overall excellence and governmental relations programs. The coefficients, in descending order, were: investor relations ($r = .53$), community relations ($r = .44$), media relations ($r = .40$), customer relations ($r = .34$), employee relations ($r = .32$), member relations ($r = .16$), and governmental relations ($r = -.28$). These coefficients were squared to provide an estimate of variance in media placement evaluation provided by overall Excellence Scores. For five of seven publics, the variance explained was greater than 10%, ranging from a low of 10% for employee programs to 28% for investor programs. Explained variance was 8% for governmental relations programs and 3% for member relations programs.

TABLE 16.3

Seat-of-the-Pants Evaluation of Communication Programs

Top communicators were asked to indicate how well each item listed here characterized the way each communication program was planned and carried out.

- Personnel working on this program can tell how effective it is by their own gut-level reactions and those of other communicators.
- Personnel in this program check its impact by keeping their eyes and ears open to the reactions of their personal and public contacts.
- Personnel working on this program prepare communications by drawing on their own professional experience.
- The impact of this communication program is checked by having personnel attend meetings and hearings of groups representative of key publics.

Seat-of-the-Pants Evaluation

Table 16.3 displays items used to measure a second approach to program evaluation. Seat-of-the-pants evaluation is the quick-and-dirty approach to measuring the effects of programs, emphasizing professional judgment and highly subjective measures of impact. Effectiveness is judged by gut-level reactions, by paying attention to the reactions of others, by drawing on professional experience, and by attending meetings with key publics. Such program evaluation provides a "soft" answer to the question of whether the program worked.

Most-excellent and least-excellent organizations were compared in their use of seat-of-the-pants program evaluation. The results are shown in Fig. 16.3. Top communicators in most-excellent organizations reported above-average use of this evaluation approach for each of the seven publics. Further, most-excellent organizations reported greater usage of this approach than did least-excellent organizations for each of the seven publics. When all organizations were examined, overall excellence was strongly linked to use of seat-of-the-pants evaluation for six of seven publics. Weak linkage was found between overall excellence and seat-of-the-pants evaluation for governmental relations programs.[4]

The "soft" answers provided by seat-of-the-pants evaluation are better than none at all. Sometimes, the scale and scope of a program does not

---

[4]Overall Excellence Scores were correlated with seat-of-the-pants evaluation scores for each of the seven publics. Positive coefficients emerged for all seven publics. The coefficients, in descending order, were: community relations ($r = .51$), customer relations ($r = .46$), investor relations ($r = .45$), media relations ($r = .32$), employee relations ($r = .31$), member relations ($r = .31$), and governmental relations ($r = .15$). These coefficients were squared to provide an estimate of variance in seat-of-the-pants evaluation provided by overall Excellence Scores. For six of seven publics, the variance explained was greater than 10%, ranging from a low of 10% for media and member relations programs to 26% for community relations programs. Explained variance for governmental relations programs was 2%.

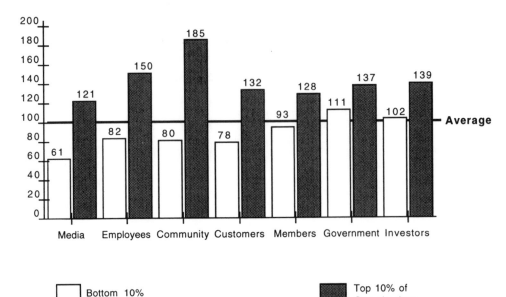

FIG. 16.3.   Seat-of-the-pants evaluation of communication programs among most-excellent and least-excellent organizations.

justify a more sophisticated approach to evaluation. Often, the realities of time and budget limit communicators to evaluating the effects of programs by the seat of their pants. Despite its many limitations, seat-of-the-pants evaluation is a useful tool.

Scientific Evaluation

Table 16.4 displays the four items used to measure scientific evaluation of communication programs. Scientific evaluation provides hard measures of program impact, using numeric indicators near and dear to the hearts of

TABLE 16.4
Scientific Evaluation of Communication Programs

Top communicators were asked to indicate how well each item listed here characterized the way each communication program was planned and carried out.

- The effectiveness of the program is checked through interviews with a scientifically selected cross-section of significant publics.
- Communications are prepared in this program after first reviewing published surveys (Gallup, Harris) on attitudes of publics involved.
- The communication effectiveness of this program is measured by comparing before-program and after-program measures of publics.
- This communication program was designed as though it were a field experiment of communication effects.

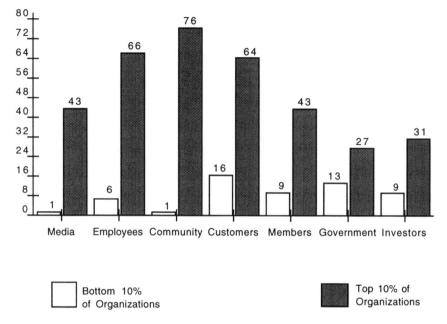

FIG. 16.4.   Scientific evaluation of communication programs among most-excellent and least-excellent organizations.

MBAs or engineers who often are members of dominant coalitions. Scientific cross-sectional surveys and before–after measures are used to determine the effects of communication programs. Ideally, communication programs are run like field experiments to precisely determine program impact.

Again, most-excellent and least-excellent organizations were compared to see if they differed in their use of scientific evaluation of programs. The results are shown in Fig. 16.4. Overall, all of the organizations we studied used scientific evaluation less than seat-of-the-pants and media placement evaluation for most publics. The reasons seem obvious. Scientific evaluation requires greater resources, demands more detailed planning, and takes more time to conduct than other forms of evaluation. Nevertheless, most-excellent organizations used this most sophisticated form of evaluation more than did least-excellent organizations. When all organizations were examined, overall excellence was strongly linked to scientific evaluation of all seven programs.[5]

---

[5]Overall Excellence Scores were correlated with scientific evaluation scores for each of the seven publics. Positive coefficients emerged for all seven publics. The coefficients, in descending order, were: community relations ($r = .60$), customer relations ($r = .59$), member relations ($r = .54$), employee relations ($r = .51$), investor relations ($r = .50$), media relations ($r = .44$), and governmental relations ($r = .30$). These coefficients were squared to provide an estimate of variance in scientific evaluation provided by overall Excellence Scores. The

TABLE 16.5
Change-of-Relationship Effects for Communication Programs

Top communicators were asked to indicate the extent to which observable evidence shows
that the communication program had the following effects.

- There was greater cooperation between the organization and the relevant public
  (symmetrical effect).
- Understanding improved between the organization and the relevant public (symmetrical effect).
- The quality of communication with the relevant public improved (symmetrical effect).
- The relevant public changed its behavior in the way my organization wanted
  (asymmetrical effect).
- A stable, long-term relationship was developed with the relevant public (symmetrical
  effect).
- Attitudes of publics changed in support of our position (asymmetrical effect).

EFFECTIVE PROGRAMS THAT CHANGE
RELATIONSHIPS AND REDUCE CONFLICT

Top communicators were asked about the effects of their communication
programs that could be supported with observable evidence. Sixteen program
effects were listed, ranging from positive media coverage to the development of long-term relationships. Top communicators used an open-ended
scale on which an effect of 100 from a program was average, 200 was twice
the average, 50 was half of the average, and so forth.

Using the same procedure we used to isolate the Excellence Factor, we
found two main effects of communication programs.[6] One kind of effect
involves changes in relationships with the target public. The items that
measure change-in-relationship effects are shown in Table 16.5. Change-in-relationship effects are potential outcomes of communication programs.
Two of the six effects in Table 16.5 are asymmetrical—they involve changing
the target public's attitude or behavior in the organization's favor. Four of
the six effects, however, are symmetrical—with these effects, the organization and the target public improve their understanding of each other, becoming more cooperative and developing a stable, long-term relationship.

A second major type of program effect is the avoidance of conflict
between organizations and key publics. These effects are shown in Table
16.6. Communication programs can be effective at helping organizations
avoid litigation, strikes, boycotts, and unfavorable legislation. Effective
communication programs can help reduce disputes and complaints from

---

variance explained ranged from a low of 9% for governmental relations programs to 36% for
community relations programs.

[6]We used factor analysis to help us cluster program effects, based on the items that top
communicators indicated belonged together in groups.

TABLE 16.6
Conflict Avoidance Effects for Communication Programs

Top communicators were asked to indicate the extent to which observable evidence shows that the communication program had the following effects.

- Litigation was avoided.
- A strike or boycott was avoided.
- Activist groups were willing to negotiate with the organization.
- There was less interference by government in the management of the organization.
- Complaints from publics were reduced.
- Desirable legislation was passed or undesirable legislation was defeated.
- There were fewer disagreements or disputes with the relevant public.

publics, as well as make activist groups willing to negotiate with the organization.

Excellence Improves Relationships

We compared program effects that changed relationships among the most-excellent and least-excellent organizations. Fig. 16.5 shows the results. The most-excellent organizations showed above-average effectiveness in changing relationships with each of the seven publics. With the exception of governmental communication programs, the most-excellent organizations outperformed the least-excellent organizations. When we examined all the organizations, overall excellence was strongly linked to changing relationships with six of seven publics. There was no linkage between overall excellence and change in relationships through governmental relations programs.[7] Governmental relations programs seem to operate somewhat independent of communication departments, often managed by noncommunicators such as lawyers. The linkage between overall excellence and most program activities often do not seem to apply to governmental relations programs.

Excellent organizations are in a superior position to provide evidence of positive changes in relationships with key publics. Excellent organizations define program objectives with impact, then set about collecting the evidence needed to see if these outcomes have been achieved. It is small wonder these organizations come out on top when asked to show program effects, supported by observable evidence.

---

[7]Overall Excellence Scores were correlated with change-in-relationship scores for each of the seven publics. All correlations were positive, meaning that higher levels of excellence were associated with higher levels of change-in-relationship effects. These coefficients were squared to provide estimates of explained variance. For six of the seven publics, overall Excellence Scores accounted for over 10% of the variance in relationship changes, ranging from 11% (media relations programs) to 26% (customer relations programs). For governmental relations programs, overall excellence accounted for about 1% of the variance in relationship change scores.

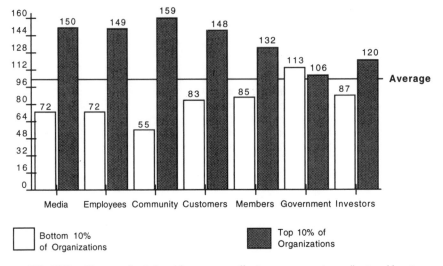

FIG. 16.5. Change-of-relationship program effects among most-excellent and least-excellent organizations.

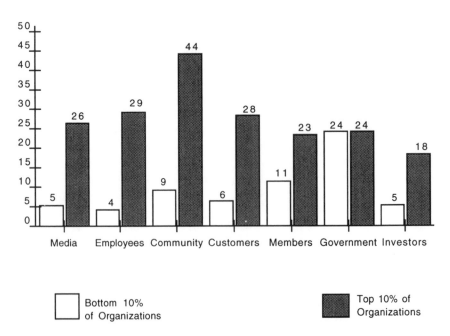

FIG. 16.6. Conflict avoidance program effects among most-excellent and least-excellent organizations.

Excellence Helps Organizations Avoid Conflicts

The effects of some programs help organizations avoid conflicts with publics. Conflict avoidance outcomes were compared for programs of most-excellent and least-excellent organizations. The results are shown in Fig. 16.6. Generally speaking, effects that avoid conflict are rare for communication programs, whether they are run by excellent or less-than-excellent organizations. With the exception of the tie for governmental relations programs, most-excellent organizations could point to higher levels of conflict avoidance than could least-excellent organizations. When all organizations were examined, overall excellence was strongly linked to program effects that avoided conflicts with five of seven publics. Overall excellence was weakly linked to conflict avoidance in communication programs for members. Overall excellence was not linked to conflict avoidance for governmental relations programs.[8]

Excellence Helps Build Symmetrical Internal Communication

Another important effect of overall communication excellence is its linkage to the structure of internal communication in organizations. The internal structure of communication, in turn, affects external relationships. Overall excellence is linked to employee assessments of symmetrical internal communication. Items on the employee questionnaire measuring symmetrical internal communication are shown in Table 10.5 in chapter 10. As the overall excellence in organizations increases, so too does the symmetrical nature of internal communication. The research team theorizes that overall excellence and symmetrical internal communication reinforce and build on each other. On the other hand, asymmetrical internal communication decreases as overall excellence increases.

As shown in chapter 10, individual and organizational job satisfaction are linked to participative organizational cultures. Overall excellence is also linked to the individual job satisfaction that comes from the intrinsic rewards of an employee's work. Employees seem to derive more intrinsic

---

[8]Overall Excellence Scores were correlated with conflict avoidance scores for each of the seven publics. Six of the seven correlations were positive, meaning that higher levels of excellence were associated with higher levels of conflict avoidance effects. The correlation between overall excellence and conflict avoidance through governmental relations programs was very weak and negative. All coefficients were squared to provide estimates of explained variance. For five of the seven publics, overall Excellence Scores accounted for over 10% of the variance in relationship changes, ranging from 10% (media relations programs) to 25% (customer relations programs). For member relations programs, overall excellence accounted for 5% of the variance in conflict avoidance scores. For governmental relations programs, overall excellence accounted for less than 1% of the variance in conflict avoidance scores.

satisfaction from their work in organizations with high levels of overall excellence. As expected, the link is even stronger between overall excellence and organizational job satisfaction that comes from external rewards for work, such as pay and recognition. Organizational job satisfaction is linked to the perceived fairness and nondiscrimination in promotions and other rewards. Employees in excellent organizations report higher organizational job satisfaction than do those in less-than-excellent organizations.

ASSIGNING DOLLARS TO COMMUNICATION EFFECTS

So far, we have shown that excellent organizations take care of the basics required to demonstrate the worth of communication programs. They start by setting program objectives that seek to affect relationships with key publics. They follow up by measuring the outcomes of these communication programs, using a variety of evaluation techniques. These techniques, in turn, provide the observable evidence that communication programs improve relationships and help organizations reduce conflict with key publics.[9] The final, most difficult step is to convert these observed effects of communication programs into dollars. We worked with 24 organizations in the case study phase to do just that.

Economists use a technical term to describe the process of assigning dollar values to program effects. They call this technique *compensating variation*. (Exhibit 16.1 provides a brief explanation of compensating variation.) When we approached CEOs and top communicators about placing a dollar value on effective communication, they were generally reluctant. The comments at the beginning of this chapter were typical. Some said our request was impossible; others just said it was extremely difficult. Still others said it was undesirable.

The Value of Communication Effects in Hard Dollars

As we continued with our interviews, however, several CEOs and top communicators were willing and able to make such an assessment after all. The chief financial officer for a community blood bank checked donation records during the peak of the AIDS misinformation period. In 1983–1984, community blood banks in other cities in the same state showed 15% to 25% drops in units of blood donated. People were afraid that donating blood

---

[9]Governmental communication programs provided consistent exceptions to strong linkages between overall excellence and use of evaluation. Most-excellent and least-excellent organizations differed little in the objectives they set for governmental communication programs. They also differed little in the evaluation techniques they used for these programs.

EXHIBIT 16.1
How to Convert Communication Effects into Dollars

In chapter 23 of *Excellence in Public Relations and Communication Management*, we outline an eight-step process for conducting cost-benefit analysis, using a technique called *compensating variation* (Grunig, 1992). For purposes here, compensating variation is the additional money an organization would be willing to pay to keep the communication program (a cost) and its observable effects (benefits). Any CEO worth his or her salt would get rid of communication programs that cost more than the benefits they provide. When we asked CEOs to make such an overall assessment of their communication departments, even those with communication programs in the bottom 10% said they get $146 back in benefits for every $100 they invest. Regarding the specific effects of a communication program, a CEO may credit the company's employee communication program with helping implement an effective total quality management (TQM) program. The employee communication program costs $500,000 annually. Would the CEO keep the program if the company had to pay an additional $500,000 to run it and receive the same benefits? At what dollar figure does the CEO say, "Enough, I'll keep the money, discontinue the communication program, and live with less-effective TQM"? That break-even point in the CEO's assessment of cost and benefit is the compensating variation for the communication program. In order to conduct such an analysis, the effects of the communication program must be known. Regarding successful TQM in this example, the benefits from TQM are due to efforts of several departments. To figure compensating variation, the CEO must have some notion of communication's contribution to the success of the TQM program, then place a dollar value on that contribution. If communication programs do not seek effects (as when objectives only involve the generation of messages), if they fail to provide observable evidence of effects (as when programs are not evaluated), then decision makers are hard pressed to figure what such programs are worth.

---

might expose them to the AIDS virus. The blood bank in the Excellence Study experienced only a 3.2% drop, or about 2,700 units. The difference was attributable to the blood bank's extremely effective media relations program. Using 1994 prices, the chief financial officer calculated that the lower-than-projected drop in donations translated into a minimum savings of $986,000. Under the worst-case scenario (a projected 25% drop in donations), the media relations program saved the blood bank $1.8 million.

As noted earlier, governmental relations programs tended to have weak linkages to overall communication excellence in organizations. One oil company, however, successfully deflected undesirable legislation at the state and federal level through its lobbying efforts. Savings to the company were substantial. In 1993, the company's efforts in support of favorable tax legislation resulted in a $20 million savings. The company was also successful in reaching compromises with environmentalists on a federal environmental bill, which would have cost the company an estimated $10 million in its original form.

The research unit in the communication department estimated a second environmental bill would have cost the company between $500 million and $1.5 billion in its original form. A third federal environmental bill would have cost the company $100 million. Compromises were eventually reached regarding these bills. At the state level, the company sought compromises in three bills involving additional regulations on oil refining. These compromises saved the company an estimated $260 million. In each case, the oil company played a mixed-motive game, seeking the best compromise (from the company's perspective) while realizing that the company must build and maintain long-term relationships with environmental organizations that supported the original legislation.

A state arts funding organization used to accept "default" funding for its many projects, according to the new top communicator we interviewed. "If you asked for $350,000," he told us, "you usually got $150,000." To turn this situation around, the top communicator worked with senior management to conduct research and present a better case to state legislators for increased funding. Based on research, the top communicator stressed message points regarding the positive impact of the arts on local economies, the importance of the arts to community culture, and the positive role that community arts projects can play in the social development of at-risk youths. These messages stressed qualities of the arts that are important to legislators.

The results included approval of a full $350,000 grant request, the first of its kind in the organization's history. The legislators, intrigued that art projects might play a role in reducing juvenile delinquency, granted an additional $25,000 to evaluate the potential impact of a $1 million project to target art projects specifically to at-risk youths. By seeking to communicate benefits of arts programs that legislators could appreciate, the arts funding organization created win–win outcomes. Arts projects throughout the state received higher levels of funding through the arts organization. Legislators were able to recognize benefits of arts projects that had not been made clear to them before. Legislators found a politically acceptable basis for supporting the arts in a politically conservative state often hostile to the arts and the artistic community. Finally, young people found forums and outlets for their creative energies that might otherwise have been directed in less socially acceptable directions.

In another case, poor communication within a not-for-profit organization resulted in the loss of $85,000 in donations. An overzealous auxiliary volunteer approached a foundation for a $15,000 contribution to the organization, and the contribution was made. At the same time, the foundation nixed a $100,000 request from the same organization, figuring the $15,000 contribution was enough. Since then, the organization has instituted better internal communication procedures to prevent such mistakes in the future.

Softer Benefits of Communication Excellence

For many CEOs and top communicators we interviewed, the effects of communication could not be converted to a dollar figure. Yet they could point to positive communication effects and assigned great value and importance to these outcomes.

One of the effects of excellent communication is crisis management. The top communicator for a medical equipment manufacturer described two incidents in which effective communication contained crises in overseas markets that could have rippled through its operations in the United States. In one incident, a European subsidiary of the company was involved in a product failure with tragic human consequences and substantial corporate liability. In the other incident, a separate corporate entity that markets the company's products in Asia attempted to bribe a government official there. Communicators and senior managers at corporate headquarters in the United States quickly implemented containment strategies, working in conjunction with local public relations firms in the European and Asian operations. The effort was to prevent these isolated incidents from becoming a three-ring circus in the U.S. media. "When a crisis happens overseas, we try not to let it get in the press in the United States," the top communicator told us. "Because that's like throwing gas on a fire. No matter who is at fault, it doesn't do any good to have half-truths from either side come back and reflect on our company." The top communicator said the containment strategies protected the organization from "huge embarrassment and financial disasters."

The top communicator at a financial services corporation told us that effective communication helps avert crises that can affect investors. "The impact [of crises] on stock prices is immeasurable," she said. "Because we are such a public company, things done or not done affect the stock prices."

Sometimes excellent communication affects how employees approach their work. Communication effects are wrapped up in organizationwide efforts to improve the quality of work. The vice president of a chemical manufacturing company told us that he could not convert communication effects into dollars. However, communication is key to helping to empower employees to root out inefficiencies. "[Employee communication] is saving us money by better enabling people who should be saving us money to go out there and get the job done," he explained. "Ultimately, that loops around and helps us make money. So employee communication is saving us money and making us money. I don't think anyone around here today would argue that point," he told us.

Sometimes communication plays an important role in building long-term relationships with the investor community. We happened to interview the vice president on the day that the chemical company's stock hit an all-time high. "The value of [the company's stock] was $150 million higher in the hands of our shareholders today than when they went to sleep last night," he told us. "Now, do I believe that today—somehow—we got some leverage from the few million dollars we spend on communication each year? Damn right, I do!"

When a new team took over the management of an ailing aerospace corporation, it instituted sweeping liquidation, consolidations, and mergers to eliminate unprofitable operations. However, such massive reengineering of the company needed to be communicated effectively through financial media to the investor community. As a result of both action and communication, stock values rose from $19 to $92 per share. Can communication effects be separated from the effects of the liquidations, consolidations, and mergers? Probably not, the top communicator told us. Could the same effects of stock prices be achieved without an effective investor communication program? Probably not, she repeated.

Sometimes communication affects the seemingly intangible qualities of an organization, such as its reputation or standing among influential people. The CEO of a state hospital association places great value on the association's standing with policymakers. Communication plays a role in the association's standing, the CEO told us, which is now at an all-time high. What's the dollar value of that standing? Neither the CEO nor the top communicator could make such a conversion.

Communication plays an important role in advancing the national standing of an engineering research agency on a university campus. "There is no way you can quantify it," the top communicator said of the agency's standing. Communication helps reduce the lag between the agency's achievements and the impact of those achievements on the agency's national standing. "The CEO is obsessed with improving that ranking," the top communicator said.

The president of a public utility told us that he doesn't regard public relations as a profit center. "But we expect them to provide a positive climate in which the organization can operate," he said.

The CEO and chairman of a major metal manufacturer expressed a similar view with regard to an industry's image. "The image of an industry affects the laws that are written, the ability to raise capital funds, and the recruiting of talented employees," the CEO said. "One way or the other, it does affect the bottom line."

The senior vice president at a gas and electric company was skeptical about any direct link between public relations and the bottom line. "If you value [communication], if you have an intuitive sense that [the benefits] are there," he told us, "then you will devote human and capital resources to it. If you don't, you won't."

Sometimes communication effects benefit the larger society. The ongoing education efforts of an association that promotes heart health uses communication to bring about changes in the behavior of large segments of the U.S. population. One goal of the organization, communicated through a network of local chapters and supported by the national office, is to reduce the intake of dietary fat. From 1976 to 1980, fat comprised 36% of the average American's dietary intake. After a sustained communication program of the association, average dietary intake of fat has dropped two percentage points. The benefits to society of reduced heart disease risk only will be realized over the decades.

A similar social benefit can be seen the efforts of a community blood bank to find bone marrow donors for victims of leukemia and other life-threatening diseases. Although bone marrow transplants are frequently life savers, only 1 person in 20,000 will have bone marrow that adequately matches that of a particular leukemia victim to permit a transplant. Further, the test required to register someone as a bone marrow donor costs $45; most medical insurance policies do not cover bone marrow registration.

In 1989, communicators for the blood bank nurtured a long-term relationship with the family and friends of a young boy suffering from leukemia. The blood bank worked with eager volunteers to mobilize both financial donations and bone marrow volunteers to register potential donors. In 1993, 30 of the 60 bone marrow transplants aided by the blood bank were made possible by the registration drive in behalf of this one little boy. The effect of the communication program in behalf of the young leukemia victim may save as many as 30 lives. What's the monetary value of 30 lives saved through excellent communication? The fact that we can't place a dollar value on this program effect does not diminish its importance.

SUMMARY

We have come full circle now, answering a major question of the Excellence Study that we posed in chapter 1. Does excellent communication affect an organization's bottom line? Of course it does—excellent communication affects the bottom line in a number of direct and indirect ways.

Excellent organizations have the expertise in their communication departments for advanced, two-way practices. These organizations have dominant coalitions that understand advanced, two-way practices and expect them from their communication department. Many such organizations have participative organizational cultures that nurture communication excellence.

These qualities of excellence are manifest in how excellent organizations run communication programs. Excellent organizations set program objectives designed to affect relationships with key publics, then evaluate these programs to measure achievement of these objectives. Because of these practices, top communicators in excellent organizations can provide observable evidence of the effects of communication programs. These effects include improved relationships and the avoidance of conflict with key publics.

In many instances, these effects can be converted directly into monetary benefits or savings for the organization. In other instances, CEOs and top communicators are reluctant to convert the outcomes of programs into dollar equivalents. The blood bank we studied declined to place a monetary value on 30 lives that may be saved through bone marrow transplants made possible through an excellent communication campaign. Sophisticated CEOs and top communicators recognize that some communication effects are critical to the overall effectiveness of the organization. They see communication effects as wrapped up in the effective efforts of several other departments in an organization, or the organization as a whole. Although they can't separate communication effects from those of the other units, they see excellent communication as essential to overall effectiveness. Stock prices, for example, cannot be separated from organizational performance. At the same time, communication plays an important role in investor relations, and these relationships do affect stock prices.

Like many things in life, all qualities of communication excellence are ultimately circular. Communication excellence affects the bottom line because senior management is smart enough to recognize the many linkages, both direct and indirect. Communicators are smart enough to set program objectives that affect relationships and reduce conflict. They are smart enough to collect evidence of observable communication effects through program evaluation. They make it easy for senior management to see linkages between communication excellence and overall organizational effectiveness.

Sophisticated communicators and savvy dominant coalitions push and pull each other to improve communication excellence, a never-ending cyclical process. CEOs in excellent organizations demand it, and excellent communicators wouldn't want it any other way.

REFERENCES

Dozier, D. M. (1990). The innovation of research in public relations practice: Review of a program of studies. In L. A. Grunig & J. E. Grunig, (Eds.), *Public relations research annual* (Vol. 2, pp. 3–28). Hillsdale, NJ: Lawrence Erlbaum Associates.

Grunig, J. E. (Ed.). (1992). *Excellence in public relations and communication management.* Hillsdale, NJ: Lawrence Erlbaum Associates.

Appendix:
How the Excellence Study Was Conducted

In 1985, the International Association of Business Communicators (IABC) Research Foundation invested in the most comprehensive study ever undertaken of the communication profession. The Research Foundation sought answers to two questions of fundamental importance to communication practitioners and to the organizations that spend (frequently) scarce resources to manage communication and public relations:

- What are the characteristics of an excellent communication department?
- How does excellent communication management and public relations make an organization more effective, and how much is that contribution worth economically?

Nearly 10 years from its inception to the final set of books reporting the results, the Excellence Study has attracted international attention. Although the Excellence Study analyzed organizations only in Canada, the United Kingdom, and the United States, follow-up studies have been launched by communication scholars in India, Greece, Taiwan, and Slovenia. Members of the research team have reported findings of the Excellence Study in speeches in some 15 nations, including many IABC chapters in Canada, the United Kingdom, and the United States. Articles about the Excellence Study have appeared in *Communication World*, *pr reporter*, the *Ragan Report*, *The Wall Street Journal*, and the *O'Dwyer Newsletter*. The Excellence Study appears prominently in the two most influential introductory texts in public relations. The study appears throughout in the 7th edition of *Effective Public Relations* (1994), by Scott Cutlip, Allen Center, and Glen

Broom, informing the next generation of professional communicators about findings from the Excellence Study. The second edition of *Managing Public Relations*, scheduled for release soon, also carries the clear imprint of the Excellence Study; the author of this text directs the Excellence research project.

LARGEST INVESTMENT IN COMMUNICATION AND PUBLIC RELATIONS RESEARCH

Why all this interest? First, the magnitude of the Excellence Study dwarfs all previous research conducted on the communication profession. The study's $400,000 budget is the largest investment ever made in the core body of knowledge for professional communication practices. The decade duration of the Excellence Study—an extension of the original 5-year estimate—makes this one of the longest continuing research projects in public relations and communication management. Indeed, the Excellence Study led Cutlip, Center, and Broom to conclude in *Effective Public Relations* that during the late 1980s and early 1990s, "The IABC Research Foundation became the major funding agency for public relations research."

Because scholars conduct the best research when theory drives the study, the Excellence Study again holds a record. The research team's 638-page book, *Excellence in Public Relations and Communication Management* (Grunig, 1992), provides a comprehensive literature review and details a unified theory of excellence in public relations and communication management.

DIVERSE RESEARCH METHODS COMBINED

The Excellence research team collected a staggering array of information. In the 1990–1991 survey of about 300 organizations, CEOs, top communicators, and a sampling of regular employees provided the research team with some 1,700 separate pieces of information about organizational communication, management in their organizations, and organizational cultures. Participating organizations included corporations, not-for-profit organizations, government agencies, and professional trade associations. In the 1994 case studies of about two dozen organizations selected from those originally surveyed, researchers conducted nearly 100 hours of interviews with communicators and members of dominant coalitions, fleshing out survey findings.

However, big budgets and lots of data alone cannot explain why the Excellence Study exerts such an influence on the practice and study of professional communication. In all research, the tools we use to answer questions limit the scope and range of questions asked. In this regard, the Excellence Study used an innovative blending of methods to answer questions that previous research strategies could not .

A BRIEF HISTORY OF PUBLIC RELATIONS AND COMMUNICATION MANAGEMENT RESEARCH

Sophisticated research about public relations and communication management has grown significantly in recent decades. The early "case studies" in public relations, which resembled war stories rather than rigorous scholarship, gave way to the influx of quantitative methods from the social sciences. Communication and public relations scholars turned increasingly to large-sample surveys and, to a lesser degree, to lab experiments. More recently, the resurgence of qualitative research in the social sciences has brought to the discipline such tools as focus groups, participant observation, and true case study research.

At the same time, our theoretical understanding of managed communication in organizations grew. Communication scholars constructed theories to make sense out of communication and public relations practices. Theories provide explanations and predictions about how communication practices are managed in organizations. As the theoretical understanding of communication and public relations grew, researchers realized they could not study communication in isolation. Communication and public relations practitioners are constrained, researchers learned, by what senior management wants from the communication department and how much management supports those communication efforts. Scholars and practitioners discovered they could not measure outcomes of communication programs in isolation of organizational opportunities and constraints. Communicator relationships with key members of senior management either expand or limit opportunities. For example, the organization's CEO may block the top communicator's participation in strategic planning because the CEO doesn't see the linkage between communication and strategic planning. Constraints also may come from the more diffuse influence of organizational culture. For example, communicator efforts to scan the organization's environment, to learn "what's going on out there," might meet with managerial indifference if the organization's culture is "closed" to the outside world.

THE RESEARCHER'S DILEMMA

In the mid-1980s, communication and public relations scholars confronted a dilemma caused by expanding theory and methodological limitations. Increasingly, researchers needed to study organizations, not individual communicators. Scholars needed to understand the context of communication and public relations practices within organizations to make sense of such practices and their effectiveness. Communication and public relations researchers have learned much by conducting mailed surveys of individual communicators in organizations, using membership lists such as *The Worldbook of IABC Communicators* (1994) as a resource to draw samples. However, such samples of individual communicators, no matter how rigorous, cannot provide the multiple perspectives that studies of entire organizations require.

At the same time, scholars needed to study communication practices in a sufficient number of contexts to build a general understanding, and to construct and test a unified theory. Rigorous case studies have enriched our understanding of how communication is practiced in some organizations. In such studies, researchers interview communicators and senior managers at length. Interviews are linked to other data such as annual reports and other collateral materials to provide rich tapestries of communication practices in context. Because of the intensive nature of data collection and analysis, case studies are often conducted on a single organization or a handful of organizations—such studies rarely include over a dozen organizations. For budget reasons, case studies typically are limited to a narrow geographic area. Often, researchers conduct case studies of similar types of organizations (e.g., Fortune 500 corporations) for comparison purposes.

But communicators work in diverse organizational settings and environments. How do findings from a case study of public relations in corporations apply to public affairs in a government agency? Could findings from a case study of American organizations apply to those in Canada or the United Kingdom? No single method, it seemed, could answer the questions the Excellence Study sought to investigate, nor satisfy the larger research agenda in communication management and public relations.

THE EXCELLENCE STUDY DESIGN

The research design of the Excellence Study took advantage of both an extensive sample of organizations throughout Canada, the United Kingdom, and the United States, as well as intensive case studies of several dozen organizations. In 1990–1991, the research team gathered information through a survey of top communicators in each organization. If more than one unit in the organization shared responsibility for communication and public relations, the top communicator from each unit completed a questionnaire. In a different questionnaire, the CEO or another member of the dominant coalition provided senior management's perspective. A sampling of employees, using a third version of the questionnaire, provided perspectives on the organization's communication and organizational culture. Thus, a typical organization in the Excellence Study completed one top communicator questionnaire, one questionnaire by a member of senior management, and about a dozen questionnaires from a sampling of employees. In all, the average organization in the Excellence Study completed over 100 pages of questionnaires!

In 1994, researchers at the University of Maryland and San Diego State University conducted case studies of about two dozen organizations from the original group. Researchers selected some organizations because they exemplified communication excellence in a variety of organizational settings. Other cases were selected because they seemed to have very few characteristics of communication excellence. The research team studied cases in all three nations, although the bulk of case study organizations were located in the United States. The large-sample survey provided researchers a detailed "snapshot" of each participating organization at one point in time. The case studies allowed researchers to explore, in an open-ended fashion, the organizational history of the communication function and the origins of excellence. Further, the passage of time since the original survey allowed the research team to examine changes in communication excellence since the time of the original survey.

This methodological strategy resolved much of the dilemma posed by the research agenda of the Excellence Study. The large sample provided the diversity of organizations to allow researchers and practitioners to extrapolate from organizations in the study to other organizations throughout the three nations studied. The multiple questionnaires completed in each organization allowed researchers to compare communicator perspectives with those of dominant coalitions. The survey of employees provided broad measures of communication within organizations, as well as measures of organizational cultures. The Excellence Study collected information about organizations from multiple perspectives, not just information about individuals.

The case studies took full advantage of research findings from the initial survey. The Excellence research team closely analyzed each organization selected for case study. The team not only knew each organization's overall Excellence Score from the Excellence Factor (see chapter 1), but could also compare top communicator perspectives with those of senior management.

This phase of research built upon the survey findings, treating each organization individually. In addition to a generic set of questions posed in the interview schedule, each investigator explored a smaller set of questions designed specifically for that particular organization. For example, why did the top communicator in one large manufacturing company report high involvement in strategic planning, when the CEO described communication's contribution as negligible? How did a small, not-for-profit organization achieve high levels of communication excellence on a limited budget? For organizations with excellent communication programs, what historical factors contributed to that excellence? Each case of excellence provided new insight. What happens to excellent communication when a new CEO pulls the plug on senior management support for excellence? The case study of communication in a state lottery provided an answer.

THE SAMPLING STRATEGY

To execute the Excellence Study, the research team developed a sampling strategy that maximized both the quality of the research and pragmatics of collecting the data. A two-step, nonprobability sampling strategy was employed. The research team first used a dimensional sampling strategy to ensure that the sample represented (included sufficient cases) organizations along two dimensions:

- Organizations representing Canada, the United Kingdom, and the United States.
- Organizations representing corporations, not-for-profit organizations, government agencies, and professional-trade associations.

The sample of organizations did not include public relations firms or agencies. Because firms represent multiple clients, provide different services for each, and play different roles, determining the relevant dominant coalition (the relevant CEO) and measuring the relevant organizational culture was problematic. However, communicators working for firms should regard the Excellence Study findings as a guide for offering additional services to clients.

SAMPLE DESIGNED JOINTLY WITH IABC RESEARCH FOUNDATION BOARD

In the beginning, the research team proposed a survey of between 200 and 400 organizations. In 1987, the research team collaborated with the IABC Research Foundation board to set projections for a single overall target sample size. Then, the board and the research team developed specific targets for each nation and for each type of organization within each nation.

TABLE A.1
Target Sample for the Excellence Survey, by Nation and Type of
Organization (August 1987)

Type of Organizations	Nation of Organization (headquarters)			Totals
	United States	Canada	United Kingdom	
Corporations	66	17	17	100
Not-for-profits	50	13	12	75
Government agencies	50	12	13	75
Associations	34	8	8	50
Totals	200	50	50	300

Table A.1 provides the 1987 target samples for each nation and each type of organization. The overall target sample size was set at 300. The research team sought 200 organizations in the United States, and 50 organizations each in Canada and the United Kingdom.

The team targeted 100 corporations in the overall sample, split proportionately among the three nations. Corporations included utilities, consumer product firms, high-tech firms, energy, industrial manufacturers, banks and financial services, insurance companies, transportation firms, health corporations, real estate developers, media/publishing firms, entertainment companies, retail businesses, food companies, and pharmaceutical firms. This category also included conglomerates, transnational corporations, and government-owned businesses.

Seventy-five organizations in the projected overall sample represented not-for-profit organizations, including colleges and universities, school systems, nonprofit hospitals, churches, charitable organizations, and public interest groups. Targets for these organizations were split proportionately among the three nations.

Another 75 organizations represented government agencies. This category included federal, regional, state/provincial, local, and political agencies. Target samples for government agencies were assigned proportionally among the three nations.

Fifty organizations represented professional and trade associations in the target sample. These targets were assigned proportionally among the three nations.

Once the IABC Research Foundation board and the research team established the dimensional sampling targets, a purposive sampling strategy was employed within each cell of the table. *Purposive sampling* means selecting sample elements that are theoretically relevant to the study. This

TABLE A.2
Final Sample for the Excellence Survey by
Nation and Type of Organization
(December 1991)

Type of Organizations	Nation of Organization (headquarters)			Totals
	United States	Canada	United Kingdom	
Corporations	108	24	16	148
Not-for-profits	39	9	10	58
Government agencies	46	17	8	71
Associations	33	8	3	44
Totals	226	58	37	321*

*Of the 321 organizations participating in the Excellence Study, overall Excellence Scores were computed for 270 organizations. Some of the data were missing for the other 51 organizations, precluding computation of Excellence Scores. Data were missing from top communicators in 21 organizations, from CEOs in 34 organizations, and from employees in 2 organizations.

nonprobability sampling technique was used in the study to select organizations with special characteristics important to the study. On the one hand, organizations were included (in their appropriate cells of the sampling matrix in Table A.1) that books and publications had identified as "excellent" according to some standard. On the other hand, organizations that had recently experienced communication crises and substantial negative publicity also were included. This strategy increased the likelihood that the organizations within each cell of the table would include those with both excellent and less-than-excellent communication programs.

Table A.2 shows the final sample of organizations that participated in the 1990–1991 Excellence survey. A total of 321 organizations participated in the Excellence Study. This figure is 7% higher than the 300 organization target. Of the 321 organizations, overall Excellence Scores were computed for 270 organizations providing complete top communicator, CEO, and employee data. For statistical analysis, however, organizations with partial data sets were fed into the computer and used whenever appropriate.

Breaking down the final sample by nation, organizational targets for both Canada and the United States were reached and exceeded. However, participation from the United Kingdom fell short of target, with only 38 organizations included in the final sample, 12 fewer than originally projected. Regarding types of organizations, the final sample included 48 more corporations than the 100 originally projected. On the other hand, not-for-profits fell 17 organizations short of the projected 75 organizations in the final sample. The final sample of government agencies fared better, with 71 of 75 projected agencies included in the final sample. The final sample included 44 associations, 6 short of the projected 50 in the original target.

ADVENTURES IN COLLECTING DATA

Any communicator who has ever conducted a readership survey knows that collecting survey data is part art, part science, and part luck! The science of survey research suggests short, short, short questionnaires. The art of survey research suggests that simplicity of design and graphics helps boost questionnaire completion. And lucky was that first survey researcher who taped a quarter to a questionnaire and urged respondents to "have a cup of coffee on me" while completing the questionnaire. The response rate was terrific! (This motivator doesn't work twice and, besides, coffee now costs a lot more than a quarter!)

Compared to a typical readership questionnaire, the Excellence Study's extensive, multi-phase collection strategy made this the survey from hell. Top communicators received a 21-page questionnaire; CEOs received a 7-page questionnaire. A 7-page questionnaire also was completed by up to 20 regular employees (12 was the average) sampled from the larger employee pool.

THE FRACTIONATION SCALE

In the Excellence Study survey, the questionnaires made use of a state-of-the-art measurement tool called *fractionation scales*. Fractionation scales ask those completing questionnaires to report how much of a particular characteristic they (or their organizations) possess. If the individual or organization has an average amount of that characteristic, a score of 100 is written down. If the amount of that characteristic is half of the average, a score of 50 is given to it. If it is twice the average, a score of 200 is assigned.

For example, the questionnaire asked top communicators to "describe the extent to which your public relations department makes a contribution to . . . strategic planning" using a fractionation scale. A score of 0 means the department makes no contribution, a score of 100 means that the department's contribution is about average for a public relations department, and a score of 200 means the department makes twice the contribution of a typical or average public relations department. The person completing the questionnaire can assign as high a score as he or she wishes.

A few top communicators declined to participate once they came head to head with fractionation scales! However, most became rather facile with fractionation scales once they got the hang of them. Overall, fractionation scales have many valuable properties that make them ideal for statistical analysis. As a pragmatic issue, however, fractionation scales complicate data collection.

SEEKING COOPERATION FROM ORGANIZATIONS

Operationally speaking, the Excellence Study survey proved extremely challenging to execute. Although few would quarrel with the value of the information collected, fewer still would volunteer to manage such a survey. Collecting the Excellence Study survey information required the cooperation of each organization's top communicator. In addition to completing a questionnaire, the top communicator often wore another hat as *internal advocate* for the organization's participation, convincing the CEO or another member of the dominant coalition to fill out the CEO questionnaire. Typically, top communicators also helped administer the organizational culture questionnaire to a sample of regular employees.

Executive secretaries and administrative assistants of CEOs also helped boost participation. Often, these "agents" would slip the CEO's questionnaire into the executive's briefcase prior to a flight to another city or country. In one Canadian corporation, the communication staff translated the employee questionnaire into French, so that their organization could participate.

Orchestrating all of these myriad activities from long distance were graduate assistants JoNell Miettinen at San Diego State University and K. Sriramesh at the University of Maryland. In 1992, Ms. Miettinen began doctoral studies in communication at Stanford University and Dr. Sriramesh joined the communication faculty at Purdue University. Their innovative solutions to intractable problems, dogged persistence, and dedicated attention to detail made the survey's success possible.

AN INVITATION TO PARTICIPATE

The strategy for collecting survey information evolved as the study continued. The first step involved soliciting an organization's participation through a mailed inquiry to a communicator in the organization, supported by a brochure extolling the virtues of the Excellence Study and participation in it. If a positive response was received, a research team member worked with the responding communicator by telephone to identify all the communication units in the organization, the names and titles of top communicators, the reporting relationships, and the names and titles of the CEO and other members of the dominant coalition. The researcher and the responding communicator also devised a strategy for conducting a mini-survey of regular employees in the organization.

Despite a stated desire to participate, many organizations balked at it, once the bundle of questionnaires arrived by mail. Of those remaining resolute in their original commitment, some could not orchestrate the CEO's continued support and participation in the end. In all, only 12% of the organizations initially solicited through the mail completed and returned all three sets of questionnaires.

THE SAMPLE AND ITS IMPLICATIONS FOR THE EXCELLENCE STUDY

Experienced researchers select a sample the way a master carpenter selects the right tool for the job. No strategy is perfect for every kind of research task; every strategy is useful in some situations. To appreciate the Excellence Study survey of organizations, it is important to keep in mind the survey's purpose and the questions driving the project. The scope and complexity of the questions investigated in the Excellence Study make this study different from the narrow research questions asked in an employee or customer survey. Consider the following questions:

- How many employees say they would prefer a video employee magazine over the current print publication?
- Do our current customers regard our products as more "reliable" than do our potential customers?

Answers to these questions will not increase our understanding of complex relations that inform us about how things work. Rather, they give numeric answers to very specific questions about how many.

To answer these questions, the researcher might draw a probability sample of employees or customers (current and potential), ask close-ended questions ("Which do you prefer most, a video employee magazine or a printed employee magazine?"), and then estimate how many employees or customers in the population would answer the question in the same way, if all of them were asked. The researcher seeks to make a statistical generalization from the sample to the entire population of employees or customers. Depending on the sample frame, sample size, response rate, and other factors, the researcher can estimate how everybody in the population would answer the question, plus or minus a certain margin of error.

Probability sampling provides communicators with a powerful tool to answer questions about how many. Because such sampling strategies permit statistical inferences from samples to populations, one might be tempted to regard these samples as superior to others. The experienced researcher, however, appreciates the strengths and weaknesses of each sampling strategy and evaluates the goodness of fit between the sampling tool and the job the tool must do.

The sampling strategy of the Excellence Study survey is poorly suited for answering narrow, inferential questions. As noted in chapter 1, CEOs of organizations with communication programs in the lowest 10% of those studied reported an average 146% return on investment in communication. CEOs of organizations in the top 10% reported a 266% return. The nature of the Excellence survey sampling strategy does not permit a statistical inference like this: "Among the most-excellent communication programs in all organizations in Canada, the United Kingdom, and the United States, CEOs place the return on investment in their communication programs at 266%, plus or minus 15 percentage points." Rather, the Excellence Study survey provides a rich and detailed analysis of communication, management, and culture in about 300 organizations. The case studies that followed the survey permitted the research team to observe communication excellence change over time, and to explore the historical roots and origins of excellence in organizations.

The information collected in the Excellence Study allow us to answer deeper questions about the how and why of communication excellence. To go beyond the organizations studied, we extrapolate our understanding of communication excellence to new organizations and settings. Through extrapolation, the Excellence Study guides us to the underlying, enduring structure of excellence that exists, in principle, in any organization. Excellence Study sampling strategy does permit the research team to answer the two key questions about excellence that drove the research project:

- What are the characteristics of an excellent communication department?
- How do excellent communication management and public relations make an organization more effective, and how much is that contribution worth economically?

HOW REPRESENTATIVE IS THE EXCELLENCE STUDY SAMPLE?

The Excellence Study provides a nonprobability sample of four types of organizations in Canada, the United Kingdom, and the United States for purposes of extrapolation. As noted previously, the nature of the Excellence Study research questions required the intensive study of a large number of organizations.

One might argue that the Excellence Study sample is representative of organizations willing to fill out about 100 pages of questionnaires by a dozen employees, ranging from the organization's top manager to regular employees. Typically, the communication departments in such organizations are more powerful than in organizations that did not participate. Recall that communicators provided the research team its path of entrée into organizations. The research team offered participating organizations an individual report of findings at the project's end, identifying and comparing communication excellence in each organization to others in the study. If the top communicator valued the research the Excellence Study would provide and also possessed sufficient political juice to convince the CEO to participate, that organization joined the other 320 in the study. If the top communicator fell short in either area, that organization was not included in the study. As detailed in chapter 3, an interest in research is one attribute of communication excellence. As outlined in chapter 6, power in the communication department is another attribute of communication excellence. For both of these reasons, the participating organizations probably have higher levels of communication excellence than do those that did not participate. (Recall that, on average, CEOs in organizations with the least-excellent communication programs placed their return on investment in communication at 146%.)

In summary, the Excellence Study sampled a sufficient number of the four types of organizations in three nations to permit extrapolation of findings to other corporations, not-for-profits, government agencies, and associations in Canada, the United Kingdom, and the United States. These extrapolations involve the how and why of communication excellence. In examining communication excellence in organizations outside the Excellence sample, these extrapolations allow us to identify the key characteristics of communication excellence from other attributes not linked to excellence. The Excellence Study tells us where to look for excellence and how to measure it. It tells us the relative importance of the characteristics that contribute to communication excellence.

REFERENCES

Cutlip, S. M., Center, A. H., & Broom, G. M. (1994). *Effective public relations.* (7th ed.). Englewood Cliffs, NJ: Prentice-Hall.

Grunig, J. E. (Ed.). (1992). *Excellence in public relations and communication management.* Hillsdale, NJ: Lawrence Erlbaum Associates.

IABC Research Foundation. (1994). *1994 worldbook of IABC communicators.* San Francisco: Author.

Author Index

B

Bell, E. C., 197, *206*
Bell, S. H., 197, *206*
Broom, G. M., 24, 31, 32, 35, *36, 37,* 41, 50, *51,*
 54, 59, *61,* 71, *72,* 85, *88,* 99, *104,*
 113, *118,* 158, 159, *161,* 196, *206,*
 237, 238, *249*

C

Center, A. H., 41, *51,* 59, *61,* 71, *72,* 99, *104,*
 237, 238, *249*
Chapo, S., 158, *161, 162*
Cohen, J., 201, *206*
Creedon, P. J., 113, *118*
Cutlip, S. M., 41, *51,* 59, *61,* 71, *72,* 99, *104,*
 237, 238, *249*

D

Dozier, D. M., 24, 30, 31, 32, *37,* 41, 43, 50, *51,*
 113, *118, 119,* 158, 159, *161, 162,*
 220, *236*

E

Ehling, W. P., 70, *72*

F

Ferguson, M. A., 113, *118*

G

Gossen, R., 31, *37*
Gray, E. R., 85, *88*

Grunig, J. E., 8, 9, 17, *19,* 31, 32, 35, 36, *37,* 41,
 51, 66, 71, *72,* 76, *88,* 98, *104,* 135,
 148, 158, *161,* 220, 231, *236,* 238,
 249
Grunig, L. A., 113, *118*

H

Hammonds, L., 173, *182*
Higgins, H. M., 28, *37,* 85, *88*
Hofstede, G., 173, *182*
Hunt, T., 31, *37,* 41, *51,* 98, *104*

K

Kalupa, F., 173, *182*

L

Lauzen, M. M., 113, *119*

M

Marker, R. K., 34, *37*
Miner, J. B., 85, *88*
Murphy, P., 47, 49, *51,* 97, *104*

P

Peters, T. J., 184, *192*
Pfeffer, J., 185, *192*
Plank, B., 70, *72*

R

Raiffa, H., 97, *105*
Robbins, S. P., 185, *192*

S

Sharp, K., 31, *37*
Smith, G. D., 54, *61,* 113, *118*
Smith, R. W., 153, *162*
Steiner, G. A., 85, *88*
Sullivan, B., 158, *161, 162*

T

Trask, G., 173, *182*

W

Waterman, R. H., Jr., 184, *192*
White, J., 173, *182*

Subject Index

A

Accredited Business Communicators, 69
American Red Cross, 6
Armstrong Cork Company, 34
Arthur Page Society, 66
Arts funding organization case study, 26
    at-risk youth program, 28–29, 45–46, 232
Asymmetrical communication, 21, *see also* Two-
        way asymmetrical communication
    department expertise, 46
    game theory, 47–50
    internal, 142–143
    model, 48
    national differences, 172
    practices, 99
    short-term gain, 212
Asymmetry, 47–50, 216
Authoritarian culture, 17–18, 131, 138–140
    communication excellence study, 164–166
    formal power, 77
    most-excellent versus least-excellent
        organizations, 144–145

B

Bernays, Edward, 41
Bhopal tragedy, 2
Blood bank case study
    AIDS threat, 187–188
    communication excellence, 1
    communication value, 230–231
    demand-delivery linkage, 102–103
    knowledge base, 26
    long-term relationships, 235
    manager/technician role expertise, 56

    strategic management and communication, 87
Boundary spanners, 14, 132
    culturally diverse employees, 151
Budgeting, historicist, 35

C

Canada
    communication excellence study, 6, 163–174
    communicator characteristics, 166–168
Canadian Public Relations Society, 66
Chemical manufacturer case study, 27
    communication excellence, 1–2
    core values, 136
    strategic program evaluation, 34
Chemical Manufacturers Association, 104, 122–123
Chief executive officer
    communication excellence, 121–129
    return on investment, 8, 248
    shared expectations, 14, 89–105
        measures, 90–92
Commission on Undergraduate Public Relations
        Education, 70
Communication
    return on investment, 8, 122, 248
    shared expectations, 7, 10, 89–105
    women and, 152–158
        Canada, 153
        demographics, 153
Communication craft, 5–6, 58–60
    traditional, 5, 21–22
        economic development agency case
            study, 59–60
        journalists-in-residence, 54
        knowledge base, 27, 53–61

253

measures, 54–58
tactical knowledge, 29
Communication department
    empowerment, 77–78
    knowledge base, 7, 10, 21–22, 25–26
        acquisition strategies, 64–72
        arts funding organization case study, 26,
            28–29
        blood bank case study, 26, 56
        college curricula, 69–72
        inventory, 68
        knowing the business, 65
        management role, 11, 23–25, *see also*
            Manager role expertise
        manager/technician role expertise, 55–56
        mentoring, 67–68
        negotiation, 63–64
        persuasion, 63–64
        professional accreditation, 68–69
        research methods and interpretation, 14,
            63–64
        research usage, 44–50
        self-study, 65–66
        strategic management, 11, 23–37, 63–64
        tactical knowledge, 29
        traditional communication craft, 27, 53–61
        two-way models, 44–50
        workshops and seminars, 66–68
    organizational change, 185–186
    power of, 75–88
        informal, 76
        manager versus technician role, 76–77
        organizational decision making, 76
    relative value, 80–82
        most-excellent versus least-excellent
            organizations, 81–82
Communication excellence, 1–19
    arts funding organization case study, 232
    blood bank case study, 1, 26, 56, 187–188,
        230, 231
    characteristics, 1, 3–4, 7
    chemical manufacturer case study, 1–2, 136
    chief executive officer, 121–129
    conflict avoidance, 218, 226–227
    crisis as catalyst, 103
    cultural diversity, 151–152
    economic development agency case study, 2
    excellence audit, 126–127
    gas and electric company case study, 137,
        188–189
    global qualities, 163–182
    heart health organization case study, 2–3
    internal restructuring, 103–104
    job satisfaction and, 218, 229–230
    less-than-excellent programs, 3, 6
    measures, 5

manager role knowledge, 23–24
    process measures, 29
monetary value, 217–236
national differences, 168–173
    asymmetrical practices, 172
    dominant coalition support, 170–171
    individualist versus collectivist culture, 173
    manager role expertise, 168–169
    masculine versus feminine characteris-
        tics, 173
    social class, 174
    strategic planning contribution, 168–170
    symmetrical practices, 172
oil company case study, 33, 187, 231–232
organizational culture and, 2–3, 7, 143–148
    culturally intense, 145–146
    ethnic diversity, 18, 131–132
    treatment of women, 18–19, 131–132
positive effects, 233–235
    crisis management, 233
    long-term relationships, 234
    quality of work, 233
    recognition, 234
public reaction anticipation, 123–126
senior management and, 5, 15, 128–129
spheres, 10–19
    core, 10–14
    middle, 10, 14–17
    organizational culture, 11, 17–19
state lottery case study, 189
strategic management and, 1–2
training, 127
universal attributes of, 4
Communication excellence factor, 7–8, 23, 207
    isolation of, 9
    manager role, 25
    participative culture, 17
Communication excellence study, 2–3, 6–10,
    121
    Canada, 6, 163–174, 237
    corporations, 166, 176–181
    data collection, 245
    design, 240–242
    expectations, 4–5
    factor analysis, 9
    fractionation scales, 245–246
    government agencies, 166, 176–181
    not-for-profit organizations, 166, 176–181
    organizational culture, 164–166
    percentile scores, 165
    probability sampling, 243
    professional-trade associations, 166, 176–181
    purposive sampling, 243
    research methods, 238–240
    sampling strategy, 240–245
    Slovenia, 174–176

United Kingdom, 6, 163–174, 237
United States, 6, 163–174, 237
Communication management role, 11, 21, 24, 107
  budgeting knowledge, 35–36
  measures, 23–24, 27, 107–108
  research knowledge, 30–35
    program evaluation, 32–35
    publics segmentation, 30–32
  responses to issues, 28–29
  strategic management, 27–28, 108–109
Communication models, 6, 44–50
Communication practices, 6
  mixed motive model, 14, 48–49
  one-way, 12, 15, 207–210
    department expertise, 57–58
    measures, 57–58
    models, 13, 40–41
  press agentry model, 13, 40–41, 208–209
    most-excellent versus least-excellent organizations, 209–210
  public information model, 13, 40–41, 208–211
    most-excellent versus least-excellent organizations, 210–211
  two-way, 12, 39–51, 211–215
    asymmetrical model, 12–13, 41, 48, 212–214
    measures, 39, 45–47, 212
    most-excellent versus least-excellent organizations, 213–215
    symmetrical model, 12–13, 41, 48, 212–215
Communication programs, 193–194
  change-of-relationship effects, 226–228
  compensating variation, 230–231
  conflict avoidance, 226–229
  environmental scanning, 199, 201–204
  evaluation research, 32–35, 217, 220–226
    benchmark, 32
    media placement, 221–222
    scientific, 224–225
    seat-of-the-pants, 223–224
    strategic versus tactical, 34
  governmental relations programs, 204–205
  impact objectives, 218–220
  most-excellent versus least-excellent organizations, 195–197, 200, 202–204, 217–236
  origins, 195–206
    historicist, 198
    strategic, 197, 199–200
    traditional, 197–198
  process objectives, 218–219
  roots, 195–198
  value of, 217–236
Communication Research, 65
Communication technician role, 11, 21–22, 53–61
  department expertise, 54–55

  measures, 54–58, 112–113
Communication World, 237
Communicator
  in advanced organizational role, 107–119
    most-excellent versus least-excellent organizations, 110–112, 115
    research activities, 115–117
  as advocate, 15, 77, 92, 246
  as boundary spanner, 14, 132
  Canada, 166–168
  characteristics, 113–114, 166–168, 176–177
  cultural diversity, 149–162
  in dominant coalition, 83–84
  gender, 114, 149–162
    discrimination, 153–155
    men versus women, 158–160
    most-excellent versus least-excellent organizations, 159
    salary gap, 158–159
    technical tasks, 159–160
  as information disseminator, 124
  journalist-in-residence, 54, 112
  as mediator, 211–212
  as negotiator, 123–124
  as organization eyes and ears, 40, 51, 89, 123–124
  reporting relationship, 83–84
  as senior adviser, 25, 109–110
  in traditional organizational role, 112–114, 124
  United Kingdom, 166–168
  United States, 166–168
Communicator's serenity prayer, 14
Comsensating variation, 230–231
Conflict avoidance, 218, 226–227
  communication programs, 226–229
Cooperative antagonists, 48, 97
Corporations
  communication excellence study, 166, 176–181
    communicator characteristics, 176–177
    manager role expertise, 179
    strategic planning contribution, 180–181
CPRS, see Canadian Public Relations Society
Crisis management, 233

D

Demand-delivery linkage, 16–17, 73–74, 102–104
  blood bank case study, 102–103
  engineering research agency case study, 103
Design for undergraduate public relations education, 70
Dominant coalition, 15
  communication department support from, 78–80, 90
    most-excellent versus least-excellent organizations, 79

conflict with publics, 33
linkages to, 107–119
shared expectations, 14, 73–74
    communicator organizational role, 74
    demand-delivery linkage, 16–17, 73–74,
        102–104
    departmental power, 73
    measures, 90–92

E

Economic development agency case study
    communication excellence, 2
    traditional communication craft, 59–60
Effective Public Relations, 237–238
Ehling, William, 71
Employees
    culturally diverse, 149–162
        boundary spanners, 151
        mentoring, 150
    empowerment, 149–162
Engineering research agency case study, 103
Environmental scanning, 14–15, 199, 201–204
Excellence audit, *see* Communication excel-
    lence - excellence audit
Excellence factor, *see* Communication excel-
    lence factor
*Excellence in public relations and communica-
    tion management,* 8–9, 19, 66, 238
    communication department, 35
    comsensating variation, 230–231
    organizational culture, 135
    research, 32
Exploratory factor analysis, 100

F

Ford Motor Company, 98
Fractionation scales, 245–246

G

Game theory, 12–13
    asymmetrical communication, 47–50
    cooperative antagonists, 48
        characteristics, 97
    mixed-motive, 47, 49, 95
        asymmetrical tactics, 98–99
    win-win relationship, 13, 48–49, 96, 99
    zero-sum game, 12, 49, 97–98
        asymmetrical practices, 98
Gas and electric company case study
    conflict over nuclear power plant, 188–189
    core values, 137
    merger, 189
Glass ceiling, 149–150

Government agencies
    communication excellence study, 166, 176–181
        communicator characteristics, 176–177
        manager role expertise, 179
        strategic planning contribution, 180–181

H

HERMES study, 173–174

I

IABC, *see* International Association of Business
    Communicators
Initial data report and practical guide, 9
Institute for Public Relations Research and Edu-
    cation, 66
Institute of Public Relations, 66
International Association of Business Communi-
    cators, 30, 90
    accreditation program, 69
    membership, 158
    Research Foundation, 9, 121, 237
    workshops and seminars, 65–66
IPR, *see* Institute of Public Relations

J

Job satisfaction, 218, 229–230
    organizational culture and, 140–141
Journalists-in-residence, 54, 112
Journal of Communication, 65

K

Kotler, Philip, 71

M

Manager role expertise, 21, 179, *see also*
    Communication department -
    knowledge base - management role
    national differences, 168–169
Managing Public Relations, 238
Media relations role, 112
Miettinen, JoNell, 246
Mixed motive model, 48–49, 95–96, 101
    two-way practices model, 101–102

N

Nestlé Company, 98–99
Not-for-profit corporations
    communication excellence study, 166, 176–181
        communicator characteristics, 176–177
        manager role expertise, 179
        strategic planning contribution, 180–181

O

O'Dwyer Newsletter, 237
Oil company case study
    communication value, 231–232
    Exxon *Valdez* oil spill, 33, 187
    1970s oil embargo, 33, 187
One-group pretest-posttest design, 32
Organizational character, *see* Organizational culture
Organizational culture, 135–148
    authoritarian, 17–18, 131, 138–140
    characteristics, 131–133
    communication excellence and, 2–3, 7, 143–148
        levels, 2–3, 7, 143–148
    core values, 135–137
    cultural change, 183–192
        communication departments, 185–186
        crises and case studies, 186–189
        power alignments, 190
        power-control perspective, 185
        shared values, 184
        total quality management programs, 191
    culturally authoritarian, 146
    culturally indifferent, 145–146
    culturally intense, 137, 145–146
    culturally participative, 146
    downsizing, 184
    ethnic diversity, 131–132
    internal communication, 142–143, 229–230
    job satisfaction and, 140–141, 218, 229–230
    participative, 17–18, 131, 138–140
    requisite variety concept, 151
    treatment of women, 18–19, 131–132
Organizations
    most-excellent versus least-excellent
        authoritarian culture, 144–145
        communication department value, 81–82
        communication programs, 195–197,
            200, 202–204, 217–236
        communicator gender, 159
        communicator in advanced roles, 110–
            112, 115
        dominant coalition support, 79
        organizational support for women, 154,
            156–157
        participative culture, 144–145
        press agentry model, 209–210
        public information model, 210–211
        strategic management contribution, 86–87
        strategic research, 115–116
        two-way asymmetrical communication,
            95–96
        two-way communication practices, 213–215
        two-way symmetrical communication,
            93–94

P

Page, Arthur W., 41, 50
Participative culture, 17–18, 131
    communication excellence study, 165–166
    employee empowerment, 77–78
    informal power, 77
    most-excellent versus least-excellent organi-
        zations, 144–145
Potter, Lester, 6
Power-control perspective, 185
Press agentry model, 13, 40–41, 208–210
    department expertise, 57
Process measures, 29
Process objectives, 218–219
Professional-trade associations
    communication excellence study, 166, 176–181
        communicator characteristics, 176–177
        manager role expertise, 179
        strategic planning contribution, 180–181
pr reporter, 237
PRSA, *see* Public Relations Society of America
Psychographics, 31
Public information model, 13, 40–41, 208–211
    department expertise, 58
Public relations, 71
    mixed-motive game, 97
    proactive, 188
Public Relations Society of America, 30, 66
Public Relations Symposium, 66
Publics, 13
    active, 31–32
    aware, 31–32
    communication programs, 195–206
    definition, 30
    environmental scanning, 199, 201–204
        formal, 201–203
        informal, 201, 203–204
    latent, 31–32
    segmentation, 30–32
        psychographics, 31
        situational theory, 31
Pure cooperation model, 48–49

Q

Questionnaire, 12
    communication excellence study, 240–241

R

Ragan Report, 237
Repper, Fred C., 205
Requisite variety concept, 151
Return on investment, 8, 122, 248

S

Senior adviser, 25, 74
  informal power, 109
  measures, 109–110
Senior management, 5, 108–109, *see also* Dominant coalition
  commitment to excellent, 128–129
  symmetrical communication, 13
Situational theory, 31
Slovenia
  communication ex~ellence study, 174–176
  gender discrimination, 175
  internal communication, 175–176
Sriramesh, K., 246
State hospital association case study, 53–54
Strategic management, 23–37, 85
  communication excellence and, 1–2, 122–124
  communication management role, 27–28
  contribution of communication, 84–88
    blood bank case study, 87
    most-excellent versus least-excellent organizations, 86–87
Strategic planning, 84–88, 115–117
  national differences, 168–170
  organization type, 180–181
Strategic research, 42
  communicator role behavior, 115–117
  formal, 44, 115–117
  informal, 44, 115–117
  measures, 44–45
  most-excellent versus least-excellent organizations, 115–116
  scanning and evaluation, 43
  types of, 43–44
Symmetrical communication, 21, *see also* Two-way symmetrical communication
  department expertise, 46
  game theory, 47–50
  goals and objectives, 32–33
  internal, 142–143
  long-term relationships, 212
  national differences, 172
  pure cooperation model, 48
  senior management, 13
  strategic relationships, 33
  symmetrical practices model, 100
  win-win solutions, 13
Symmetrical practices model, 100
Symmetry, 47–50, 216

T

Tactical knowledge, 29
Tactical research, 42
Top communicators, *see* Communicator

Total quality management, 78, 191
Two-way asymmetrical communication, 12–13, 39, 95, *see also* Asymmetrical communication
  department expertise, 46
  dominant coalition demand, 95–96
  measures, 95
  model, 41, 48, 212–214
  most-excellent versus least-excellent organizations, 95–96
  shared expectations, 94–102
Two-way model, 49–50
Two-way practices model, 101–102
Two-way symmetrical communication, 12–13, 39, 95, *see also* Symmetrical communication
  department expertise, 46
  dominant coalition demand, 92–94
  model, 41, 48, 212–215
  most-excellent versus least-excellent organizations, 93–94
  shared expectations, 92–94
  symmetrical practices model, 100

U

U. S. Department of Labor, 18
  Bureau of Labor Statistics, 151
    Employment and Earnings, 152

W

The Wall Street Journal, 124, 237
Win-win solutions, 13, 48, 96
Women, 18–19
  communication and, 152–158
    Canada, 153
    demographics, 153
  empowerment, 149–162
  gender discrimination, 153–155
  glass ceiling, 149–150
  mentoring, 150
  organizational support, 153–158
    mentoring-advancement activities, 156–157
    most-excellent versus least-excellent organiations, 154, 156–157
    nondiscrimination policies, 155, 158
    work environment, 156–158
  stereotypes, 2
The Worldbook of IABC Communicators, 240
World Health Organization, 98

Z

Zero-sum game, 12, 49, 97–98